RUN to the ROAR

RUN to the ROAR

Coaching to Overcome Fear

Paul Assaiante and James Zug

Portfolio / Penguin

PORTFOLIO / PENGUIN
Published by the Penguin Group
Penguin Group (USA) Inc., 375 Hudson Street,
New York, New York 10014, U.S.A.
Penguin Group (Canada), 90 Eglinton Avenue East, Suite 700, Toronto,
Ontario, Canada M4P 2Y3 (a division of Pearson Penguin Canada Inc.)
Penguin Books Ltd, 80 Strand, London WC2R 0RL, England
Penguin Ireland, 25 St. Stephen's Green, Dublin 2, Ireland
(a division of Penguin Books Ltd)
Penguin Books Australia Ltd, 250 Camberwell Road, Camberwell,
Victoria 3124, Australia (a division of Pearson Australia Group Pty Ltd)
Penguin Books India Pvt Ltd, 11 Community Centre,
Panchsheel Park, New Delhi–110 017, India
Penguin Group (NZ), 67 Apollo Drive, Rosedale, North Shore 0632,
New Zealand (a division of Pearson New Zealand Ltd)
Penguin Books (South Africa) (Pty) Ltd, 24 Sturdee Avenue,
Rosebank, Johannesburg 2196, South Africa

Penguin Books Ltd, Registered Offices: 80 Strand, London WC2R 0RL, England

First published in 2010 by Portfolio / Penguin, a member of Penguin Group (USA) Inc.

1 3 5 7 9 10 8 6 4 2

Copyright © Paul Assaiante and James Zug, 2010

Foreword by Tom Wolfe published by arrangement with the author

Photographs by Jonathan Lester Photography

LIBRARY OF CONGRESS CATALOGING IN PUBLICATION DATA
Assaiante, Paul.
Run to the roar : coaching to overcome fear / Paul Assaiante and James Zug.
p. cm.
Includes index.
ISBN 978-1-59184-364-1
1. Coaching (Athletics) 2. Fear—Prevention. I. Zug, James, 1969– II. Title.
GV711.A85 200
796.07'7—dc22
2010022347

Printed in the United States of America
Set in Electra   Designed by Francesca Belanger

To Matthew, Scott, and Kristen,
who taught me that love is unconditional

TRINITY COLLEGE
v.
PRINCETON UNIVERSITY

22 February 2009

Jadwin Gymnasium, Princeton, New Jersey

Trinity	Princeton	Winner	Score
#1. Baset Ashfaq	v. Maurico Sanchez	T	8–10, 9–3, 9–5, 2–9, 9–5
#2. Gustav Detter	v. Kimlee Wong	T	5–9, 5–9, 9–6, 9–1, 9–3
#3. Manek Mathur	v. Christopher Callis	T	9–10, 10–8, 0–9, 9–1, 9-2
#4. Parth Sharma	v. David Letourneau	T	6–9, 2–9, 9–7, 9–0, 9–7
#5. Randy Lim	v. David Canner	P	2–9, 10–8, 9–5, 9–1
#6. Supreet Singh	v. Hesham El Halaby	P	9–5, 9–10, 9–4, 4–9, 9–4
#7. Andres Vargas	v. Kelly Shannon	P	8–10, 7–9, 9–4, 9–3, 9–2
#8. Vikram Malhotra	v. Santiago Imberton	T	9–3, 10–8, 9–4
#9. Rushabh Vora	v. Peter Sopher	P	8–10, 9–2, 10–8, 9–4

Order of Play:

COURT ONE
#3. Manek Mathur (senior; Mumbai, India)

#2. Gustav "Goose" Detter (senior; Malmo, Sweden)

#1. Baset Ashfaq (junior; Lahore, Pakistan)

COURT THREE
#6. Supreet Singh (junior; Mumbai, India)

#5. Randy Lim (sophomore; Penang, Malaysia)

#4. Parth Sharma (sophomore; Jaipur, India)

COURT FIVE
#9. Rushabh "Roosh" Vora (senior; Mumbai, India)

#8. Vikram Malhotra (freshman; Mumbai, India)

#7. Andres Vargas (sophomore; Bogotá, Colombia)

INJURED
Chris Binnie (sophomore; Kingston, Jamaica)

CONTENTS

FOREWORD

Over and over they've tried it—*they* being entire regiments of television producers, directors, lighting technicians, fiber-optic engineers, robot software gurus, computer swamis, grips, gaffers, and construction crews—over and over they've tried to turn squash, the racquet sport, into TVisible entertainment. I've seen them. They love the idea! The possibilities—*infinite!* Squash is the fastest intercollegiate sport in the world, if you consider defense as well as offense. Baseball's fastest pitcher, Nolan Ryan, could throw the ball a shade above a hundred miles an hour. Tennis fans gasped when Pete Sampras hit 130 mile-an-hour serves. But professional and Division I college squash players routinely hit a ball just 1⅝ inches in diameter 160 miles an hour or more. They rocket it into ricochets off any or all of four walls plus the floor inside a two-story enclosure, creating bewildering trajectories. What with the bursts of speed, the lunges, and abrupt changes in direction required to defend against such shots, the top players wind up with thighs as massive as a speed skater's or a racing cyclist's. They have to have the aerobic fitness of boxers and Olympic wrestlers, since a one-on-one squash match can go on at top speed for two hours. Soccer players? Compared to squash players, soccer players spend most of their time on the field loitering . . . expertly, of course.

Sadly, I have also seen our TV troops as they straggle home after the fray . . . eyebrows lowered and wrapped around the nose . . . ditches down the middle of the forehead . . . mumbling . . . defeated by the very thing they came to capture: the speed, strength, and gymnastic bravura of the players, the velocity of that damnable little ball, the dizzying ricochets . . . these three, all at once . . . demanding purple-dimension jumps from one camera to another camera to another camera and another camera and another—at a speed that baffles even the best TV sports directors.

The absence of the TV eye has largely spared squash from TV sports' three STDiseased, shanks-akimbo harlots: Cheating, Gambling, and Greed. *Greed*? There's no money in squash! None! Top-ten squash professionals fly to major international tournaments in herd class, at brain-grating off-peak hours, no-food flights, aboard AAAs (Almost An Airline) on the order of Aeroflot, Song Air, and Carnival.

But the TV darkness has also deprived millions of sports fans of the most astounding story they have never heard . . . the story of the hottest and statistically most successful American college coach ever—by far—Paul Assaiante, and the dynasty—the most omnipotent in the history of intercollegiate sports—he has created at Trinity College in Hartford, Connecticut.

As I write, he and his boys are riding the crest of twelve straight undefeated seasons and twelve straight Division I national championships. Their won-lost record over that stretch is 224–0. No other team in any college sport has ever come close. The second-longest streak is the University of Miami tennis team's 137 straight half a century ago.

In the pages before us Paul Assaiante tells the Trinity saga himself. Before I knew it, I was devouring it in job lots. *Run to the Roar* is one of those rare sports books, like Michael Lewis's *Moneyball*, that quite effortlessly starts you thinking about life far beyond the confines of the sport itself. Assaiante provides a lesson in twenty-first-century global psychology. He describes how he turned athletes from nineteen countries and every continent on the globe except for Antarctica, all of them ambitious and many of them hot-dogging egotists, into brotherly loving, team-spirited, one-for-all-and-all-for-one creatures within their own ranks . . . and implacable warriors on the court.

This sweet science, as it were, was the outcome of a single, simple, direct order. One day in 1996, Trinity's then-president Evan Dobelle called Assaiante into his office—they barely knew each other—and said, with very little backstory, I want you to go forth and assemble a squash team that can compete with the Ivy Leaguers. At the time

Harvard, Yale, and Princeton—especially Harvard—dominated the sport. The meeting lasted all of two minutes.

As Assaiante was leaving the room, the president called out, "And don't mess this one up!"

Assaiante had never heard of the game of squash until he was twenty-seven and found himself forced to coach the army squash team at West Point, like it or not. He had graduated from that well-known training ground for coaches Springfield College, barely thirty miles north of Hartford, in Massachusetts. Now he was offered the job of tennis coach at West Point. Seven highly regarded coaches had turned it down. Assaiante soon found out why. The contract came with two riders, or jokers, depending on how you looked at it: the tennis coach had to lead his boys on a cross-country run every morning at reveille—and coach the squash team, too. Assaiante took a deep breath and signed anyhow. He didn't want to be anybody's assistant coach any longer.

By that day in 1996 in Evan Dobelle's office, Assaiante had coached squash at West Point, Williams, and Trinity for eleven years in all. While he was at it, he had learned to play the game himself and won two New York State regional championships. But his most important asset was what he had learned, en passant, coaching the U.S. national team in international competition in Europe. In Europe one day, a lightbulb went on over his head. Wherever the British had stayed long enough to build squash courts—Australia, India, Pakistan, Egypt, Zimbabwe, Nigeria, South Africa, Canada, Malaysia, even Bermuda, not to mention England and Scotland themselves—the players were superior to ours. The British had left here too soon. He didn't have to look far to find the most promising young international junior players. Their competitions took place in Europe at the same time. They were all conveniently on view in one place.

Assaiante became a great recruiter . . . out on the Old Colonial trail. He was charming and good-looking. He always had the sunniest disposition, broadest smile, and readiest laugh in town, whatever town, whatever continent. He knew each prospective recruit's own history backward and forward. He knew squash technique forward and backward and had proved it as a player. He was well-spoken . . . and not *too* glib . . . yet definitely glib enough. In fact, he struck the cynically inclined as too good to be true, like Meredith Willson's *Music Man* or *Huckleberry Finn*'s Duke and Dauphin. But he proved to be the real thing. He was straightforward to a fault. He developed a genuine personal interest in every recruit and maintained it as long as the young man was at Trinity—and often long after. You will get to know many of their stories in these pages.

Assaiante's decoding of squash's British Colonial secret paid off in 1999, the first year of the streak. Seven of Assaiante's international players, along with two talented Americans, routed Harvard, Yale, Princeton, Penn, Dartmouth, Brown, and Cornell. The Ivy League's hold on squash was broken—*just like that.*

Right away the Ivies made known their resentment of Assaiante's international players, even though they themselves had been recruiting abroad for a century. In 1980 Cornell's entire ice hockey team was made up of Canadians. In 2004, after Trinity's sixth straight undefeated season, the *Harvard Crimson* created a big stir with an editorial calling Assaiante's monarchy "The Evil Empire." On February 27, 2005, Trinity clenched its seventh straight championship by defeating Harvard at Harvard's own Murr Center courts. The moment the match ended, Assaiante's assistant coach, James Montano, handed out navy T-shirts to the Trinity team. On the front, in bold gold letters, each T-shirt read, THE EVIL EMPIRE; on the back, WELCOME TO THE DARK SIDE. The Dark Side! By now the two coaches couldn't help but get a laugh out of this Evil Empire business. Well before that moment in 2005, the Ivies no longer thought their own joke was funny. They were out combing every former British colony on the globe for squash players themselves. By 2006 they had *loaded up* . . . Oh, yeah.

But I especially remember that night at Harvard in 2005. Lest you think I have any bias in Trinity's and Paul Assaiante's favor, let me make one thing absolutely clear. I was with my son, Tommy, the moment James Montano handed him his EVIL EMPIRE T-shirt and congratulated him on the match he had just won.

—Tom Wolfe

Prologue

Over the millennia on the African savanna, lions have developed a hunting technique. The oldest lion in the pride is often infirm. She is a great-grandmother. She has lame legs, rotten teeth, a scabby coat. She cannot hunt. But she still has lungs and can still give a deep-throated, primeval roar.

When the pride spots a herd of antelope, she heads into the tall grass while the rest of the pride spreads out in the bush in the opposite direction. The old lion roars. The antelope instinctively gallop away from the roar and slam right into the string of younger lions.

The antelope should run toward the roar. To survive this kind of attack, they would have to confront the instinct to flee from their worst enemy. They would have to confront their fears head-on.

This is the core message I bring as a coach. The normal reaction of people on and off the athletic field is to fear matches, contests, performances. Practices are easy. It is the public recital that is unpleasant. They turn from the challenge and thereby run into the proverbial young lions of mediocrity, underachievement, and, ultimately, failure. My biggest challenge as an educator is helping my athletes conquer their fears, their anxieties, and their worst nightmares. In moments of tension and crisis—when the lion roars—I teach them to understand that safety is actually found in moving forward. There is just an old lion lying in the grass, familiar, toothless, and unthreatening.

I started the 2008–09 season like every season, talking about running to the roar. It was the last day of October. League rules prohibited me from officially coaching until the first of November. That meant a party. One of the keys to my success was making Trinity squash seem like a big-time college program. I got new uniforms each year. I had a highway sign erected to proclaim our championships. (It was updated each year, except when a Dartmouth fraternity came down and stole it.) We get invited annually for recognition to Fenway Park and the Connecticut governor's office. I try to make them feel a part of something majestic and eternal.

As if we were Duke basketball, I hosted a Midnight Madness party the night before practice was allowed to begin. Because it was Halloween, it transmogrified into a costume bash. About a third of the students on campus came—more than eight hundred bedecked and bedazzled kids. As one of the few national championship teams in town, Trinity squash was huge: dozens of students came to some of our practices, players received standing ovations in the cafeteria, a crowd of two hundred would gather in the parking lot to greet the team coming home from the nationals at two in the morning, eighty kids would sign up for the campus championships (open to all students who weren't on the team) even though they had to pay an eight-dollar entry fee. The Halloween party was the classic event of the fall at Trinity.

Lady Gaga's "Poker Face" blasted from the stereo at the top of the bleachers—"*bluffin' with my muffin*"—and kids danced on every one of our courts. Mary Poppins was flirting with Thomas the Tank Engine, who was laughing with Buzz Lightyear, who was gossiping with Tinkerbell. Kids had painted their faces and glittered their bodies. Masks flew in the warm air. Everyone was young and happy and hopeful.

At the stroke of midnight, the team entered court 1. I introduced all twenty-two players: Spider-Man, a springbok, Dr. Seuss's Thing One and Thing Two, a cricketer in white flannels, the Hamburgler. A glorious mob surrounded the court, cheering and clapping. I awarded a new racquet to the person with the best costume—this year it was someone who looked like Dick Cheney, or rather someone who said he looked like Dick Cheney if Dick Cheney were twenty-two years old and a hundred pounds lighter and had been born in India.

I sent the team out to play mixed doubles. The small, white clock above the championship banners said it was nearly three in the morning when the last kid left the courts and I turned out the lights.

Fourteen hours later we started. All Souls' Day—the first practice.

The kids straggled in, the sugar high of Halloween gone. Some came a few minutes early, dressed to play; others stumbled in barely awake. With the autumnal wind blowing away the last gasp of Indian summer, some were bundled up in sweatshirts, but most came wearing the usual collegiate garb of flip-flops and T-shirts. They planted their bags on the gray-carpeted bleachers outside my office and slumped to a seat.

It was a motley crew, the sons of sailors and engineers and ball-bearing-factory owners and architects and diamond miners. I looked at them for a minute, waiting for them to become silent. Their faces were every shade of white, brown, black, but their eyes were all startlingly similar: expectant, searching, unblinking, open. I didn't say anything at the Halloween party the night before. That was the message: that at the core we were here to have fun. We started with fun. Plus, as a fifty-five-year-old, it would've been hard for me to keep a straight face lecturing the Hamburgler.

"We are a family," I said. "We are the biggest mishmash of people, but we still care about each other. Win, lose, or draw, we walk away from this season as a family."

I then paused and looked at each kid, one by one, before going on in a lower voice. "Most coaches at the first practice of the season ask you what your goals are. I don't do that. Goals are easy. You can write them down in a flash. And you're all good enough, talented enough, dedicated enough, that you'll reach most of those goals, whatever they are.

"I don't care about your goals. I care about you. I want to know what you are afraid of. What is holding you back from excellence, from achieving and fulfilling your potential? What is the worst thing that can happen? What do you fear?"

The upperclassmen shifted on the bleachers, wry smiles blossoming on their faces. They had heard it before. They knew what was coming next. I told my annual story about the old lion on the savanna. I asked, "What are your fears? What are your anxieties, your doubts? What will hold you back? What will hold us back? What sunk the Titanic was not the tip of the iceberg that you could see. It was what was underneath, out of sight. We've got to get the source of your issues. What seems unsolvable? Let's confront your fears. Let's run to the roar."

No one was moving now. Their eyes were focused on me. "Life is not just about peaks and valleys, about wins and losses. Life is about the journey. You hear that all the time. You've got to absorb that. You've got to know that. The journey has to become the destination, because there is no true destination. There is no end point. There is no goal. All rivers run to the sea and yet the sea is not full. Life goes on; accept what life gives you. The sun rises the morning after you win the championship or lose in the first round. A billion people in China are getting up right now, and they couldn't care less about a bunch of kids in Hartford, Connecticut, bashing a ball around a box."

And then we spent the rest of the practice talking. The captains spoke first, then the other upperclassmen, then the freshmen. We followed that hierarchy because we had to throw some cold water on the freshmen's egos. They were national champions in their own countries, and the only way to get them to buy into the team, rather than playing for themselves, was to create a subtle pecking order. But at the same time, we wanted everyone to talk. No one ridiculed, no one teased. It was real sharing.

This was the most important practice of the year and we didn't hit a ball. Most coaches opened the first practice with a lecture about goals, maybe a pep talk, and then scattered everyone to go through drills. That was not my approach. The biggest challenge I faced was helping these boys conquer their fears so that when the lion roared—when the match got close—they would not sprint away; they would confidently hold their ground and then go toward the pressure. They would want the ball. They would not be scared. They would face the old lion.

We sat on the bleachers. Manek talked about how over the summer his grandfather had been killed by a swerving truck while walking on a sidewalk in Hong Kong. Goose talked about wanting a 4.0 grade-point average and the subtle pressure he felt not from his parents, he said, but from himself. Parth talked about coming to America, how he had to do right for the family name. Burchy talked about his triskaidekaphobia, how his fear of the number thirteen meant he had to play 12 on the ladder. Burchy laughed so hard he could barely spit out the word and everyone cracked up. It got serious again. Many of the boys talked about the anxiety they felt about squash, about pouring so much into their game for so long. An hour went by, then another. Finally, we stopped.

Now, four months later, I see the effects of that first practice. A string was plucked and all season it vibrated. Today, the guys are not scared of the challenge. They do not dwell on the score or the scorching shouts of the crowd or the pressing doom of what it might mean if they lose. They are free from fear. They are running to the roar.

I am the winningest coach in collegiate sports history—for 224 consecutive matches over the past twelve years, my Trinity men's squash team has gone unbeaten.

No other team has achieved the same sustained level of greatness.* Streaks are hard. Reaching 224 is very hard. There are sixty other colleges trying to knock us off each winter, sixty other athletic directors

---

* The next-closest streaks for collegiate sports are 201 wins by Yale men's swimming in 1940–1961; 137 wins for Miami men's tennis in 1957–64; 92 wins by North Carolina women's soccer in 1990–94; 88 games by UCLA men's basketball in 1971–74; and the University of Oklahoma's 47 straight football wins in 1953–57. Interestingly, Notre Dame ended North Carolina's, UCLA's, and Oklahoma's streaks. Current win streaks of note are 102 straight wins by Penn State women's volleyball and the 78 by Connecticut women's basketball.

allocating resources, sixty other coaches recruiting around the world, plucking the best players from the fifteen million who play squash.

There should be no streak. When I first became a squash coach, at Army in 1977, I had never heard of the game; the job came with Army's tennis coaching position. I literally knew nothing about squash. Not only have I led my teams in creating the longest winning streak in college sports history, but I have done so while learning the game myself.

The story that follows here begins and ends with a dual match against Princeton in the finals of the nationals as we go for win number 202. If we win, it will be our eleventh straight national championship. It is a dramatic contest. The dual match consists of nine individual matches, and each match is extremely revealing. My Trinity men play in a crucible of pressure that burns away all the clichés of what it means to be a good leader and exposes my strengths and weaknesses as a coach. They reveal essential life lessons.

This is not a book about squash. It is about leadership. It is about pride, about instinct, control, about anger management, about talent, about mentoring. These are universal issues that every parent and every coach faces. This is not easy. At times it is tragic, disappointing, painful. I have made horrible mistakes. I have suffered and I have made others suffer. And those moments have taught me more than the victories.

It ends up being not at all about numbers and streaks and wins and losses but about how you feel about it. If you feel fear, you will live with regret. You will fail. You will not learn. You have to feel brave and calm. You have to run to the roar.

People always asked me, "How do you do it? How do you win? How do you survive the anguish in your life?" This is the answer.

It is Sunday, February 22, 2009, in Princeton, New Jersey. It is the day of the finals of the national intercollegiate team tournament. In our four-month regular season, we have played sixteen colleges. We had faced Princeton in Princeton on Valentine's Day and won the dual match five matches to four, the sixth time in our eleven-year unbeaten streak that we escaped with a 5–4 dual-match win.

We do not want another nail-biter. But just eight days later, we are back at Princeton, which is hosting sixty colleges in this year's national team tournament. After easy 9–0 wins over Dartmouth in the quarters and Harvard in the semis, we are now 18–0. At this moment our unbeaten streak stands at 201 consecutive wins. We have not lost since February 1998. In the finals we are once again playing Princeton.

In the past few seasons, Princeton has been our number one challenger. They have three great seniors and a couple of remarkable underclassmen. This is their chance to dethrone the champions. Once again we are playing them on their home courts. It's as if we're Ohio State and we have to play USC in the Rose Bowl and then eight days later return to Pasadena and play them again in the BCS Championship.

The morning starts at our hotel. We wake the boys around nine— these kids could sleep until the middle of the afternoon if I let them—and we trundle off to the Princetonian Diner, on Route 1 just south of town. I like to give them plenty of time at the pregame meal. They get out into the world, see the passing parade, talk to waitresses who have never heard of squash. It is humbling and helpful—they realize that life will go on regardless of today's results.

I also want to whisk them out of the hotel before they turn on the television. The media blitz has been especially intense this year. In the past, the *Hartford Courant* had covered us each week, and occasionally we'd pop up in the national media; for instance, in 2008 *Sports Illustrated* published a piece on us. But this year has been unusual—NPR, ESPN Radio, CNN, and the *New York Times* did stories on us—and today of all days, ESPN is airing a new five-minute segment on our team. As most college athletes would be, our players are thrilled to make it onto ESPN. But I'm not: the last thing I want is for the boys to see themselves on national television just hours before they get on court.

I wake up early and watch the segment, which airs hourly on

SportsCenter, with the other coaches. It opens with ESPN declaring that this is "the greatest streak of them all." The first image is of my hands, with the camera slowly panning over the ten championship rings on my ten fingers. I think, *Oh, God, they can't see this.*

We hustle them out of the hotel and drive down the road to the diner. Disaster: there is a line out the door—a couple of other visiting collegiate teams have arrived just before us. When we finally sit down, everyone asks for the same meal they ordered eight days ago—most of the Indian kids do their usual pancakes-and-ice-cream combos—but the food doesn't arrive for another ten minutes. We are still on schedule, just not ahead of it, but the kids don't see it that way, and they start to fidget and complain.

After we escape the diner, we drive over to Jadwin, Princeton's gym. We enter by the basketball court and take the elevator down to the basement. We put our gear in the Zanfrini fencing room near the courts, and immediately dozens of friends flood in—classmates, fraternity brothers, parents, cousins, girlfriends, and alumni. The well-wishers and glad-handlers are wonderful to see, but with every hello, with every Trinity squash hat with a number on it, the pressure mounts. In almost every other collegiate sport, there are physical barriers between the players and the crowd before and during the contest. In squash, we have no way of separating ourselves. The locker room is too small. The courts are right next to the bleachers, and if you want to watch, you've got to mingle.

I shoo the crowd out. Suddenly, it's quiet—a little too quiet. The usual collegiate banter—the casual profanity, the verbal preening, the jokes—is missing, and it worries me. Some players have put on their iPods, white snakes dangling from their ears. A few guys are sitting on couches winding blue tape on their grips with a crisp steadiness—preparing their weapons as they have done a thousand times before—or carefully wrapping bandannas around their heads. Others stretch on the floor, legs splayed, feet in the air. No one is talking. I fear that the guys have disconnected from the mother ship of reality and drifted into a black hole of pressure. I want a little bit of tension—if there is no anxiety, then you don't care—but I don't want too much. Bill Russell threw up before every game—that's over the top. I want them to run to the roar, but would rather not have them vomit on the way.

I walk around and mix up the room. I get Dick Druckman, the team's photographer, to shoot a picture of Roosh stretching like Plastic Man. I kid Goose about the Scandinavian rock on his iPod and commiserate with Supreet about the dry omelet he had at breakfast and ask Charlie whether his mother has arrived yet and quote a line from the film *300* to get Manek to smile. I briefly review game plans but mostly try to emanate calm. James Montano, our assistant coach, is a whirlwind of movement. He lugs in bottled water and athletic tape and hands out new wristbands that look like oversized white Chiclets. I like for James to talk to the first three guys on the court and pump them up with little motivational quips.

My speech is short. Anything more than a minute and it becomes forgettable. I want it seared into their minds so that six hours later they can still hear it. Last week I had told them to forget about the streak and show Princeton what is feels like to play champions.

"This is the hardest thing to do, but we have forged a team," I say in almost a whisper. "No one has held back. There is no fear. We have instilled in each other a responsibility for the guy on the court next door. There's a spider web of commitment. You are never going to give up because the guy next door is never going to give up.

"Princeton's had a good season. They are good. They almost beat us here last week. On the surface they believe they can now beat us. But they still have doubt. They can't beat us. They will have made adjustments. It will be a closer match than last week. Don't panic when it is closer. Don't get spooked. Adjust to their adjustments. Don't worry about the crowd. You have Princeton's undivided attention. This is the ultimate sign of respect.

"We must send a message early in the match that it is futile, that they cannot win. You must punch them in the nose early and make them think, *Oh, no, it will be too hard, too much work, to win.* Remember, they can't throw anything at you that is harder than a challenge match. I want you to smile out there, but don't show me the smile. I want to see the back of your heads—don't look out at the crowd. Stay in the moment; don't give in to the moment. Stay in it. And remember, when it is close, you'd better be giving it your all, because your teammate on the court next door is diving, bleeding, giving it his all.

"We will always be brothers. Bring it."

The team leaves the room and heads in to court 1 for introductions with the Princeton team. When we walk onto the court, the murmuring crowd bursts into a deafening, teeth-rattling roar. It is a bestial din. It's a tidal wave that has toppled over onto us. We are drowning in whistles, shouts, chanting, applauding. More than a thousand people are roaring only feet away from my players, and many more are watching this on the Internet or following minute-by-minute reports on Facebook. We are in the sunless bowels of a gymnasium three stories below the frozen ground.

It's midwinter and yet, in typical undergraduate nonchalance, the Princeton students are wearing nothing but T-shirts and shorts. The Trinity team lines up along one side wall, the Princeton team along the other. For a minute, I can't hear a thing Bob Callahan, the Princeton coach, is saying to me. When I am introduced, I am lustily booed. When it quiets down, I say, "I haven't been booed this much since I saw my ex-in-laws." Everyone cracks up.

I feel a wave of tranquility splash over me. For the first time in weeks, I relax. The final dual match of the season has begun. It is the first time I can control my contribution to the outcome and stop worrying about the uncontrollable factors: the boys' emotions and attitudes, their injuries, their fears.

Amid much cheering, the players are announced and walk to the middle of the court to shake hands. Afterward, we gather in a huddle by the front wall. I always let the captains do the talking. I give my pep talk before introductions; after that point, the dual match has begun, the crowd has roared, the players have seen their opponents, and everyone is too wired to absorb anything profound.

One of the captains, Goose Detter, turns to the glass back wall and gestures to the cluster of bombsquaders on the bleachers. It is a slow sweep of his arm, and it sums up the season. He is saying, *Come on, you're on this team*. The bombsquaders are the junior varsity kids, the scrubs, the boys who don't appear in the newspapers or television. They are all in street clothes and, a dozen strong, come bounding in to the court to join the huddled human amoeba. We have all twenty-two guys at the weekend. Only the top ten play (and only the top nine count), but we bring the entire team. Since we get only six hotel rooms, the bombsquaders are sleeping on the floors, four or five to a room. But they are there in the huddle. No other team has their bombsquaders.

Goose says, "We are never going to be here again. Let's fight for our brothers. One. Two. Three." Then a deep, bassooning roar, "SIMBA!" woofs out of the court. It echoes out of the gym and across the Princeton campus and into the New Jersey woods, and then we begin.

CHAPTER ONE

Ownership: Manek

We contest nine matches over the course of the afternoon and the first three—the number 3, number 6, and number 9 players on each team's ladder—go out to play, number 3 on court 1; number 6 on court 3; and number 9 on court 5. As I go down the lineup, I feel that Manek Mathur, at number 3, is a wild card; the match could swing either way. The first two games show that to be true, as he and Christopher Callis from Princeton split them in about forty minutes of top-notch squash.

Callis is a shaggy-haired, burly freshman. He looks like a lacrosse player. He grew up in Philadelphia and is perhaps the top American in the college ranks. Like many of the players in the dual match today, Manek and Callis had encountered each other on the international tournament circuit. They had first played each other in the 2006 world junior championships, in New Zealand. The United States has never been a global power in squash, and Manek's attitude that day was that of the sophisticated townsman encountering the proverbial country bumpkin. The southpaw from Mumbai told himself that he was not going to lose to an American. He went out and chopped Callis up in four games, the final one an emphatic 9–0 whitewash.

But city ways can be learned if you are hungry and determined. Callis improved. He entered Princeton, one of the top collegiate programs, and eight days ago, at our Valentine's Day dual match, he surprised Manek with a four-game victory. Callis frittered away a 7–5 lead in the first game, losing 9–7. In the second he was down 8–5 but smacked some stunning drop shots to win 10–8. He took the third easily and held off Manek in the fourth 10–9. It was a close battle, and if you had seen nothing more than the cold agate of the score in a newspaper, you would think that Callis had done something remarkable.

Instead of being discouraged by the loss, Manek was just glad to be upright. He never attempted to diminish Callis's victory; he never made excuses, but he did have an excuse. He had gotten the flu earlier that week: coughing, runny nose, high fever. He not only missed practices but didn't leave his room for a couple of days. On the Saturday morning of the dual match, he had dragged himself out of bed, light-headedly tossed some squash gear strewn around his room into a bag, and hauled himself to the courts. He hit a few balls and got on the bus, miserable and drained. He drank Pedialyte the whole way down to New Jersey, trying to get hydrated. In Princeton, he ate his first meal in a week, felt a bit better, but after the second game, he knew he had little chance against Callis. The pace was too fast. Callis made him twist and reverse directions, and Manek, running a second behind the action, couldn't catch his breath.

Considering all that, Manek was sanguine about their rematch. He trained very hard all week, got all the toxins out, and recovered his strength. Like many Indian squash players, he had a highwayman spirit. He was willing to gamble, take risks, put on a show. He thrilled at the unexpected. He had a smooth swing and great finishing ability and seemed able to switch to a new level of precise length whenever a match tightened. But his life had to be set: he needed his fitness, he needed his health, he needed his courses to be going well, and he needed everything to be solid with his latest girlfriend. If a piece of the puzzle was out of place, he would get skittish.

Before today's match, I tell him he has to go out strong, that he has endured incredible hardship of playing so high on national championship teams. I tell him to be patient, to accumulate advantages and then shoot. I also asked him to crack his backhand crosscourt to keep Callis from slapping forehands into the front wall nick. He nods and goes out and plays adroitly but without passion. Both games go into a tiebreaker. Callis wins the first and has a game point in the second, up 8–6. Manek goes on a tremendous spurt, winning the next six points to get out of danger—and avoiding a 2–0 deficit, which would have been hard to recover from (especially in light of how he ends up performing in the third).

But Manek is struggling. If Callis hadn't tinned a couple of balls, the second game would have been his, too. Manek is not dictating the play, but rather responding to Callis's brilliant strategy. He is an animal in a cage, unable to get out and run free. I have miscoached him. Callahan has gotten Callis to play at half speed, lifting balls crosscourt, lobbing—anything to get it wide and deep—and then attacking. His attack is particularly tough: he hits a straight drop to Manek's forehand and then volleys Manek's response (usually a cross-court) with a crushing forehand. Callis is winning too many points with his straight drop-and-volley, one-two combination. Rather than using Manek's strengths, I have neutralized him by asking him to do things he shouldn't be doing. He should be shooting first. If you own a shotgun, why leave it in the closet?

After the second game, I sit down with Manek outside the court. I start to give him some Gatorade. "I can't drink it, Coach." He is too nervous to take a sip. I tell Manek to get out there and attack early, to speed up the pace and not be defensive.

Instead, he disintegrates. Callis wins the third game 9–0. It takes more than seven minutes, so it isn't embarrassingly quick, and Manek wins four of the seventeen rallies. But he's down 2–1 and lucky to still be out there.

Squash is not a vegetable. Boys at an English prep school called Harrow invented it in the 1850s. It arrived unceremoniously in the United States in 1884, when a master at St. Paul's School in Concord, New Hampshire, relying on a college classmate who had played this new game at Harrow, built four open-air squash courts. The game took hold first in Philadelphia, where U.S. Squash, the governing association, was founded in 1904. Intercollegiate squash began in 1923, when Harvard played Yale. A country-club sport primarily for the nation's elite, squash began to reach the masses in the 1970s, when commercial clubs sprang up. Today, more than a quarter of a million

Americans play squash every week. There are two dozen after-school youth enrichment squash programs, which spend a total of ten million dollars annually and reach more than five thousand underserved kids. More than sixty schools from around the country compete in the men's collegiate nationals. Pro tournaments are staged on portable glass courts in iconic locations like Grand Central Terminal in New York and Millennium Park in Chicago.

It is a tough game. The court is cramped, slightly smaller than a racquetball court, thirty-two feet long by twenty-one feet wide. (Until the 1990s, American squash was played in a court eighteen and a half feet wide, using a bulleting fast ball; the old American game was colloquially called hardball, and the international game, which is now standard, was called softball.) Each match is best of five games, and each game goes to nine points; if you reach 8–8, then there is a tiebreaker of one or two points (the player who first reaches 8 gets to decide; the final score 10–8 or 10–9 if he chooses "set two" and 9–8 if he chooses "set one.")

A key part of the scoring is that only the server can score points, and to get the serve you first have to win a rally. Thus, games can go on and on; players can alternate serves without scoring a point—sort of the way volleyball used to be. This kind of scoring is usually called hand-in, hand-out, or hi-ho (the person about to serve is said to be hand-in, while the receiver is hand-out), and has a built-in defensive mechanism. You can be down, say, 7–2, but stay in the match by winning the rally every time your opponent is serving. It's a lot easier, when you are losing badly, to win half the rallies rather than all the rallies.

Otherwise, squash is simple: keep the ball from bouncing twice on the floor and keep it in the court. (Unlike tennis, if the squash ball hits a line, it is out.) The ball must hit the front wall once, and can hit the floor only once. However, it can hit any number of the other walls—but not the ceiling—before or after being struck by the racquet. On the front wall, there is a nineteen-inch-high line; all balls must hit the front wall above that line. Below the line is the tin, usually a sheet of metal that makes a distinctive sound when struck by the ball. The racquet is the same length as a tennis racquet but has a smaller head and thinner neck and weighs about the same as a badminton racquet. The ball is made of rubber, and is squishier, smaller, and less bouncy than a tennis ball.

The essence of squash is to dominate the center of the court without impeding an opponent's access to the ball. When a player is in the way during a rally, the opponent can ask for a "let" and they replay the point; if the opponent had an opportunity to make a winning shot but for the first player's obstruction, then he is awarded a "stroke" rather than a let and wins the point. Skillful players strike the ball so as to keep it close to the side walls. A well-placed shot can hug the side wall or slam into the "nick," squash lingo for the seam where the side wall meets the floor. A shot hit into the nick usually rolls out onto the floor and is unplayable. The service boxes on the floor form a T, which is the power position on the court, a kind of line of scrimmage. Players basically compete to dominate the T during a match, and the player who controls the T, who pushes his opponent to the corners, generally wins the point.

It is an incredibly aerobic, fast-paced sport. Herbert Warren Wind, the great golf writer, loved the game, having picked it up at Yale. He was particularly enamored with the legendary Khan family from Pakistan, as he wrote in the *New Yorker*: "Indeed, watching the two Khans go at each other in a prolonged rally for a big point in a tight match is something like watching the speeded-up film of an old Keystone Cops sequence, the two wraiths darting in and out of the corners and making a succession of acrobatic 'gets,' each one more fantastic than the one before, as the tempo of their movements and their strokes keeps mounting until the action becomes almost a blur. I have seen few things in sport that can compare to it for sheer velocity and excitement."

Scoring-wise, the Trinity versus Princeton final has a historic side to it, for it will be the last time an intercollegiate dual match uses the nine-point hi-ho scoring. The collegiate coaching fraternity has voted to switch the following fall to eleven-point scoring—it is a point-a-rally, or PAR, system that the pros adopted a few years ago to make their tournaments more accessible and spectator-friendly and shorter (better for television). In an effort to make the game uniform (part of squash's vain campaign to get into the Olympics), every level of the game worldwide has switched to the eleven-point PAR scoring. Today we will depend on the capacity with hi-ho scoring for comebacks: our players will steady the ship, rally by rally, taking risks only when serving, and slowly grind out rallies when receiving.

You start a sport for no reason but happiness. The first time you do it might be by chance at a playground or a schoolyard or it might be orchestrated by a parent, but those initial moments are inevitably unscripted. You play for a couple of minutes. You hit or kick or toss a ball or wobble on your skates or jump in the air. It's fun. There's nothing more, no streaks, no requirements, no score.

Your parents, excited about your having an interest, latch on to this passing fancy. Happiness is a great thing; they want you to have more. They get involved. They pay for clinics, a private lesson, a first tournament. You improve. You need a more competitive pond in which to swim. You get more coaching, more tournaments, summer camps, weekend clinics. You get more gear, more posters, more books. At some point, there is a subtle change. You notice the involvement of others. You discover that the sport is important—to your parents, to your classmates, to your friends. You begin to see yourself differently. For each of my players, there was a moment when they viewed themselves not as someone who played squash but as a *squash player.*

Billie Jean King once spoke to me about the roots of her success. Her father, a fireman, had a second job, and her mother worked as a receptionist at a medical center and sold Avon and Tupperware products, so they could afford to pay for her early tennis lessons. From the beginning her parents showed her that they valued her tennis career and were extremely dedicated to ensuring her success. But they also had their own lives and careers, as well as a younger son, Randy (who went on to play baseball in the majors). Billie Jean had to save her own money from chores to buy her first racquet. Her tennis tournaments were not all-consuming. Her mother and father didn't attend her practices and more often than not were absent from her matches.

Moreover, she did not have a real coach in these early years: until they linked up with Alice Marble when Billie Jean was fifteen, they made do with the instruction at the Long Beach city recreation department. The combination of guiding, not pushing, parents and not having a coach led Billie Jean to take ownership of her sport. She had to rely on herself to learn the game. She had full responsibility for her performance and behavior. She was making the ultimate decisions about what she was doing and why.

It doesn't matter what the game is; ownership is possible. A world-famous oboe teacher I know in New York has a rule about the students he teaches: they must find their own way to the studio where he gives lessons. After the first initial visit, the parents are not allowed to drive or escort the child. The child has to come unattended. A friend of mine had to bike three miles each way to her daily field hockey practice, even in the rain or snow. When she climbed Mt. Everest years later, she finally understood what it meant to push herself rather than have someone push her.

A parent must hold on to their child with a loving, open hand, not a clenched fist. The metaphor I like is that it's the parents' job to put gas in the car and teach the child to drive, but then they have to let the child drive himself, alone, thinking and reacting for himself. The child can never simultaneously reach his potential and be happy if the parent is driving the car.

Manek is a senior, a captain of the team, tall, sinewy, and long-limbed. He has matinee-idol looks—one of his nicknames is GQ—which are completed by his luminescent smile, broad shoulders, earring, and thick, wavy hair. Sometimes he talks about trying to break into the Bollywood film industry in his native Mumbai, India, or into the music industry, as he is minoring in music. He is a stage-door lion. The female fans at Trinity flock to his side after matches and at parties. Manek is often the star disc jockey at fraternity parties and has even opened for visiting rock bands. Yet Manek has tried for four years to own his squash.

Manek grew up obsessed, like most Indian boys, with cricket. He was an all-rounder: he bowled (medium-fast pace, often tricky in a lefty), batted, and even kept wicket, all at a first-class standard. His idol was the slashing leader of the Indian national team, Sachin Tendulkar, regarded as the best batsman in the world. Manek lived with his parents, paternal grandparents, and sister. His father ran the family business of exporting textiles from southern India to Europe, and sport was the common weekend activity. They played at the Bombay Gymkhana. Once, the club hosted a professional men's squash tournament, and Manek, thrilled by the artistry, told his father, "I want to play squash," and had his first lesson. He was eleven.

After playing for a couple of years, he got serious. Very few teenagers in India took more than one sport seriously. The three-sport high-school athlete was virtually unknown. He had to drop cricket and devote himself entirely to squash. Giving up his beloved club, he moved to the Cricket Club of India. The CCI was the old heart of Indian squash. The country's first great player, Abdul Bari, was a pro there before and after Partition—Bari reached the finals of the British Open in 1950. In the 1960s, Anil Nayar came out of the CCI, winning both the national men's and junior's titles in the same year as well as the Drysdale Cup for taking the British Junior Open title. The best young squash player in the world, Nayer went on to star at Harvard and capture the U.S. national title twice. Manek was very good at a very young age. He was ranked in the top four of his age group each year and once made it to the finals of the under-nineteen nationals. He trained twice a day, at seven in the morning before school and in the late afternoon. He was in the newspapers and on television. He represented India. His identity was Manek the squash player rather than Manek, a guy who likes movies, follows cricket, and oh, by the way, plays squash a lot.

Because of a quirk in league rules, I had a precious opportunity each year to instill a sense of ownership in players like Manek. The guys came to campus in late August, with classes starting right after Labor Day. Yet the New England Small College Athletic Conference (NESCAC) decreed that I could not coach until the first of November. So we had two full months—more than a third of our season— during which the boys were on their own. The rules forbade me to hold practices or to get on court with them.

This period became a nine-week course in ownership development. The team, led by the captains, devised the weekly schedule. I didn't approve it or consult with them about it. They figured it out by themselves and told me what they were doing. They set their boundaries and agendas. They put in their time. They did off-court training runs, biweekly sessions in the weight room, Friday sprints on the track. They drilled. They practiced. They hit alone. They did not play matches or tournaments. They did not calculate or measure or delineate. Why are you playing this sport? This was a question many of my players had never been asked. I talked about the day-to-day enjoyment of stretching the body, challenging the mind, acquiring new skills, and improving as a person. I always said that I couldn't care less about the short-lived result of beating some rival player or team. It was not about some streak. It was about living a life to the fullest.

I was not absent. My office was right near the courts (it used to be a court itself), so I poked my head out and licitly chit-chatted with the guys as they rummaged in their bags or tied their shoes. They came in for impromptu discussions, in little groups or alone. I got to know them as individuals, not as my players. I let them lead. I was not worried about their blowing off squash. They tended to be high-achieving, type A perfectionists and were unable to just go through the motions. It was a question of trust and communication. If they wanted to win, they would have to motivate themselves. At crunch time, the team that played for a coach would fail.

Amid the sweaty runs and hours on court, the team gelled. They fell in love with one another and developed a sense of team, and they fell in love with their sport and rekindled a passion for what had become

a profession. I even insisted that the little ritual of freshman initiation—
which most teams performed at the start of the season—come after
the season-ending banquet in the spring, weeks after our final dual
match. I didn't want anything to disrupt the good vibes at the start of
the season.

After the third game, with his 2–1 lead, Callis looks confident. Bob
Callahan has told him exactly what he should do, and his success
early in the match has buoyed his spirits. Conversely, Manek comes
off court looking confused and disorganized. He has just lost a game
at love and is down 2–1. He sits in a folding metal chair in the low
hallway behind the courts. He towels off the sweat. His breath is shal-
low. I say, "Okay, this is like last year against Harvard in the semis,
when Niko hit you. You've got to wake up again." He gives me a short,
imperceptible sigh.

To play for yourself is one thing—it is so specific. To play for your
country is another—it is too abstract. But to play for your peers is real
pressure, and he is flailing.

Manek had been a raw, blue-chip recruit, still seventeen. In 2006
he flew to New York from Mumbai with Sahil Vora, his best friend's
older brother. Sahil was a junior at Trinity and returning to campus
after a couple of weeks' holiday. When they left JFK, they passed a
Toys"R"Us. Sahil said, "You go there," pointing to the store, "and do
all your shopping." It took a second before Manek realized Sahil was
joking.

He had a hard time adapting to school. He played number 6 or
number 7 on the team, going 14–2, but things that came naturally to
the other students—such as the conveyor belt in the lunchroom where
you placed your tray—were exasperatingly foreign to Manek, who had
never been to America before and was still quite young. About a week
after his matriculation, we played at a high-end private club in New
York. After playing, we all shed our clothes and tromped into the giant
Turkish bath steam room with just towels wrapped around our waists.
Manek had never been in a steam room. He had scraped his knee during

the match and had a bandage on his leg. I said to him, "Manek, you can take that off," pointing to his leg. He misunderstood me, and looking around for a second, he dropped his towel to the floor. A gale of laughter swept over the steam room and he quickly pulled his towel back around his waist.

In some circles Manek had been considered high-strung as a junior, proud, defiant and prone to petulant behavior. When he arrived at Trinity, one of his first questions was, "When are the intercollegiates?" He didn't understand the team aspect; he had never been on a team for longer than a couple of weeks. He had heard about the Trinity dynasty from Sahil and other Trinity players who had come from Mumbai—the Juneja twins, Rohan Bhappu and Akhil Behl—but he didn't grasp the scale and scope until a month after his arrival.

In his first season, his hallmate and fellow freshman Gustav Detter had miraculously saved a couple of match points in a close 5–4 dual-match victory over Princeton. A demimonde of half-wild schoolmates hugged and shouted for hours after the match. When Manek and Goose finally arrived back at their dormitory, it was after one in the morning. They got to their hallway and stopped. A couple of dozen classmates were dancing in the halls, which were festooned with dozens of congratulatory posters, notes, streamers, balloons. An enormous Swedish flag covered Goose's door. The classmates dragged the boys out to a fraternity. No one got to sleep before dawn. When they got up, Manek and Goose headed to a late breakfast at Mather Hall. They walked into the cafeteria and the entire room rose and gave them a raucously loud standing ovation. Manek realized what the program meant to the campus, that this was like the national cricket team in India, only in microcosm.

Manek's defining moment had been in the 2008 semifinals of the nationals. In our dual match against Harvard, he had lost the first game to Niko Hrdy, a physical, bruising Cantabrigian. Niko had been playing number 5 two weeks before and had been beaten by our number 5 in three games. Now it looked like Manek, at number 3, couldn't take him. After the first game, Manek slumped on a chair.

He complained about the court—some of the older players had told him how they hated the new four-wall glass-court at Harvard, and he had absorbed the negativity—and I backed off. In leading, you have to know when to force the issue and when to withdraw. It was the end of a long season, and Manek was evidently scraping the bottom of his barrel. He had no energy left to fight for a match he felt he should win easily. I walked away.

Tied with Niko at 7 all in the second, Manek leaned in after hitting a drive, and Niko smacked him in the head with a follow-through. It all happened in a flash, and it was hard to see where the racquet caught him—in his head or his shoulder?

With a convulsive yip, Manek went down in a heap, instantly felled, not moving. Manek's sister, Shefali, rushed into the court. A medical school student, she was attending her first college squash match. She shouted, "He's been knocked out." As she was saying this, Manek opened his eyes. We crowded around him, talking to him, asking what hurt. He was seeing stars, a bit of blood pooled in his mouth, and a welt was purpling on his right cheekbone. But he was soon breathing easily. We walked him off the court. He sat on his chair and drank some water. Niko came over and asked if the match was going to continue. Manek said, "Yeah, sure."

"I am asking for a stroke, then."

Manek looked at me as if this was a joke. We were so dumbfounded at Niko's insolence that for a couple of seconds no one said a word. I then turned to Manek and said very quietly and slowly, biting off each word, "Go get him."

He summoned a surprising reserve of inner strength and thrashed Niko. The ball zigzagged all over the court, always exactly where Manek wanted and always out of Niko's reach. The points were short and brutally, openly one-sided. Manek blew through the rest of the second game and then the next two 9–2, 9–2.

Today against Princeton, Manek doesn't have the luxury of a wake-up call coming in the form of a racquet smacked on his face. Reggie

Schonborn, our assistant coach, tells him, "Make this an athletic contest. Go out and have some fun. You're the better athlete." Then we briefly talk tactics. Callis is an attacking player, so we go over the need to attack more, put him on the defensive, to upset his rhythm. We don't seem to be getting anywhere.

After ten seconds of silence, I start again. "Listen, the match is probably over. But at least lose while being Manek. You aren't playing like Manek Mathur. Samurai, Manek. Samurai." Samurai is a code word created by James Montano for Manek to stop worrying about results, about the streak, about the score. Samurai warriors in ancient Japan would fight freely once they accepted defeat. They were tranquil when faced with inevitable defeat. Manek is going to lose. Callis is starkly outplaying him; there is no doubt. But relieved of the burden of winning, Manek can now play with freedom in this final game. He can play his game. He simply has to change the way he feels about what is happening.

There are always outside forces that crowd your mind: your opponent's backhand volley, the referee, the ache of your hamstring, the looming assignment, your girlfriend's anger. There is only one thing that you have total control over: the way you feel. The score is the score. You can't change it. But you do get to decide how you feel about it. You get to decide how you will react not only to the match while it is happening but also before and after, how the victory or defeat will color your day and your life.

I always told the boys before the first big dual match of each season: "In ten years you will not remember the score of each of your games against Yale. I know it sounds crazy, but you won't. You will remember how you felt."

I told them about my first big squash match. It was a professional squash doubles tournament at the posh Buffalo Tennis & Squash Club in 1987. It was a big deal. There was a black-tie dinner-dance at the Knox estate hosted by Seymour Knox, a squash player who owned the Buffalo Sabres. The Buffalo newspapers covered the event with reporters and cameramen and even printed betting odds. Mine were twenty to one against. My partner and two opponents were all insiders who had grown up in this scene. I was in way over my head, on and off the court. Twenty to one was generous.

We were playing in a refrigerator. The ball died in the icy front of the court. We won the first game, stealing it in overtime. In the second, our opponents started to pepper me with blistering drives and sneaky drop shots. Out of my element, I cracked balls into the tin. I heard the crowd and felt small and alone out on the wide white expanse of the court. We lost the game 15–4. In the third I recovered a little and we stretched them to overtime, but again my inexperience showed and I made a couple of unforced errors during the crucial final points.

We left the court for the break after the third game. As I toweled the sweat off my face, my partner stomped up and down the hallway, furious at losing the game. "I should put sweats on," he blurted out. "I'll bring a chair on the court and have lunch. I'm not seeing a single ball. They're hitting everything at you. I don't know whether you're going to hit the ball on the strings or the frame or where it's going."

As he was venting, I saw a little boy playing in the dim winter light of the hallway. It was Clive Caldwell's son, John. Clive was a leading squash pro; his son was born with severe mental and physical handicaps. He was sitting on the floor pushing a tennis ball. The ball rolled to the wall and came back to him. John was smiling. He was happy.

I said, "See, Clive's son there? We're out there doing something we love and getting acclaim, and this is a big deal, the quarters of a big tournament—and yet we're feeling sorry for ourselves. Can you imagine what this kid would give to have this experience?"

We went back in and the rest of the match was like a dance. The mood was different. We were still fighting hard and willing every point to go our way, but somehow we were free. Our perspective had changed. The court was warm with our energies. I saw the ball clearly. I moved in a calm, easy rhythm. My shots sometimes went for winners, and sometimes our opponents got to them and hit something equally brilliant. We won the fourth game. In the fifth and deciding game, each point slid past in slow motion. We danced into another tiebreaker. They managed to get away and win by two points.

Afterward, I was elated. We hugged each other. The crowd roared with cheers and applause. They had witnessed something very special: four guys playing at a peak of performance. We had lost, but at that moment it did not matter. I felt more alive than I had after any victory in my life. Looking back I am glad this watershed moment came in defeat. I learned to not be afraid of losing, to not fear defeat or victory. In those fourth and fifth games I learned about perspective. I learned not to fight or flee in the face of pressure but to revel in it. I learned that it was only a question of changing how I felt. On that cold Saturday in Buffalo, I learned to lose.

For years, I had on my wall a 1983 newspaper clipping about Julius Erving, the great Philadelphia 76er. Dr. J had been close to winning the NBA title, going down to the Lakers in six games in the 1980 finals (the series that featured his famous baseline drive in game four) and then suffering a couple of stupendously bitter defeats to the Boston Celtics. Something he said just months before he finally got his championship was the essence of learning to lose: "The pain that was suffered, the feeling of having backs turned on us, that's still with this team. But the positive side is carried with us, too. We have the scars, but we also have the glue. I don't feel incomplete or inadequate in any way because I haven't won an NBA championship. I don't lie awake and think about it. I know I've given my best to the public, and the rest is really out of my hands. I can accept that."

Another player in the same situation might be bitter and resentful. It's a choice, in the end. A few years ago, after the breakup of my second marriage, I went to a tattoo parlor in East Hartford. I flipped through some of the sample binders and, finding the perfect design, had the man ink it on my upper back between my shoulder blades. It was the Chinese symbol meaning "choose happiness." Both words were equally important.

As Manek warms up for the fourth game, I see he has his balance back. He is innately a positive person. Confident, he pops his shoulders down from his neck, the tension flowing away. He is looser. His head is up while he waits for the ball during the warm-up, and when he gets it, he's blistering it down the wall. I can see that although he's down 2–1, this might not be the end. He looks up at his mother in the gallery and smiles. Arati has been in town all week. It is her first visit to see her son. The whole match, she holds my fiancée Julia's hand. At this moment she is much more nervous than her son.

The odd thing, Manek later tells me, is that he begins to have random flashbacks during points. Little pictures jump up, and he thinks about what one of his earliest coaches in India used to say: that if you work hard, it will come back to you.

Manek grinds it out. He doesn't play perfectly, but he plays happily. He doesn't get discouraged when he loses a point or overly elated when he wins one. His grinding slowly overwhelms Callis. The points are long, then staccato short, then long again. Callis is increasingly tired. He had a brutal match yesterday, coming back from a 2–1 deficit to beat Rochester's Hameed Ahmed in five. The match had lasted an hour and forty minutes, and it's around the eighty-minute mark today when he begins to fade. The last two games take just a dozen minutes.

The fourth game is punctuated by a couple of outstanding points, in which Manek performs miracles: He digs out balls that he has no business touching. His legs splay, his left arm elongates, and he keeps the ball in play. The first one, at 2–1, is like a nail in Callis's coffin. After a series of great gets, Manek slashes a clean winner past Callis.

In the fifth, Callis starts out strong and gets it to 2–2, but then he wilts. He wins just two more rallies in the match. At 7–2, Manek is close to the front wall, far out of position. Callis hits a screaming ball. Manek blindly flails at it, all reflex, and manages to hit it for a winner. It is astonishing. "Great hands," I murmur. Only a relaxed player can pull off such a trick.

Manek wins the match. He and Callis hug. He then windmills

both his arms, exhorting the crowd, and then tugs at the TRINITY emblazoned on the front of his shirt. He comes off the court, tears in his eyes, and presses his sweaty torso against mine in a bear hug. I don't say anything. This is his last match ever for the team. I want to let him savor it.

In the tunnel by the court, he slumps on his chair and his arms envelop his head. Baset Ashfaq, our number 1 player, who's six feet five and 220 pounds, comes barreling down the tunnel looking for someone to encourage. He sees Manek crumpled in his chair. He starts screaming, "C'mon, GQ, you have to push forward! You have to attack! You can't lose to this guy!"

Manek lets him go for a while and then interrupts. "B, it's over."

"It's over?" Baset asks. "Don't say it's over. C'mon, dude, you're there, you can do it."

"It's over."

"It's two all, right?"

"No, no, It's over. I won."

"Dude, you're kidding."

"No, I won, nine–two in the fifth. It's over."

Baset gives him a pat on the shoulders and sheepishly retreats down the tunnel, in search of another teammate in need of inspiration. Manek buries his head in his towel again. It's over.

CHAPTER TWO

The Power of Now: Supreet

College squash was a full-time occupation for my players. Thirty-four years ago, when I joined the intercollegiate coaching ranks, kids played two or even three sports in college. As late as the mid-1980s, for instance, Greg Zaff, at Williams, was an All American in both tennis and squash. Training for squash back then amounted to an occasional sprint around a track or a gallop up the steps of a stadium—no weights, no Nautilus, no nutritionists, no star drills, no psychologists, no marathon sessions on the stationary bicycle or treadmill. A squash player got on court around Thanksgiving and got off a couple of weeks before St. Patrick's Day. Even if they wanted to play in the summer, they couldn't: squash courts were not air-conditioned, and in the heat and humidity the hard, pelletlike ball bounced too high, and the walls sweated. The courts were always empty half the year.

Now, they played all year round. They took a break after the season ended, but then squash was such an integral part of their routine—a daily ritual like a morning cup of coffee—that inevitably an invisible magnet yanked them back to the courts. The squash facility—the courts, the bleachers, my office—was their main hangout spot. They studied here. They talked on the phone or texted or Facebooked here. Often a fun doubles game would break out. They spent the spring hitting informally with teammates and in a couple of tournaments, as well as working on deep, off-court training; in the summer, they went overseas to play more tournaments or trained with top coaches and players in exotic locales, or they worked at one of the many American summer squash camps. Squash was not a pastime in between soccer and tennis. A sizable minority of my players went on to make a career in the game, either as teaching pros at local clubs or as pros on the world tour, but for many this was the climax of a long athletic journey.

When a child begins a sport, the ratio of practice to competition is about 30 percent to 70 percent; as the child matures in the sport, that ratio is slowly flipped until at the elite levels it reaches 99 to 1. The growth of a player depends largely on managing that movement away from regular competition toward practice—away from the destination and toward the journey. The match happens every day, then once a week or once a month; for some Olympians, it's really once every four years. Practice, on the other hand, happens almost every day. The opportunity for learning—the teachable moment—is at practice, not matches.

Since my players get on court more than two hundred days a year, I have to ensure that my official practices brim with meaning. Practices tend to blend together. I fight this as hard as I fight anything. Under my regime, every day is different, every week is different. Consistency is the hobgoblin of little coaching minds. I start practice at different times and run them at different lengths: we'll have a Sunday morning training run and no practice on Monday, a three-hour session on Tuesday afternoon and a fifty-minute burst on Wednesday evening. I hold some practices first thing in the morning, so that the players will absorb my tenet that squash practice is a crucial part of their schedule, not some frivolous hobby tacked on at the end of the day.

I make practice the point of Trinity Squash. We travel toward a distant, exciting place called a national championship, and we use the date on the calendar—in 2009, it was February 22—as a lodestar as we move through the year. But we focus on the modest piece of earth in front of us. It's like building a railroad line. You survey the land. You sketch a blueprint. You spread out the maps. You draw a line from point A to point B. You look at the mountains you have to build over or blast through, the rivers you have to bridge. And then you lay down the track.

Practice can be boring and difficult. No one gets a trophy for practice. Acquiring skills is tedious. Grooving a shot—creating muscle memory—is frighteningly dull. But muscle memory is the carbon of sports, the element that has the highest melting point on the periodic table. It always stays solid, even in the cauldron of a close match. I remember one afternoon when I was a child that our yellow rotary telephone wasn't working and a workman was standing in our kitchen, fiddling with it. I watched from a stool. He put the phone to his ear and without looking dialed a long-distance number to test it. I was amazed—he did this so often that he could find the numbers from memory.

Matches are easy. My boys enthusiastically pour their energy into competition. It's natural. They live in a binge-and-bust cycle. They pull all-nighters to write papers. They drive nine hours to see a girl-friend for ninety minutes. They eat breakfast at two in the afternoon. But this is not how life is for an adult. In the real world—no matter what the field is—there are daily performances: emails to respond to, schedules to follow, meetings to take, calls to make, memos to write, managers to answer, staff to supervise, children to feed, food to buy, dishes to wash. No one hands out medals when you drop the kids off at school or complete a report. We have practice at nine in the morning for the same reason you have a big meeting at that time. There is no off-season in life. It's about doing the right thing when there's no audience. Practice is not a dress rehearsal but an actual performance. It teaches you how to live.

John Wooden, the basketball coach at UCLA, spent more time planning each practice than the practice actually took, in an effort to make each one interesting and relevant. I work harder than the players, not physically during practice, but before and after practice: planning, plotting, reviewing video, and talking individually. I monitor the ministeps, the behind-the-scenes work that leads to a beautiful, sturdy, functional, seamless track appearing in the wilderness.

At practice I treat my players like seedlings, juvenile plants bending toward the sun. I do not cut them down. I do not worry if all the skills are not meshing, if their backhand crosscourt drops look awkward or if their forehand volley boasts (an advanced two-wall shot) fail almost every time. I encourage experimentation. I want failure. I used to say that if everything were perfect, something would be wrong. You want uncertainty, you need doubt, you demand obstacles. You never achieve perfection, and you don't want to. Perfect is the enemy of good, and good is good. The things kids want are approval, joy, and success; the thing kids need is the freedom to fail. Practice is the perfect place to learn how to not be perfect. To execute your shot under pressure, you need to know the boundaries. You need to know how far you can go, so you can pull back and play within your margin of error.

They are still students. They are trying to learn. Someday they'll be able to fly down the track faster, but they can't do that right now. Just keep chugging, I tell them. The scenery will still flow past. When girlfriends or exams trouble them, I say that the squash court should be a refuge; the four walls can be a safe house where they don't have to think about the outside world. It's a place where they can fail.

One trick I have is to take advantage of their imaginations. College kids, more than any other segment of our population, are rife with desire. They want and anticipate. They hum with passion. To harness that overactive imagination, I use visualization. A lot of coaches screen video for match play. I do it for practice. I started this when I was coaching gymnastics at West Point. We'd watch film for hours a day, first watching ourselves and then watching the Japanese national team, which was the best in the world at the time. Little by little the two images would meld in the mind's eye. So at each practice at Trinity, each player digs into the enormous cache of tapes I hoard: videos of them solo practicing, of them doing drills, of every match they've played. They see body language, reactions to winning or losing a point, footwork, racquet preparation, and tendencies. But just as important, I always have them watch five minutes of a pro player, someone that has the same style. This is my version of the Japanese national team. They can watch the pro and visualize themselves playing calmly, deceptively, brilliantly.

They have to work their butts off. There's a saying I picked up at West Point: It is really hard to quit the first time, not so tough the second time, and by the third time it becomes a habit. If they took a shortcut in practice, then they might try one in a match. Every year, players ask me to postpone a challenge match (an intrasquad contest that helps sort out our ladder): they have a niggling injury, a cold, or a looming term paper. I tell them: You don't get to reschedule life's challenge matches. In the real world, you often have to produce when you do not want to. You go to work with a cold because you have a big presentation and can't call in sick. You have to complete that project, hand in the contract, and feed that baby. You accept that you are at 50 percent of your normal self and learn how to get 100 percent out of that 50 percent. You can't reschedule life.

How do you focus players on the immediate rather than long term? The power of now. I demand each player be fully invested in each practice and in each part of practice. I ask them to give full attention to this time we're spending together. For our seventy minutes together: no texting, no gossiping, no wandering off, no goofing around. It's a cliché, but I ask them to treat each day as if it were the last day of their lives, to consume every second as if it were water and they were dying of thirst. Trinity Squash is about doing *everything* like it means everything.

When I was coaching squash and tennis at West Point, I had a kid named George Geczy. An army brat, the son of a high-ranking officer, he was a special kid, with a concentrated stare and an acetylene voice. He was not a great tennis player; when God was handing out tennis skills, George was in the men's room. In the winter of freshman year, he got knocked out during a boxing class, and X-rays revealed a brain tumor. It was lucky that he had gotten knocked out; otherwise they would have never discovered the tumor. Doctors operated on him that night. He recovered enough to travel to Germany, where his father was stationed. Because of residual damage from the tumor, the doctors said, he would have trouble walking for the rest of his life.

The following September, George came back to West Point. He walked with a cane. He forgot names. He did pushups agonizingly slowly. For a second time, he went through all the plebe-year hazing. In the spring he came out for the tennis team. He couldn't run, he couldn't walk. There was no way he could hit a tennis ball.

But George was driven. I couldn't say no and kick him off the team. I remembered how, in my freshman year of college, I had appeared at Springfield College after a couple of years of gymnastics training as a schoolboy on the weekends. Springfield had a rich tradition in gymnastics. Frank Wolcott had run Springfield's program since 1955, and by the time I arrived on campus in the fall of 1970, he was firmly entrenched as one of the nation's great gymnastic coaches—so great that he rightly judged my abilities and cut me after I tried out as a walk-on. He kindly said I could try out the next year. I refused to listen. "You'll have to call security every day, because I intend to keep coming," I told him. "I'm going to make the team." Wolcott agreed to name me the "manager" of the team and let me attend practice. By the end of the season, I had made varsity.

In the same vein, I named George manager and assistant coach, assigning jobs like collecting towels and carrying the ball hoppers. In his sophomore year, he threw away the cane and was able to get on the court, so I asked him to feed balls to players. Then he became a hitting partner for the junior-varsity guys, and then a doubles partner when someone was late. George came to every practice. He lifted weights. He hit hundreds of balls. He worked relentlessly. In his junior year, he played doubles in a couple of junior-varsity matches at the beginning of the season, and by the end of it, he was at the top of the JV. The team elected him captain for his senior year, and he played on the varsity.

Today is the present. They call it the present because it is a gift. You have to open up the gift and use it.

On court 2 Supreet Singh, our number 6, is enduring a titanic match with Hesham El Halaby.

Nothing could sledgehammer a player more than appearing on court at the start of a dual match, especially this one. The crowd is so pumped up that the first few points of Supreet's match are as deafening as the roar at a Super Bowl kickoff. After each point, kids yell.

"He's flustered." I'm thinking, *Hey, they've played six points; he can't possibly be flustered yet.*

It's not just Princeton fans. For Trinity Squash, the Sunday of the nationals has become our program's annual homecoming, and usually about three or four dozen former players, wearing their championship rings, crowd the stands. They are sometimes a bit cocky, but even worse are the current undergraduates, who can get unruly and don't care. A horde of them loudly hoots at Princeton fans, griping about not being able to get into the gallery, hassling people with seats. I sweep them deep into the tunnel. "We are going to win this match," I scream at them, "and I don't want your horrible behavior to be what everyone remembers. One more inappropriate comment and I will escort all of you out of Jadwin." Later on, I actually kick out a Bantam fan who is berating the referee in a vicious way.

Meanwhile, Supreet loses the first game. In the second, he is up 8–6; he lets his lead slip away but calmly snags the game in the tiebreaker. At 9 all, he hooks a ball from deep in the right back corner crosscourt and it is just perfect. It nicks—catching that spot where the wall meets the floor—along the backhand side and Hesh is unable to play it. Eight days ago, he tumbled badly against Hesh, going down in three close but clear games. He is taller than Hesh, but Hesh is thicker, bigger, stronger, and Supreet is having a hard time getting around him.

After the second game, I remind him of his match against Harvard. In 2007, Supreet was a freshman, and soon after his arrival on campus he found himself at the heart of a bitter dual match against our archrivals. It was a messy day. Playing at Harvard had always been tough. There was their great history and, despite now playing in an entirely new squash facility, their courts still oozed tradition. Moreover, the Cambridge crowd was sometimes less than genteel. In our 1997 dual match (which we lost 7–2), the crowd started getting on Charlie Saunders, our number 4 player. He was down 2–1, 13–8, about to lose. It was momentarily silent, then a student harshly shouted: "You're fucking this up, like you've fucked up your whole life." Saunders didn't know the fan from Adam, but it unnerved him. Although it became a joke on the team, it still rankled everyone to remember the patronizing comment, which seemed like it could only have come from a Cantabrigian.

The Murr Center was a madhouse in 2007. About twelve hundred fans were there in face and body paint, holding up elaborately designed signs, and yelling at the top of their lungs. They were very aggressive. They shook empty plastic jars loaded with pennies. It was unreal: the noise, the swirling mob on the thousand-foot-long bleachers. We felt like we had stumbled into a nest of angry hornets and were running out of arms to swipe at them.

The refereeing was regrettable.* All of the players on both teams, with the voracious crowd right on top of them, were intimidated and once in a while gave questionable judgment calls to their teammates. In one match, Roosh Vora had a match point. His opponent asked for a let on a ball well out of reach. The referee, a Harvard player, gave him the let. They replayed the point. Again, the rally ended with a clear winner for Roosh, yet the Harvard player asked for another let, and his teammate gave it to him. The assistant coach at Harvard, a quiet, kind Pakistani named Mohammad Ayaz, then opened the door and said, "No let," and shook hands with Roosh, ending the match. It was unusual, to say the least, to have Ayaz, a coach, intercede in a match like that.

Harvard's ladder was also out of whack. This happened to all teams at one point or another, often in the early stages of a season, because

---

* Until the mid-1990s, the players on court refereed their own matches. No one adjudicated any calls. After a number of incidents, we adopted a new system in 1996: for even-numbered matches, the home teammate was referee, while the visiting teammate was "marker" and kept and called out the score; for odd-numbered matches, the roles were reversed. This meant that two players who had just spent an hour bashing each other had to sit side by side in the gallery and work together to manage a match. It was not as good as playing without a referee or having professional referees, but it did lend a do-unto-others balance to the dual matches.

of the unique variables of the challenge-match system. Here it led to a bizarre result: each of the nine matches was a 3–0 blowout. This was unprecedented in a dual match that ended up with a close 5–4 final score. With four victories for each team, it came down to Supreet, Trinity's freshman at number 7, playing in his first big dual match.

Supreet was as cool as ice. His opponent was Niko Hrdy, the bruiser who a year later would have that run-in with Manek. Hrdy fist-pumped after winning points and moaned like a horror-flick change-ling after losing them. Supreet was steady the whole match, oblivious to the tension. The first game was close. Supreet was down 7–2 but clawed his way back and won it. After the game, Supreet toweled himself off next to the court. None of us knew him that well. What was his psyche? Was he was one of those guys who need a full exposition on the game that just happened, or did he loathe advice and analysis? James Montano, our assistant coach and chief motivator, went over to him.

"Supreet, you know, it is four all. You've got to win."

"Okay, coach." He paused. "Then I will win," he said evenly.

He turned and walked away.

James came back. "What did he say?" I asked, worried that their conversation had been so short that Supreet was angry, that James had said something wrong.

"I told him it was four all. He said, 'Then I will win.'" We shook our heads. *Who was this guy?*

In the second game, Hrdy again went up, 7–3 this time, and again Supreet coolly pricked Hrdy's bubble with some long, wall-scraping drives. He was almost predatory out there, tracking the ball with a killer instinct. He won in three. It became a legendary line, repeated a thousand times: "Then I will win."

Jadwin is sui generis. Princeton opened its signature gymnasium in 1969 as a mother's lament: Stockwell Jadwin was a Princeton student who died in 1928 just after graduation in a car accident; when his mother passed away, in 1965, she donated twenty-seven million dollars to the university in his name. Adorned by a conical, scalloped roof, the gym somewhat resembles the Sydney Opera House. Herbert Warren Wind described it as "a Brobdingnagian armadillo." It is a huge facility, with five levels that house eight football fields' worth of floor space (about a quarter of a million square feet). Two floors below ground is a warren of tunnels, stairwells, and eleven squash courts, as well as the Zanfrini Room—the world's largest fencing room.

Forty years ago it was a state-of-the-art squash edifice; now most other schools' facilities have superseded it, in large part because of a technological advance that occurred just after Princeton built Jadwin: the glass wall. Every new squash court has a back wall made out of glass so that spectators can look through and watch from the same level as the players. Additionally, top-flight programs boast a show court with glass walls on the front and sides. At Trinity, we have eight glass-backed courts and two show courts with three glass walls. Jadwin's show court is its only glass-backed court. The gallery—the spectating space—is so cramped that Bob Callahan, Princeton's coach, resorts to ferrying around a stool to stand on. In forty years, the armadillo has sadly become archaic.

It gives Princeton a tremendous home-court advantage, though. The show court's gallery, where the number 1, 2, and 3 matches are being played, is almost entirely enclosed and sealed off, so with five hundred passionate people crammed into a space designed for half that number, it becomes a deafening, roaring pressure-cooker. For me, this is the loudest gallery I've ever heard. Moreover, for the number 4 through number 9 matches, the courts we use are two of the old ones. They are not glass-backed courts. The bleachers rise literally just above the back-wall line. Spectators are therefore perched on top of the court, with no wall to block the sound or to offer a psychological barrier. It is even more of a primal scene than the show court: a chanting mob right on top of the two gladiators.

Having split the first two games, Supreet and Hesh divvy up the next two, each winning one at 9–4. Supreet goes up 4–1 in the third and, with the little breathing space, starts to attack. Hesh, anxious to stem the tide, returns a serve to his forehand by hammering it into the front wall–side wall nick—he is going for a winner off the serve. It shows impatience or it shows boldness; the difference is only in whether it's successful. Supreet, in his usual postserve pattern of loping toward the center of the court, changes direction and hurls himself toward the front. He can't reach the ball and ends up sprawled on the court in a spread eagle. He quickly hops up, and for half a minute he and Hesh pace around the court. They first point to some sweat on the floor, and the referee, Meherji Madan, a professional hired up from Washington for the weekend, asks, "Can someone find me a towel, please?" so they can wipe off the sweat. "A towel, a towel," a couple of the Princeton kids say mockingly. Then Hesh notices a slight cut on Supreet's right knee and Madan orders Supreet to get it wrapped, as it is against the rules for a player to be bleeding on court.

The crowd splutters about him being a hemophiliac. About four minutes elapse. Supreet loses the momentum. He comes back on court and immediately tins a forehand volley. Gathering steam, Hesh wins the next eight straight points; Supreet doesn't even serve once. A river of sweat pours down the center of the back of Hesh's shirt.

In the fourth, Supreet cools him off. Hesh dashes to a 2–0 lead on some lucky shots. Twice Hesh comes over to tap him on the back, a universal sign of apology. The match has been played with pretty good sportsmanship and hardly any ticky-tacky fouls. Both men are calling balls down on themselves. Hesh then tins a couple of service returns. He stalls for time to catch his breath, cleaning his goggles with his shirt, drying his grip in his shirt, and bantering about strokes with Madan. With Supreet up 4–2, Hesh lightly nicks him on the face with his racquet. More delay. A minute later Hesh breaks a string on a racquet. Some more delay. Hesh is looking unhinged; he is tinning a lot of shots. Supreet, his rubbery legs allowing him to almost pogo-hop to the ball, runs it to 9–4.

It is 2–2 and now we head into the deciding fifth game. Supreet towels himself off and says that he is calm, but I can see the grip of tension. Unlike two years earlier at Harvard, he now is more aware of the stakes. He knows too much.

No one on our team understood the beauty and importance of practice more than Supreet. He spent three or four hours after practice grooving a shot. Three or four hours—that could be deadening. When most players did solo work, they had a tendency to get bored and resort to what they liked to do, which was usually what they did best. This reinforced the good parts of their game, but by avoiding the weaker areas, they made their game more lopsided. Supreet, I noticed, practiced with purpose.

He was a loner. Growing up in Mumbai, he was a Tae Kwon Do master as a child, earning a brown belt by the age of thirteen. His dad had him try golf, badminton, and Ping-Pong before Supreet went to a pro squash tournament, saw the great Jansher Khan play (Khan won a record eight World Opens), and begged to try squash. He started at a small, obscure squash club that had just one court. The floor was often slippery from humidity and dust, and only a handful of people ever played there during a given week. For two years, Supreet played alone. He taught himself the game, learning a little from his father but mostly from trial and error. It was how he developed his unusual grip, with his thumb and forefinger both high on his racquet—his father and he didn't know any better. After two years, his father connected with some golf buddies and got Supreet a playing membership at Otters, one of the leading squash clubs in Mumbai. Supreet remembers the date of his first practice at Otters, finally playing with other kids.

It still was not easy. He was short of money. His father had been an underground telephone line contractor, but suffered financial setbacks when Supreet was young and never fully recovered. Squash was a sacrifice. Supreet played with ratty sneakers and his father's old racquet and he sometimes glued broken balls back together.

He spent two years on scholarship at the Siemen's Squash Academy in Chennai. He was an accomplished junior but never the best. In the semis of his last national juniors, he got bageled: 9–0, 9–0, 9–0. While lackadaisically attending a local university, he tried to make it as a professional. He scraped together money for coaching; sometimes the coaches, knowing his situation, worked with him for free. He got to 165th in the world but could not afford to travel, so he foraged for ranking points at second-tier tournaments in India and Pakistan. In the eyes of the NCAA, he had not forfeited his amateur status, since his expenses were greater than his meager earnings.

When he arrived at Trinity, he was already twenty years old, cerebral and mature. He was a Sikh. Over time, we had almost every major religion represented on our team: Hinduism, Islam, Zoroastrianism, Judaism, and Christianity of a dozen different types. But before Supreet, I knew little about Sikhism. During one private run-to-the-roar session, he told me about a decisive break from family tradition when as a child he had stopped wearing the signature Sikh turban. Nonetheless, some years later his family made the pilgrimage to the sacred Golden Temple in Punjab, and he was a strict vegetarian and teetotaler. Like many Sikhs, he wore bracelets and necklaces, and he had two rings on his left hand, one made of gold with an emerald stone and the other silver with a red coral stone. His parents had given him the rings for good luck. The jewelry led to his nickname: Bling.

The rings had an interesting denouement. During a spring break, he was swimming off at a beach in Mexico when one of them slipped off. He stood on the beach and looked at his hand with one of the empty fingers. He threw the other ring into the waves. When he came back to Hartford, James Montano asked him about the missing rings. "Coach," Supreet said simply, "I gave them to the ocean. That is the situation. They are lying in the Pacific."

Today that coolness, that ability to move on and not dwell in the past—*I gave them to the ocean*—is missing. Somehow, Supreet's racquet work is faulty. He makes errors, shots that would have been winners if they were an inch higher or lower. When he serves, he pokes at the ball with a short-armed, stiff-wristed, flat stab. He's not in the groove and he walks around with his head down.

On the other side, Hesh is a senior. He is also the younger brother of Yasser El Halaby, who won four straight national individual championships before graduating from Princeton in 2006. Both Hesh and Yasser played in the 2006 Atlas Lives dual match. This was an epic contest; in the last match of the day, with the dual-match score at 4–4, Yasser blew a match point against Gustav Detter. Hesh walked Yasser out of the Trinity gym that night as tears flooded down his brother's face. He felt the pain. In the finals of the nationals a few weeks after the Atlas Lives dual match, we again beat Princeton with another nail-biting 5–4 score. Yasser and the freshman trio Maurico Sanchez, Kimlee Wong, and Hesh won at numbers 1 through 4, but the bottom five lost, in a show of Trinity's depth. Since that month three years ago, neither he nor his brother had fully healed.

Yasser El Halaby is still a legend. Four straight intercollegiates—no man has ever done that. Bob Callahan brings Yasser out during the player introductions and the crowd cheers wildly. It can't be easy to have such a famous brother. Lantern-jawed, Hesh looks a bit twitchy out there. During a rally he changes his grip, moving his hand up and down the handle after hitting the ball. Sometimes he flips the handle a full revolution the way players tend to do in between points—not during the point. He often has barely any follow-through on his swing. When he is tired, he bends down when receiving serve, grabbing the bottom of his shorts like basketball players used to do when they lined up for a teammate's free throws. But he is a tremendously skilled player: as a sophomore he played number 2 and was ranked seventh in the nation after the season. Hesh has slipped as a senior, with tasks like finding a job and grappling with his senior thesis taking away some of his focus on squash. But he is extremely formidable at number 6.

In the stands, it is mayhem. His friends are standing after many of the points, applauding loudly and fist-pumping as they grin at the Trinity supporters. They yell "Bullshit," or "Horseshit," or "Why, why?" after every let request Supreet makes. They chant "Hesh! Hesh!

Hesh!" Yasser is exhorting him in Arabic. It reminds me of last season, when Supreet was playing in the first round of the intercollegiates. The Naval Academy had set up a portable glass court in a field house, and more than twenty-five hundred people—mostly midshipmen in dress whites—came in to watch Supreet take on a Navy senior who was not nearly as good. They were ringing cowbells and singing "Semper Fidelis." It was the largest crowd in U.S. squash history. I said to Supreet, "Don't look out at the sea of blue and white. Be calm in the glass court, in the eye of the hurricane."

He said, "Coach, there is no place I'd rather be." He was living in the power of now. He was going to forget all about the crowd. That was what I thought. He then went out and laid a stinker, losing 9–1 in a welter of errors. He came off the court looking like he had just lost his house in a storm.

I said, "Okay, now where do you want to be?" We laughed and it broke the tension. Then we looked up and saw the middies filing out. They thought the match was over after one game, and their commander had ordered them to the next activity on their schedule. The gym suddenly seemed empty and Supreet won the next three games easily.

Today, the crowd isn't going anywhere. Hesh has a new gray shirt on. Oozing testosterone, he swaggers again in between points. He trips going past Supreet to a short ball and lightly tumbles. He goes off court for treatment. He comes back and bludgeons a flat footed volley into the nick. He is up 8–2. Supreet saves a match point. Then another. A couple of long points end in lets. A sixty-stroke rally ensues. Supreet wins it. It's now 8–3. Another long point and it's 8–4. Is he coming back? More lets. Hesh then boldly cracks a backhand volley off the serve into the nick. He comes in from the left—anything to end the bad luck and win the match point. Let. Another let. Hesh is jumping, like a tennis player, when he hits the ball, his chest to the front wall, his arm finishing high in the air. He tins a boast. Back to Supreet's serve. Again Hesh tees off on the serve and slams the ball into the nick. Then another let. It has been two hours since they got on court to warm up. This game alone has lasted almost half an hour.

It ends anticlimactically. Hesh hits a boast. Supreet gets to it. Hesh catches the ball in his left hand, assuming the ball was down. They both look at the referee. Madan calls the ball down. The crowd stands and roars. Hesh has redeemed his brother.

Part of the obstacle to living in the day-to-day—in the now as opposed to the past or future—is narrative. Worrying about what has happened or what will happen, you tend to end up writing a story in your mind. You anticipate the result and how you'll feel about it and what people will say and who will do what. If you come in to the match thinking the story is that you should win and then you get behind, you will think, *Hmm, maybe the story instead will be how I blew this easy match*. It becomes self-fulfilling. I tell my players: "Never write the story in your mind while you are warming up. You must live in the moment with an open mind." Teenagers succumb to internal narratives all the time. It's called simplistic thinking. They make up a story and it becomes reality. They have a fight with their girlfriend. They call and she doesn't pick up. They text; still no answer. What could she be doing? They decide she's cheating on them, run through all the possibilities and eventualities, and soon it becomes not a theory but fact. They march over to find her and break up.

Supreet had never played Hesh before this February, but I think that deep down he thought he couldn't beat him. Hesh, everyone said, was too good to be playing number 6, and Supreet internalized some of that. His reputation preempted anything Supreet experienced on court.

Every coach has an unspoken measuring rod, the one pupil who has the requisite qualities of grace, talent, drive, and generosity. Mine was Preston Quick. My first great American recruit, Preston grew up in Denver. His father, Taylor, was a good player and leader—he was president of the U.S. squash association in the 1990s. Preston took up the game early and got some coaching from the resident genius at the Denver Athletic Club, Hashim Khan.

This was like saying you had a young boxer coached by Muhammad

Ali. Hashim had learned the game as a barefoot boy playing on open-air courts in Peshawar, Pakistan. He went on to win seven British Opens and became squash's first global celebrity—*Life* magazine did a major profile on Hashim's first tournament in the United States. In the 1970s, Hashim moved to Denver and coached at the DAC. Preston was his last star pupil and Hashim's legendary calmness rubbed off on Preston.

Preston had a crisp-as-a-fall-apple stroke and a balletic fluidity around the court, dancing sideways as if he was en pointe. But he struggled with a nemesis. All through his junior career, he ran up against Dave McNeeley, from Philadelphia. Dave was a wonderful player, tall, with a precise style. He could slow the game down, and even though Preston was a far better athlete, Dave could dictate the pace and control the match. There was also a slight divide in squash terms. While Preston saw himself as an outsider, coming from Colorado (Hashim or not), Dave grew up playing at the most storied country club in the nation, Merion Cricket Club; attended one of the great squash schools, Episcopal Academy; and even had a court at his house. Moreover, Dave was the first American junior to embrace the softball game, the international version of squash. With a passionately involved father, Dave had private coaches, traveled to the junior tournaments in Europe, and took squash seriously in a way that Americans never had before. Dave was the number one junior, winning the national juniors three straight times—something that had not happened since the 1950s.

Preston worked hard but also tried his hand at other sports. He played varsity tennis for four years and in his senior year won the state doubles championship. While in high school he flew to Baltimore to play in the national squash doubles championship; he was by far the youngest player in the tournament. (Squash doubles has a different ball and court, besides the element of teamwork, so is almost a separate sport.) In more than thirty matches as juniors, Preston did not beat Dave once. Now in college, Preston still could not conquer his nemesis. In Preston's freshman year, he lost to Dave in a tryout for the national team, which was going to the world championships. Then he lost to Dave in the men's national championship—the SL Green, which is open only to U.S. citizens. Dave even won SL Green in 1999 as a junior, a stunning achievement.

In Preston's sophomore year, he had five match points against Dave and still lost. He walked off the court totally shattered. Breaking my rule about talking with a player after a losing match, I put my arm over his shoulder and said, "You will never lose to Dave again." I just could see it. He was that close, and a slight push of confidence would enable him to rewrite the story.

I was right. He beat David a dozen straight times—he never lost to him again. Bursting with belief, Preston went on to win the SL Green singles and doubles twice. He just needed that little push.

In my own squash career, I needed a shove, too. For three years in a row, I lost in the finals of the over-fifty national squash tournament, all to the same guy, Chris Burrows. He was a great athlete—he climbed the Seven Summits—and I just couldn't imagine defeating him. Finally, I let it go. I told myself that beating Burrows didn't matter, that my squash career couldn't be based on that. In the next nationals, free from that self-imposed anxiety—I had subconsciously rewritten the story—I beat Burrows in the semis. He shattered his racquet in frustration early in the first game and I knew that he felt pressure, not me. Up 2–0 and holding a match point I was winded and losing steam. If I didn't win now, I thought, I wouldn't have enough for a fourth game. My heart was pounding, my legs shaking. Suddenly, I heard a voice: "You can do it." It was Kristen, my daughter. Her voice bumped the past and the future out of the way and I won the point.

I told my players to live in the present, to live as if their hair was on fire. "The only people for me are the mad ones," I told my boys, quoting the renowned passage from Kerouac's *On the Road*, "the ones who are mad to live, mad to talk, mad to be saved, desirous of everything at the same time, the ones who never yawn or say a commonplace thing, but burn, burn, burn, like fabulous yellow roman candles exploding like spiders across the stars and in the middle you see the blue center-light pop and everybody goes 'Awww!'"

The problem was that my son Matthew truly lived in the present. He was a roman candle and all he did was burn. He just saw the front of his nose and no further, the end of the day and no further. He would do anything to get rid of the discomfort and pain of the future and the past. He was incredibly short-term, always focused on just what was going to happen in the next few minutes. He was a heroin addict and heroin addicts would say anything to make the immediate crisis go away, even if it would inevitably worsen things in an hour or day.

Like most parents, I tried anything to help him survive. I gave him rides. I bought him clothes every time he got out of prison. I paid insurance on a car for years before finding out that he had sold the car to a friend for cash and never bothered to tell me. "Dad, I need sixty dollars to take the bus back to the rehab place." "Dad, my friend's car broke down. I need thirty-five dollars to pay for the tow." I probably wired five thousand dollars through Western Union to Matthew, all of which, I guess, ended up feeding his need for drugs rather than solving any problem.

I tried to heal him by placing him in a rehab center. Since I couldn't afford a fancy private one, I used state-run institutions. One quirk was that there was often a waiting list for treatment, and sometimes I needed to keep Matthew alive for a week or two until he could get into a facility and start to detox. Basically, he needed to continue to use heroin while living with me. In the summer of 2003, I had gotten him a job at a garden center while we waited for a bed to become open. We were heading there one Sunday morning in June when Matthew said, "Daddy, I need my fix." So he directed me to a street about a mile from the Trinity campus. I pulled into a bank parking lot, empty cars in a couple of the spaces. He got out and walked away. I thought a police officer could pull into this parking lot and ask me what I was doing. What would I say? It was lunacy.

It was Father's Day.

"You are a father, not a drug escort," I told myself. I had tears in my eyes and anger in my throat. Ten minutes later I saw him walking back. He got back in the car as if he were doing nothing more than fetching a stick of butter from a neighbor. Without saying a word, I drove him to the garden store and went to work.

During another stay, he was looking on the mend. He mowed lawns for a landscaping company He was seeing a therapist twice a week and was on some antidepressants. They were making him a bit sleepy—once he nodded off at the dinner table. But it was a steady life. One afternoon, he came home and asked if he could borrow my car. "I want to go into town and see some friends."

I said, "Fine, but be back by eight o'clock."

At eight I was looking out the window. Matthew never had a cell phone, so all I could do was wait. Nine o'clock. Ten o'clock. At ten thirty, I saw my Honda Civic pull up Firetown Road. Behind it were four police cars, lights flashing.

"Daddy," Matthew said, jumping out of the car, "sorry I'm late."

"Matty, what is going on here?"

Before he could answer, the police were in our driveway. "We've got a report of someone driving erratically on Route 10."

"He's my son, officer," I said, defending Matthew. "He's on some antidepressant medication. I'm afraid he didn't take the right amounts."

"Is everyone okay?" the officer asked, looking from Matthew to me and back to Matthew. "Are you all right with all of us driving away?"

"Yes, officer, he's in my custody," I said. The police left.

We went inside. Matthew said, "Daddy, I'm sorry I was late. Thanks a lot," and he went to bed. In the morning, I went to get in my car. On the driveway I found four bags of heroin. He had emptied his pockets when he jumped out of the car.

I went back into the house and woke him up. "Pack your bags. You are outta here." I drove him to a YMCA shelter on Bushnell Park. Everyone knew him there—he had been to the shelter a half-dozen times before.

For half a year, Matthew worked in the Buildings and Grounds

Department at Trinity. Suddenly, it was a family affair: I was on the faculty at Trinity, my daughter, Kristen, was a sophomore, and Matthew was a janitor. Although that was an unusual juxtaposition, we were thrilled. Kristen liked seeing her brother as he raked leaves or drove a John Deere tractor, and I liked knowing where he was. We saw him every day or two. Then things started to disappear—he was stealing— and he sometimes showed up late for work or not at all. Eventually, he got arrested and that was the end of the Trinity job for him.

After he finished a monthlong prison sentence, he lived near the campus. One time, I was driving the Trinity Squash van to a squash match at Harvard. I saw Matthew on the corner of Babcock and Broad, about a quarter mile from the campus. I rolled down the window and he came around. He smelled like cigarette smoke—stale, unwashed.

"Lend me some money. I need some food," he said with a raspy voice. He knew that I would cave with all my players watching. I gave him sixty bucks from my wallet.

"Talk to you soon, Matty," I said as I rolled up my window. The van was quiet the whole way to Cambridge.

CHAPTER THREE

Seniority: Rushabh

The squash team was side by side on stationary bicycles. Twenty guys. Every player started and finished biking at the same time. Because of differences in fitness, talent, and dedication, each player ended up traveling a different distance. Squash was a team effort—everyone pedaled together—but the contributions were unique. The genius and the epigone, the exuberant and the mirthless—all were in the same room biking. Some were sprinters and fell off at the end. Others were compilers, going steadily along. A couple had a finishing kick. One guy wore headphones and ignored everyone else. Another stared straight ahead. A third constantly glanced at the other bikes to see where they were. Some got nervous as the finish line approached.

Equity, not equality. You have to treat each guy fairly but not equally. They are not equal. My number 1 player is different from my number 20 player. I have to individualize my work. When I was coaching at West Point in the midseventies, I could get away with placing my entire team in one box. Not in the twenty-first century. Now society is thin-sliced and focused on self-expression, self-actualization, and self-empowerment. Reality television was around in the seventies—the famous Loud family documentary, *An American Family*, aired in 1973—but thirty-five years later, life in America is a reality television show. Each player needs attention. Now I have to acknowledge my number 1 player's ego and my number 20 player's ego, and I have to treat those egos in different ways. I have to make each one special. And I have to be consistent.

Each player—by background and temperament—is unique. Jack Barnaby, the longtime Harvard squash coach, published a wise book about squash in 1978, just when I began coaching the game, and I have never forgotten a quotation from it: "The greatest limitation found in teachers is a tendency for them to teach the game the way they play it. This should be avoided. A new player may be quite differently gifted, and the teacher's personal game may be in many ways inappropriate to the pupil's talents. A good teacher assesses the mental and physical gifts of his pupil and tries to adapt to them. There is no one best way to play the game."

If everyone is different, then how did you organize a team? I find that seniority is a key principle. I like the idea of waiting your turn. This gives the guys incentive to work hard for four years, knowing that they might be rewarded in the end. I like experience. When you are coaching young people, the difference between eighteen and twenty-two years of age is enormous; that additional 10 percent of maturity and training and familiarity with match-play pressure could very well be what turns a defeat into a victory. I like the image of seniors going out for their last home match amid the cheers of the fans. I don't mind the freshmen being dogsbodies and plebes and doing the little extra things like carrying the trays in the cafeteria or putting up flyers on campus bulletin boards or obediently going to the back of the van. I do not like a freshman driving a senior off the ladder.

Captains are a critical part at Trinity. I run a hierarchical squad, and the captains—always seniors—take on an almost legendary load of responsibility. Yale traditionally has just one captain; he wears a white sweater for the team photo, while everyone else wears blue sweaters. I would never have been able to coach at Yale. I need at least two and usually three captains. For the 2009 season, I had four—Goose, Manek, Roosh, and Charlie Tashjian. They ran the preseason practice schedule. They figured out which player was late and why. They sorted out the traveling arrangements when we had two vans. On the metaphysical level, they provided a permeable but consistent boundary between the boys and me, so that I could be the coach and administer discipline, while ensuring that communication flowed freely and abundantly. I need to be somewhat isolated from the team. I have to be able to make tough decisions and not have the boys attribute it to a particular friendship. It can't be personal.

Each captain receives an early morning phone call. I phone each captain individually every day. Usually the call is around seven. (This makes me extremely popular with my captains' roommates.) Sometimes we'll talk for just three or four minutes, but often we talk longer. They tell me what the scuttlebutt is, who's doing what, saying what, feeling what. It's often just minutiae, but knowing the inconsequential details about my players enables me to head off problems before they become consequential. It was a West Point–style leadership derived from seniority, from experience, from daily hard work, from class, not simply from your position on the ladder. In 1999–2000, Duncan Burns was a captain, even though he played number 17 on the ladder, and Marcus Cowie was not a captain, even though he was number 1.

I also lean heavily upon the assistant coaches. James Montano is a giant figure for the boys, someone the players can go to when I've made a difficult decision. Reggie Schonborn is a technical genius. He can plot tactics. He can spot weaknesses. In the past, I had some great assistants, including Joe Pentland, who came back after graduation and was a loyal, helpful presence. In 2009, with James and Reggie, I had a second layer of insulation that prevented me from becoming too close to my players.

Seniority also proves central to handling the insanity of challenge matches. Like most individual sports that play as a team (golf, tennis, fencing), we use challenge matches—intrateam contests to determine rankings on the ladder—to help decide who plays where in dual matches. College squash players attach fundamental importance to where they are on the ladder. They think of themselves as a number 2 or a number 7, and their whole life falls apart if they drop down the ladder. Some of it stems from the fact that in many clubs' locker rooms, the fulcrum of conversation bends around where you land on your ladder. Inevitably, "What number did you play?" is the first question a player is asked about his college career, and he always answers with his highest spot.

Moreover, players put so much stock in where they are on the ladder that they often perform differently based upon their position and their perceived place in the hierarchy: if they're a longtime number 2 challenging up at number 1, they'll play brilliantly; if they're a long-time number 3 playing down at number 4, they'll play nervously.

In the teammate-versus-teammate interplay of challenge matches, I saw some of the worst fears manifested. The clichéd ethos of "all for one, one for all" commonality was fine for 95 percent of the season, but challenge matches could decimate guys psychologically. When I was coaching at Williams, I had a player who was a brilliant dual-match player (he never lost to Harvard, for instance) but awful at challenges. He was frightened to death of losing his place in the lineup and automatically came up with ailments. If I made him play, he was usually so tight that he would lose. Yet in dual matches against other schools, he played at his normal level, way above the guys he had lost to in challenge matches.

This is not uncommon. Challenges are so weirdly intense that some players—the obsessive, driven types—do better than their more laid-back teammates and win matches they should lose. Sometimes playing styles are synchronized so that one player just can't beat another, no matter how much better he is. The strangest things of all happen when one guy is bashing his best friend or roommate or fraternity brother—or all three. When I draw up a schedule, I can predict with certainty which challenges are going to a fifth-game tiebreaker despite a vast gap in skills. The matches often deteriorate into naked aggression. Players are as territorial about their spot as a wolf is about his patch of mountainside. The guys push and shove. They claw for each point. Elbows fly. Racquets smack teeth onto the floor. Players ask for bad lets (and we coaches end up having to referee challenge matches, because otherwise it would get ugly). They moan at calls. They hit double bounces. These are chippy ninety-minute marathons. Every time we have challenge matches, dozens of students come to watch: it's a spectator sport, a collegiate version of cockfighting

Sometimes these are good battles. It's practice with pads on and the only way of recreating the taut, gut-sucking tension of a dual match. It also provides a nice space for leadership. One year, Eric

Wadhwa and Tommy Wolfe, two Americans, were battling it out for the number 9 spot just before the nationals. It inevitably went to a fifth and deciding game. Early on in the fifth, Simba Muhwati, then just a freshman, had yelled out "Come on, boys!" Normally, no one cheered during challenge matches.

Simba was an unusual case and just the perfect guy to change our approach to challenges. His father, a policeman in Zimbabwe, had started Simba on a police athletic club's squash court when he was six. He played every Saturday, and if he won his matches in the morning, his father gave him lunch at the club's restaurant; if he lost, they went home for lunch. After high school, Simba took a job at a Harare bank doing foreign exchange. He did this for three years, until a local friend, Shaun Johnstone, who had come to play at Trinity, connected the two of us. I sent him an email and persuaded him to change courses. In two months, he applied to Trinity, got in, obtained his passport (his dad pulled strings to cut the six-month wait time to two weeks) and then, just after Christmas, ran into a roadblock. The U.S. embassy didn't believe he would return to Zimbabwe—he had no assets, his parents didn't own anything, and he had taken out a loan from his bank to purchase an airplane ticket—and denied his visa application. I called Senator Joe Lieberman's office, and in a few hours they had faxed the embassy in Harare a sharply worded letter.

It was New Year's Day, snowing and twenty two degrees, when he landed. It was the first time he had been to the States, and he was wearing a T-shirt, a tracksuit, and flip-flops. He had one bag and twenty dollars in his pocket, money that a friend at the bank had given him. James Montano put an old team jacket on him (Simba would wear it every winter until his senior year). He walked outside and had a borderline asthma attack. The cold air literally took his breath away. Now, at his first challenge match, Simba was showing some leadership skills that no one had expected from a freshman, let alone one who came from such a background. It was revelatory.

I didn't trust challenges. Many years there were guys in the wrong places. Everyone on the team knew it, but the sacred system of challenging each other made it problematic to change anything. In February 1999 half my team quit when I tried to do something about it. It was three days before our Harvard dual match, and I had four guys scrambling around in the number 5 through number 8 spots. They had played one another repeatedly and the results were a mess. I told the team that Charlie Saunders, a senior, would play at number 5. It would be Charlie's last regular-season dual match against our fierce rivals. I wanted him to be able to find redemption after his demoralizing sophomore-year loss. He was one of our captains. And he had posted some good results against other teams. Early in my career, I didn't use dual-match results as a variable—something I began doing later—which besides helping lessen the insane pressure of challenge matches gave me the room to move people to their correct spot on the ladder. (I started telling the guys that our official schedule didn't include challenge matches, only dual matches against other schools. That was why we had a team. Beating Princeton was more important than beating each other.) There could a virulent domino effect when players got moved, and with Charlie at number 5, a freshman from Mumbai, Guarav Juneja, would be pushed out of the top nine.

That night I got home to a voice mail message: six of the boys on the team were quitting. It was all the Indians and southern Africans, all underclassmen. Three before Harvard and I didn't have a team. I had been disrespectful to them. Guarav Juneja had won his matches; he should be number 9. Case closed. If I didn't agree, they were not going to play against Harvard. (Some of them were additionally annoyed because earlier in the winter, I had vaulted Preston Quick up to number 2 above a couple of guys he had lost to in challenge matches. Quick had reached the finals of the Price Bullington, an annual autumn tournament in Richmond; in the quarters he beat Tim Wyant in overtime in the fifth, and Wyant was a top player. Despite a couple of fluky challenge-match losses, the Richmond results indicated he was the second-best player on the squad—as he was the previous year. But since the players didn't know I was formally using nonchallenge match results as factors in deciding the lineup, they saw it as unfair.)

I had meetings with the captains (Saunders, Ian Conway, and Joe Pentland), and we then had one marathon session as a team. I listened. I didn't want my ego, bruised as it was, to get in the middle of it. I made them comfortable enough to share their thoughts. Undergraduates were instinctually jaded, so it had to be a caring atmosphere. After an hour of talking, Rohan Juneja, Guarav's twin brother, got up. "It is clear that Coach does not understand how things get done in Bombay," he said. "We clearly do not understand his system, how things get done here in Hartford. But we are in Hartford, not in Bombay. We are here and we need to agree to do what he asks. If he was coaching in Bombay, he would have to agree to do what we are used to."

We beat Harvard 8–1. We called this episode of insubordination the Indian Revolt, and it seemed to seal the idea that seniority was a good thing. When the Indians were seniors, they too relished the little nods to rank and ritual that came their way.

Usually the problems emerged from the ends of the ladder, at number 1 and number 9. In 2000 I recruited Michael Ferreira, a talented and very personable South African with an unorthodox two-hand backhand. About two weeks into the season, before any challenge matches, he came into my office. It was a typical weekly session I did with all the freshmen: discussing his adjustments to the States and to Trinity, his classes, his parents, his goals. "I think you'll fit in around number five or so on the ladder," I told him, when he asked about the ladder.

"No way, Coach," Ferreira immediately blurted. "I should be higher."

"Well, I'm thinking five is right for you."

"I've had a hit with everyone. I've known Akhil and Coetzee and Lefika for years. I know I should be number one."

"You're a freshman and this is where you'll start off, and maybe you'll get higher, but you probably won't play number three this year, not as a freshman."

"I really think I can play number one."

"One?"

"Yes, Coach, I should be number one. I want the opportunity, if I win my challenge matches, to get to number one."

We argued back and forth, and it got heated. I didn't know Ferreira that well and had no inkling about his massive inner drive—a competitiveness that bordered on arrogance. He had moved to England when he was twelve to better his squash game. I later discovered that he used to pore over the monthly ranking lists that came out in England. He had been a part of the English junior training squads that included some future top-ten players. On the other hand, he had no inkling about the team aspect of Trinity squash. We had been national champions for only a couple of seasons. No one talked about a streak yet. The meeting ended badly, with each of us dropping F-bombs and Ferreira storming off saying he was quitting.

I was very disappointed at myself, getting engaged in a heated argument with a new player and, moreover, not knowing enough about his personality to avoid it. And I should have made the challenge system open. Seniority was one thing, and I was right to give the benefit of the doubt to the older players, but if he was clearly better than the rest, then, yes, he should play number 1. We met again the next day, and, backing down, I agreed that if he could keep winning, he could challenge up to number 1. In the next four weeks, he went from number 5 to number 2, winning three straight challenges. Then just before our dual match at Harvard, our number 1, Jonny Smith, came down with the flu (as did Rohan Bhappu, at the other end of the ladder). We were seriously depleted, and I was nervous having a raw freshman play number 1 in a rough, unfriendly environment. Ferreira proved me wrong, as he gutted out a tense 3–0 win over Harvard's Deepak Abraham.

It was an indelible performance and a key result in a grinding dual match. (We were tied 3–3 going into the final cycle, but we quickly took the first two, rendering Nick Kyme's match against Shondip Ghosh, by now in its third game, meaningless; Ghosh did win 3–1 to make the final dual-match score 5–4). Afterward, I told the team that Ferreira was the man of the match, that I was very proud that he backed up what he had said. Ferreira then played number 1 the rest of the season and went undefeated.

He had trouble, though, giving way the next season, when we brought in Bernardo Samper, a Colombian superstar. Samper was the better player, in my mind, based on dual-match play against other schools. He did better in the intercollegiates, winning the national title as a freshman, while Ferreira's best result was reaching the semis once. Samper also went on to a pro career, reaching fifty-seventh in the world. Yet Ferreira, a year older, managed to claw his way to victory in some of their challenge matches and then insisted on playing number 1. Stupidly, I kept placing Samper against Ferreira in challenge matches, which greatly frustrated our number 3 player, Reggie Schonborn, another South African, who wanted a shot at playing number 1 or at least number 2. (Reggie also had pro inclinations, and after graduation, he reached eighty-first in the world before returning to Trinity as an assistant.) The tension was not awful—Ferreira and Samper were both fantastic kids who got along well and were roommates, and Ferreira and Reggie could be heard in the van discussing Boeremusiek in Afrikaans—but it did upset the equilibrium between the team and the individual.

In 2007, I had another seniority issue about who was going to be number 1. Shaun Johnstone, a senior, wanted to start the new season where he had ended the previous one, as the number 1 player—regardless that Baset Ashfaq, on paper the greatest recruit in college squash history, had just arrived on campus and looked much better. Shaun, like Simba, was from Zimbabwe. He was an eye-popping athlete. He was five feet eight and could dunk a basketball with one hand. He had played number 1 most of his junior year (after playing number 8 as a freshman—an incredible rise for our team). He wanted seniority.

After I posted the draw for the intrateam tournament that always started the season, with Baset seeded one and Shaun seeded two, Shaun sent out a teamwide email. Within a few hours, the electronic bitching and moaning had clogged my in-box. John Wooden used to say that in one minute off court you could undo something you worked on for six hours on court. Only a series of individual and group meetings averted a crisis. And I ended up seeding Shaun at number 1.

It was stupid. I should've let Baset beat Shaun rather than placing the freshman at number 1 before any matches. Shaun deserved the benefit of doubt. Ironically, Shaun was right, because he actually beat Baset in a challenge match a couple of weeks later and for a few dual matches played number 1. Moreover, the tiff over the seeding revealed a larger issue: Shaun felt distant from me and the team. I had to put more into communicating with Shaun, to keep him in the loop, treating him like an experienced veteran. I had taught him to respect seniority, and he now was teaching it to me.

In the 2009 season, the challenge-match system exploded. On the day of our challenges just before the first Princeton dual match, Randy Lim tried to get out of his match. He couldn't, and when he got down 2–0, he stopped trying to win. The third game lasted just two minutes. He was crying afterward. Next door, Binnie and Roosh were two toddlers in a sandbox: yelling, pushing, close to tears. I pulled them off the court in the middle of the match: "No one is in control here. You are showing no respect." It went to five games and both guys were angry when it was over.

I sat the team down on the bleachers in front of the national championship banners: "Look at those banners. That is a dozen years of Charlie Saunders, Preston Quick, Bernardo Samper, Mikey Ferreira, Jonny Smith. Those guys would have found it incomprehensible to quit. How can you quit? I am not going into battle with a bunch of quitters. I am pissed off at you guys who let them quit. How can you accept this? Baset, you won the Drysdale Cup. But you didn't say anything today? What kind of leadership is that? I can accept losing. I cannot accept not trying. I cannot accept bad sportsmanship. Supreet, you were dabbing your knee, wasting time. Get tape on your knee. You say, 'I don't want to play with tape on my knee.' Well, if this were the Princeton match, you'd be playing with tape on your knee. Roosh and Binnie. Can anyone clear? Or do you have to interfere with every shot? Great for drama, shit for squash. You guys were playing so close to each other you might as well be wearing the same pair of shorts.

"You think you're special. You're talking about streaks. You guys have done nothing. That streak is in the past. We are not one ninety-seven–zero. We are four–zero. The past seasons are the past. You are talking about rings, shirts, hats. National champions. I am the only one here with ten national championship rings. I am disappointed in myself. I disgust myself. You disgust me."

Then, with a laceratingly cold look, I eyed them for about thirty seconds, staring darts. The best way to avoid being picked out was to nod in agreement, and each guy on the team was nodding furiously, like some bobble-head toy. I had their attention.

I said, in a low voice, each word a whole stark sentence: "So. National. Champions. Get. Out. Of. My. House."

That night I got a half-dozen emails. "Coach, I am so glad you did that." It was a cathartic moment for them. Disappointment freaked them out. Disappointment was worse than anger. They didn't get too bothered about anger. They could blame me and my temper, my inability to think straight. Guilt they pushed away. But disappointment killed them. If I was giving 100 percent, they hated it when I knew they were not matching it.

Chris Binnie, our regular number 9, was a soft-faced late bloomer lacking in confidence. A sophomore from Jamaica, he had grown up playing at the Liguanea Club in Kingston, a colonial relic (it was founded in 1910 and only expats were members until independence in 1962) that was featured in the James Bond film *Dr. No*. The Liguanea, with six courts, dominated Caribbean squash.

Binnie's father worked for PricewaterhouseCoopers and used to play squash, as did his mother. So at age six he was introduced to the sport and by ten was taking lessons, but he played a lot of cricket (a huge sport in Jamaica), and his real love was soccer. He played goalkeeper. Unlike most of the Trinity players, he rated squash as the third-most-important sport in his life when he was a teenager. He had become the top squash junior in Jamaica but had been stuck behind Bryant Cumberbatch of Barbados. Then he beat Cumberbatch in the Caribbean under-seventeen championships and got more serious.

He struggled in his first season at Trinity. He was number 13 on the ladder, lower than he expected. He was nervous, always trying to impress me. But his grades were good and we all looked forward to his sophomore year. But that summer, he went back to Jamaica and didn't pick up a racquet, and then in the fall, he was the backup goalkeeper on the Trinity soccer team. and he only got over to the squash courts a half-dozen times or so and missed out on most of the captains' practices. After New Year's, he tweaked his right hamstring. He didn't practice for a week and then did soft practice the second week, moving gingerly around the court. How much of the injury was psychological, I didn't know. He was quiet and kept to himself, the antithesis of the clichéd Jamaican with dreadlocked hair and Rastafarian ebullience. I felt he walked a little on eggshells, not sure of his place socially. Having been AWOL most of the fall, he didn't know the jokes, the references. He wasn't in the front of the van, giggling and needling.

He picked his game apart and putt it back together, as a soldier will with his rifle. James Montano, our assistant coach, used to joke that for many guys you would offer nothing but a few phrases of advice when you counseled them in between games, but for Binnie you should bring an encyclopedia. Reggie, our other assistant coach, developed an agreeable working relationship with him and became the between-games advisor and practice mentor. Binnie seemed to flower under Reggie's influence as his sophomore year wore on. They both loved to pick at the minutia of squash—how a player's feet moved as he retreated from the front wall or the right kind of service return. But Binnie lacked confidence to just go out and play. By this time of year, everyone had niggling injuries, and either you played or didn't play. It seemed to me he was using the injury as a crutch. We had a sign in my office that said, PAIN IS WEAKNESS LEAVING THE BODY. In Binnie's case, it was hard for him to let that pain leave.

I decided to keep him in his spot on the team for the first dual match against Princeton, on Valentine's Day. He bulldozed his way to victory over Peter Sopher, a sophomore from Washington. Binnie won the first, third and fifth games without losing more than two points, while giving up two close games in between. But he had looked a bit bewildered during the match, not by the squash but by the crowd. Hundreds of hostile fans hung right on top of him and yelled, "Play the game" every time he tried to talk to the referee about a decision. It was claustrophobic. He was up 4–0 in the fourth, close to clinching the match, but the intensity of the crowd bore down on him, and he frittered away the game. Before the fifth, Goose and Reggie reminded him that he had asked to play in the dual match and had to come through—which he did.

The team got back to Hartford late Saturday night. Within hours of returning, Binnie began a concentrated workout regimen to prepare for the nationals the following weekend. As if to make up for all the lost training from the previous summer and autumn, he trained on Sunday morning, Sunday afternoon, Monday morning, Monday afternoon, Tuesday morning, Tuesday afternoon, and Wednesday morning. Normally, no one underwent two-a-days late in the season, but I let him do it because I thought it would boost his emotional immune system and inject a little confidence. On that last morning, he was hitting with Reggie and made an awkward turn and felt the hamstring twinge. He stopped the training and rested. "I don't know if I can play, mon," he said, when I asked about the injury.

The national team tournament has a three dual-match draw—each of the sixty-odd squads gets ranked and slotted into an eight-team flight. We were seeded number one and played the number eight team, Dartmouth, on Friday. Against the Big Green, Binnie looked a bit tentative, his leg strapped up with tape. In the third game, up 6–1, he lunged for a short ball and felt it twinge again. He could barely put any pressure on his right leg and drop-shotted each time he touched the ball, trying to end the match quickly. On Saturday against Harvard, he got it strapped again but looked even worse. Everyone else won 3–0, but he lost a game and was clearly struggling with his movement. He had previously pulverized his Harvard opponent, but this day he looked out of sorts. He was unable to stretch to balls up in the left corner. He nibbled on his necklace in between points and ran tentatively, as if he expected the earth to give way.

After the match, I had our trainer, Ivo Wessling, talk to him about his hamstring and make an assessment. Ivo said it was weakened and threatened his mobility, but that Binnie could not injure it more by playing. We sat on the floor outside the courts. "You at seventy-five percent may be better than Roosh at a hundred percent," I told him, "but Ivo thinks the injury is sizable. I can tell you think so, too. You are at fifty percent."

"Don't worry, Coach," Binnie said. "I'll be okay tomorrow."

It was not convincing. "There will be no tomorrow," I said. "I'm going to pull you out of the dual match."

A cloud of confusion quickly spread across his face. He was relieved that he wouldn't be letting the team down by playing at less than 100 percent. Yet he was disappointed at all the training in the winter now going to waste. He didn't complain. Perhaps it was his long experience as a soccer player, where substitutions occurred. I was impressed and relieved that he didn't dig in and bad-mouth me and hurt team morale.

Of all the players I had ever coached, Binnie was the most like me. I was insecure. I doubted my athletic skills and my friendships and never really felt comfortable in my own skin. I used injuries as an excuse.

My younger sister, Michelle, and I grew up in the Bronx. Our father worked as a general manager at a celluloid factory called Hudson AS Photographic. Both sets of our grandparents had emigrated from Italy to the United States around the turn of the century. We lived in a tight-knit Italian-American enclave on Nelson Avenue in the Bronx. It was pretty typical: aunts and uncles and cousins always around, a big Sunday pasta dinner. My father's father, a cobbler, died when I was young, but my grandmother, Nonnie, ruled as the matriarch on Nelson Avenue. My mother's mother died of tuberculosis when she was a little girl, and my mother had been raised by an aunt who had three children of her own.

We were just a fly ball north of Yankee Stadium. When I was little, my father would take me to Macombs Field under the shadow of the stadium and race me around the quarter-mile track. He would run backward and beat me. I thought he was the greatest man in the world.

I was short for my age. When I was eighteen, I was five feet four and weighed about one hundred pounds. I harbored a little Napoleon complex, with a chip on my shoulder. I had started gymnastics as a sophomore in high school in large part because it was a sport where size didn't matter. It was a very rudimentary program at Pearl River High School—when I was thirteen, my parents had moved out of the city and into a sleepy suburb near the New Jersey border. The mid-sixties were not a high point for gymnastics in the United States, and at Pearl River we had no mats, a smattering of ancient equipment, and the vault was in a low-ceilinged hallway: you ran along the brown tile floor past classrooms and then did a scissor kick, or even, if you were feeling brave, a handspring.

Gymnastics was a sport that seemed to touch me. My body started to fill out and toughen, and a little six-pack appeared on my stomach. On Tuesday nights my parents drove me to Little Ferry, in New Jersey, where I worked out with an older, more advanced group of athletes. My mother sat in the bleachers and knitted sweaters—she kept her head down, as she got nervous if she saw me catapulting through the air. My father sat with his elbows on his knees, watching every move. On the way home, we dissected the practice.

Collegewise, I exhibited not one iota of promise or potential. My grades were mediocre. I tested poorly and had scored under one thousand on the SATs. My college guidance counselor told me I would not get into any college in the country—"You are not college material," he bluntly told me. Therefore, I applied to all the top gymnastics schools in the country—Wisconsin, Iowa State, Southern Connecticut, and Springfield—thinking gymnastics might open doors that my grades would not. When I interviewed at Springfield, the admissions officer asked why I was also applying to Southern Connecticut. I told him that I was going to be on Southern Conn's gymnastics team. (It was coached by Abie Grossfeld, a gymnastics legend who was the U.S. men's Olympic team coach.) The officer looked pleased, and I later found out that Springfield accepted me solely because they thought that if Grossfeld was interested in me then I must be good. In the end, I was rejected by Wisconsin, Iowa State, and Southern Connecticut— Grossfeld had never heard of me.

Once I made the team at Springfield, I was like Binnie in between the Princeton dual matches: Trying to make up for lost time, I practiced on weekends, during holidays. I lifted weights at dawn. I ran on icy sidewalks. The passion from my first days on the mat was still there, but it evolved into something deeper, not an infatuation, but more a narcissism. Gymnastics plugged into my insecurities. There was no perfection. No one, not even Nadia Comaneci, ever got perfect tens every time. You could win a meet but you could never be perfect. And I was not even close to perfect, so I didn't feel valuable. I was sprinting to a finish line I would never reach.

My sophomore year, I managed to work my way up the ladder to the top of the junior varsity squad. Frank Wolcott, the coach, was a stickler for rules. One day—this was 1971—he demanded that the top gymnast on the team, Jimmy Martin, a defending national champion in the rings, get a haircut before we leave for the nationals. Martin refused. I received a call at seven in the morning saying I needed to be in the van in one hour. I was replacing Martin, and my first varsity competition was the nationals. I was too innocent to know what was going on and came in thirteenth, ahead of everyone else on the Springfield team.

The next season I competed in the Easterns a major annual tournament in Boston. I came in first in the pommel horse and third in the rings. I remember nailing my dismount from the pommel horse, standing stock-still, raising my aching arms, my hands still chalky, and thinking, *Yes*. It was a joyful ride on the bus home with the team that Sunday. When we got back to campus late in the evening, I went to the gym. Nationals were in a week, and just like Binnie, I felt an overwhelming urge to train. I slipped in to the locker room, changed into my shorts and T-shirt, and jogged out to the mat to rehearse my floor routine. As I lay there stretching, in the dim half-light, the echoing voices of students trailing into the night, I suddenly remembered that I had left my trophies on the bus.

Monomaniacally, I would not allow myself any good feelings or any sense of satisfaction about gymnastics. Fearing failure crippled me emotionally to such an extent that I experienced a series of psychosomatic injuries at Springfield. I sprained my ankle. I wrenched my knee. My shoulder froze. I found a level of safety in being injured. I figured out a neat trade: I would work harder than anyone else in practice, but with my injuries I didn't have to perform in the meets; I hoped my coaches and teammates would see my work ethic in practice and my prematch injuries and say, "Bad luck that he can't perform in a meet." I was running away from the roar.

HERE LIES A MAN WHO MADE A DIFFERENCE. That is what I want carved on my tombstone. But too often I think my epitaph will be IT SEEMED LIKE A GOOD IDEA AT THE TIME.

I hated to make a last-minute change, but I desperately needed a win at number 9, and so just before the last dual match of the 2009 season, in the finals of the nationals, I switched my players. Through the eleven perfect seasons, our number 9 slot had been automatic. We almost never lost at 9 in any close match since the streak started. James and I, when we talked about an upcoming match, started down the ladder from number 9 because it helped us to begin our calculations with a win. We always found very good players who could anchor our team and come out with an early win. It took a fighter to survive the challenge-match system and get that final spot.

Rushabh Vora was the quintessential number 9. Loquacious and exuberant, he was the team clown, the extrovert. He was full of mischievous bluster and useful, ribald advice. He was volatile. Like Binnie, he had parents who both played squash, and on Sunday evenings he and his older brother Sahil would go with them to the CCI (Country Club of India) and muck around on empty courts while they played next door. When he was six and a half he started playing seriously. When he was eight, he went to Hong Kong for a tournament and lost in the semis of the under-ten draw. Roosh got good. He beat his mother, then his father. He was ranked in the top four of his age group each year, and reached the semis of the Indian junior nationals.

Sahil was already thriving at Trinity, but Roosh applied early to Penn because he wanted to go to the Wharton School. By the time he found out he wasn't getting into Penn, it was too late to apply to Trinity. I sent him to the coach at Franklin & Marshall, where Roosh played number 1 his freshman year. He liked F&M, but at the nationals he suddenly decided to transfer to Trinity. He was standing with some teammates and saw the Trinity team saunter in to the building before our first dual match. I tried to keep our team away from the courts as long as possible. I wanted to mystify, not familiarize. Everyone stopped and watched, as if this were a Western and the villain had just walked into the saloon. We had an aura of toughness.

He wanted to be a part of it. He had never visited Trinity, even while at F&M, but he had heard stories from his brother and his best friend growing up, Manek Mathur, and after seeing our entrance at the nationals, it was a done deal. He transferred at the end of the school year and played number 8 as a sophomore. Sahil was a captain and played number 4.

The 2007 dual match at Harvard, during Roosh's first year at Trinity, shocked him. He had beaten his opponent, Verdi DiSesa, in three, but had not adjusted to the verbal abuse, the screaming, body-painted, sign-waving Harvard fans. After that dual match, he had the fanaticism of the convert. He surfed the Web to find any references to the team, especially anything negative. If a player got bad-mouthed, Roosh attacked back.

He worked at UBS in New York the summer of 2008 before senior year and was thrown for a loop the following winter when UBS, because of the Great Recession, had put his return offer on hold. He scrambled for a job, sending out his résumé and going down to New York for interviews. Most weeks he was down in New York more than at practice. It ended up being too hard to schedule challenge matches and thus, for the first time in years, there had not been a war over the 9 spot. Binnie was at 9 and since Roosh was at 10, it didn't seem to matter if he was not as fit as he should be.

On the Saturday night before the finals, I tell Roosh that he's playing in the Princeton dual match, and he's thrilled. He instantly says, "I will win." An hour later he sends me a text: "We need four wins from the other 8 tomorrow. I will give you the result at 9." I texted him back: "You've never let me down so far." But he's nervous, and all night, in a room he's sharing with a half-dozen other players, he can't sleep. Instead, he clicks his tongue and says, "I'm going to win." Still, in the morning, he's his jaunty old self.

As his match starts, Roosh looks unsure of himself. He has not practiced in ten days. He's got that buzzing, tired look you get when you're sleep deprived. The crowd is chanting, "We've got Sopher, we've got Sopher," and he looks around cautiously. Peter Sopher was a sophomore from Washington, DC. He and his twin brother were two leading juniors and, with their grim-faced determination and curly shock of black hair, looked almost interchangeable. Sopher had lost to Binnie on Valentine's Day, 9–2 in the fifth. He is excited about playing Roosh rather than Binnie.

Charging out like a bull at a rodeo, Roosh bucks to an 8–4 lead. But he can't get that last point to clinch the game. Sopher patiently hangs in there. The year before, Sopher had looked nervous when he played Trinity in the finals of the nationals. He had rushed in to the server's box and started the point with a sort of stop-action stutter. Today he is tranquil, more mature, no hurrying down the platform to catch a train.

Roosh, on the other hand, looks like the panicky freshman. A national championship is on the line. He pounds three straight balls into the tin. They have an awful sound, an enormous, ringing splat. The score is suddenly knotted at 8 all. Roosh scoops up the next two points to get the game, but he's exhausted. *If this is how hard it is to win a single game,* he is saying to himself, *how can I win the match?* All the confidence of the night before has drained away. He is confident he'll win because he's got the experience, but he's slightly worried about his fitness. For some reason, he felt winded after just one game. This had never happened before.

"Listen," he says when he comes off court. "I am tired."

The next three games are a nightmare. The crowd is chanting, "Peter Sopher," *clap, clap, clap-clap-clap.* Roosh slaps more than a dozen tins, off the return of serve, off wide, easy openings. He goes down guns blazing, but he seems to have forgotten about how points are won. Two of the games are lopsided. One goes to a tiebreaker, when Roosh has an 8–4 lead but squanders it.

After the first shift of three matches, Princeton is up 2–1. I later learned that Sopher and the Princeton team was glad I had switched Roosh in for Binnie. They thought that this gave them a better shot at winning at number 9. It was a terrible blunder. I should have decided this weeks ago, not the night before.

In his own eyes, Roosh did not have a perfect career at Trinity. He was an All American and, having never lost in a dual match, he had tremendous pride in Trinity's depth. He felt that the guys at the bottom of the lineup should never lose. We won at 9. That was the mantra. And today we have lost at 9.

CHAPTER FOUR

Love Wins: Vikram

It was like a barometer in a coming storm. Nicknames were my gauge for when a team was gelling. By late fall, the japes, the goofiness, the chummy camaraderie hopefully had manifested itself in the fact that no one called each other by their given name. James Montano, our assistant coach, had a knack for appropriate monikers. Randy Lim, a tiny cannonball from Malaysia, was Shark and then Yakuza, for he talked with a wink and a gangsterlike patter. Parth, who was even smaller than Randy—our sports information staffer, Dave Kingsley, generously listed both of them at five feet seven—was Tsunami. Vikram, a preening, clothes-conscious Indian, was either Rum, a take on the second syllable of his name, or Bollywood, the old standby for guys from Mumbai. Vargas, from Colombia, was El Gato Grande, the big cat. Charlie Tashjian, whose rumpled hair, drooping eyelids, and loose shirttail made him look like an unmade bed, was Shaggy. Supreet, covered with Sikh jewelry, was Bling. Manek was GQ or Muscles. Baset became B and then Killer Bee. It was perfect, because he was a sloe-eyed giant. Last year I don't think he was early to a single practice. This fall he lost his sweatpants within two days of getting them. He sent around an email. Mary, the team manager, fifteen inches shorter than him, replied: "I have to confess. I have them, Killer Bee." She was in Rome, studying abroad.

Gustav was Goose or Gandalf the Great or Wizard. He was from Sweden and flew slightly apart from the pop-culture slipstream. In the fall of his junior year, he and Roosh studied abroad in China. He sent a photograph of himself on the Great Wall. His hair was unusually long, a white-blonde mane waving above the ancient gray crenellations. The emails started humming. Goose was now Fabio. "Coach, who is this Fabio?" came an email from Goose. "Is he porn star?"

Besides James, our assistant coaches were not immune. Reggie, who graduated in 2006 and now was an assistant coach, came from South Africa, where you were called what you were named. He was Regardt. He never was Reggie until the day he landed at JFK, and then he was never Regardt. Simbarashe, a dreadlocked whirlwind from Zimbabwe, was obviously Simba. He was a lion: he was fourth on the all-time Trinity wins list. He was now an unpaid assistant coach (he ran out of eligibility before he graduated). Until his final match, he had thought his nickname was no more than a play on his first name. At the nationals against Princeton, he had come off the court down 2–0. I said to him, "Simba, you are Simba." He gave me a blank stare. "You've heard of *The Lion King*?"

"No, Coach." Simba grew up in Zimbabwe, far from the clutches of Disney.

"It's a movie. There's a lion. His name is Simba."

"Okay." He didn't know why I was talking about some obscure American film.

"Lions tear apart tigers. Go in there in and rip him apart." He smiled, walked back into the court, and won the next three games.*

Team chemistry is a mysterious, alchemical, fragile thing. It's like the sun: it always affects your little ecosystem, whether it's cloudless or rainy or nighttime. It's always there, but if you stare too closely at it, you'll go blind, and if you try to sneak up to it and touch it, *blam*, you get burned. You can try to create a positive love fest, but a single glitch could ruin it.

---

* Montano's nicknames have a long history. Among Trinity alums: Eduardo Pereira, a Brazilian, had the soccerlike one-name nickname Dado; some of the boys liked to call him HB, for Humongous Brazilian. Bernardo Samper was El Matador. Michael Ferreira was the Sheriff. Rohan Juneja was ITC (Indian Tom Cruise). Neil Robertson was Gates (as in Bill). Tommy Wolfe was T-Money. Peter Scala was Yoda. Jacques Swanepoel was Red or Big Red. Charlie Saunders was Kramer (from *Seinfeld*). Tosh Belsinger was Tosche Station (from *Star Wars*). Yvain Badan was Swiss or Vampire. David McDonough was Shampoo. Eric Wadhwa was Rambo. Cyrus Appoo was Virus.

I encourage players to take a semester off to study overseas during their junior year. They return with expanded horizons and deeper maturity, which helps greatly on and off the court. Often they go together in little United Nations cells: in the fall of 2009 we had three boys from the team—Gedd DiSesa from Philadelphia, Randy Lim from Penang, and Andres Vargas from Bogotá—living together in a flat in Shanghai. My players are here for the full Trinity experience, and if the institution supports and maintains these programs, then I need to. And besides, I know it's a once-in-a-lifetime opportunity. I never got the chance to study abroad—that wasn't the norm for Springfield in the early seventies—and when my daughter, Kristen, graduated from Trinity in 2006, she unequivocally stated that her junior fall in Rome was the greatest experience of her four years.

But it comes at a huge cost. Normally, when they return it takes a while to sandpaper the rust off. They usually get injured and stay injured—they're so eager to catch up they get nicked up and don't take the time off to heal. Moreover, they haven't been with the team all fall, so the reintegration process often is bumpy. They don't know the freshmen, for instance, and locating their own place on the ladder and in the team's emotional hierarchy can be difficult.

I once had a player at West Point with a verbal tic. He would only use the first person singular when talking about the team. I would ask him about the next match, and he would say, without thinking, "I am playing Dartmouth." It drove a lot of guys nuts and erected an artificial division—for some it was like fingernails on a chalkboard, and for others it was annoying simply because guys on the team were annoyed. I called the player on it a dozen times but it never changed. At the end of the season, the team gave me a clock that said, THANK YOU, COACH ASSA ANTE. They deliberately misspelled my name because I had spent the year proclaiming that there's no I in team.

There is an *I* in win, and balancing the individual and the team, especially in college squash, is devilishly difficult. There are very few top-tier sports where the players never physically join one another in the field of battle: in swimming or track, teammates push each other from the next lane; in tennis they play doubles together; in golf they're sometimes paired together and can line up putts for each other. In intercollegiate squash, each man plays singles and is isolated in his own walled box, like a monk in his cell. He can't see his teammates next door. So to believe in the team, they have to believe in something that on the surface makes little difference to their game. Moreover, none of the overseas guys had been on a team for longer than a fortnight.

Sometimes they just can't buy into it. This is especially true of players from overseas. One day in the winter of 1997, out of the blue, a videotape arrived on my desk. It was sent by Dave Talbott, the jovial Yale coach, with a note: "Dude, check this out." The video was a promotional film of Zafi Levy, a young player from Israel. A couple of Israeli squash players had come to play at U.S. colleges, most notably Jonny Kaye at Harvard in the early 1990s, but Israel was a squash backwater. Zafi was in his twenties, having completed high school and then his three-year army service. The video featured thumping music, shots of him lifting weights and swimming, as well as some clips of him playing squash. It was like a train wreck. I didn't know whether to avert my eyes or keep staring.

In terms of team chemistry, Zafi became one of my biggest coaching failures. From the first day, he was not at ease. He was too old, too complicated, and too uninterested in the collegiate life, especially the social component. Once a fellow freshman was in the Trinity co-op buying a Trinity jacket. Zafi came up to him—they had never met—and told him that he knew a place that made the same kind of jacket, only cheaper. The freshman said, "Gosh, but I want something that says *Trinity* on it—that's the point of the jacket." Zafi didn't understand.

He had Christmas dinner with me and my family, which was punctuated by an awful phone call: the fiancée of a fellow Israeli squash player had died in a plane crash. The friend called Zafi with the news. This shook him up. After New Year's, when the other boys came back,

Zafi stunned me by saying he didn't want to practice anymore with the team. He felt it was too social and not focused enough. He wanted to follow his own routine and train on his own, when it worked with his class schedule. He could push himself better on his own. He found the team too soft, too social. We had a team meeting and a vote. By a small margin, we agreed to let Zafi do his own thing as long as he followed two rules: he had to come to every team meeting and he had to play every assigned challenge match. Zafi ended up practicing solo for hours at odd times, and many days would go by without another teammate seeing him.

The situation was a canker in the rose. I needed to step in and exercise leadership. A vote? What was I thinking? Democracy was for countries, not squash teams.

At first, it looked like we would get away with it. Our team looked good and for the first time in history had a real shot at winning the national championship. So much had changed since I had arrived in Hartford three years before. In my first home dual match against the Crimson, in 1996, about two hundred friends and family members came. It was the usual crowd, pretty good for college squash—Trinity had a reputation for a large number of fans, especially attractively knowledgeable women, because they had gone to high schools with squash programs and usually knew players on both teams. But by 1998, word had evidently gotten out that Trinity Squash was up to something. The day of the Harvard match, the place was mobbed. More than a thousand people had come to Ferris Athletic Center to watch—alums, local squash players, parents, and a ton of fellow students. Seating became tight. Kids were coming up to players and asking for autographs. Fans pressed against the back walls, banging on the glass in between points. It was so crowded that in between games players couldn't walk out of the court and down the hallway to the lone water fountain, because they wouldn't get back to their court in time for their next game.

Jumping out to an early lead, we snagged four of the first five matches. The biggest difference from past years was that we had real depth—not mediocre prep-schoolers in the middle of the ladder and converted tennis players at number 8 and number 9. (In fact, Charlie Saunders, who had played number 2 as a freshman, was now at number 5 as a junior.) We won 6–3. The loss snapped the Crimson's eighty-nine dual-match win streak. Trinity had never beaten Harvard before, not once in seventy years.

We thought it was a watershed moment, but ten days later, at Princeton, we cratered. It was the last dual match of the regular season, and the pressure to win was dazzling, especially because Princeton had lost to Harvard. If we could beat Princeton, we would have an undefeated regular season and the top seed at the nationals. But we tumbled, 5–4. Zafi Levy crumbled 3–0 to Princeton's number 3, Danny Rutherford.

At the end of the month was the nationals, held at Princeton. Evan Dobelle, Trinity's president, had his assistant, Maureen, call me from San Francisco. "Evan wants to know when the finals are."

My vocal cords tightened. "We don't know if we'll make the finals."

"What do you mean?"

"We have to play Princeton in the semis, and we just lost to them a week ago—and this is on their home courts. We might not win."

There was a long pause on the line as Maureen explained the situation to Evan. She came back on the line. "He wants to know when the finals are."

We went down to Princeton for the nationals. In the semis, we crushed the Tigers 7–2. That was satisfying. The next morning, February 28, 1998, we took on Harvard in the finals. Having beaten them once, we should have beaten them again and taken the national title. But any sport with young people is unpredictable. Harvard was well coached by Bill Doyle. A former Trinity star, Doyle had worked nearby when I was the head pro at the Apawamis Club in Rye, New York. We were close friends and doubles partners and had often gone on training runs in the empty back roads of Rye and Greenwich.

It was a neutral court and we had barely any student support. We went up 2–0 after the first cycle, then dropped the next four matches, as three of our guys lost to players they had beaten three weeks before. At number 1, Daniel Ezra pounded Trinity's Marcus Cowie 3–0: in the first game, Marcus was up 14–11 but could not put it away, and then he lost the second and third games without much resistance. As each match drew Harvard closer to the magical number of five wins, their team grew more and more animated. They started mobbing their players when they exited the court, to the extent that Trinity guys sometimes thought that their match had clinched Harvard's win. The dual-match score seesawed to 4–2 in favor of Harvard. Then we climbed back to 4 all.

This was exciting. We had a chance. But the last match was Zafi at number 3 against Harvard's Tim Wyant. Our team was not there for him. Most of the guys had mixed feelings about what was happening. They wanted to win the nationals, but still harbored ill will toward Zafi because of his behavior. No one came with me to counsel him between games. He lost in three. It was the last time we lost a dual match.

The reason we finally became national champions in 1999 and the reason we haven't lost ever since is not recruiting or luck or better technical knowledge or tactical advice. There is no secret, mysterious formula. The reason is time. I get into the office earlier in the morning than any other squash coach in the country and I leave later in the evening than any other squash coach in the country. I put in the time with the boys. I hang around all day in my office, before and after practice. I spend time with them away from the courts, away from the campus. I know the boys.

I get older each year, but my constituency remains the same, a narrow slice of eighteen- to twenty-two-year-olds. The gap between them and me widens each year. I don't act like an old man: I have a tattoo. I have ESPN Radio playing continuously in my office and know

more sports trivia than is healthy. and on van rides I put the radio on
KISS 95.7 FM, Hartford's pop music station. But I have to consciously
work to keep up with their culture. I can't teach them if I didn't know
them. Knowing players is a further challenge because they're mal-
leable. They can change so much in the forty-five months that I work
with them. They arrive as callow teenagers and leave as mature adults.
During their four years, they're figuring out who they are, and while
that happens I have to make make sure I find out what makes them
tick. Usually what makes them tick is quite different from what made
kids tick when I was last in college in 1974.

I call them every morning. A couple of years after getting to Hartford, I figured out a way to generate a telephone call to the entire
team. This was before cell phones and iPhones and BlackBerrys, and
each player just had a land line in his dormitory. I got to work around
six or half past six and would record the message and shoot it out to
the twenty guys: "Good morning boys. It's Monday morning. Beautiful cold weather in Hartford and the birds are just starting to come
out." Then I would tell them the schedule for the day, remind them
what to bring (racquets would be going out that day to get strung, etc.)
and what we would be focusing on at practice and when to be where.
I would usually end with a quotation or a favorite line. "Remember,"
I'd say, "be a duck: calm on the surface but paddling like mad in the
water below."

On Tuesday, I'd broadcast a new group voice mail, and so on for
every day of the week. At practice each day, no matter how inured the
team got to the daily calls, the boys would comment upon them. The
calls showed that I cared, that from the moment I woke up and until
the moment I went to bed, I was thinking about the team. When cell
phones became common in the middle of the last decade, I started
sending daily texts. Usually by eight in the morning, I have sent them
three or four messages. In 2009 each one ended with 11—we had won
ten straight national titles and were going for our eleventh.

I also see them in person as much as possible. My office is a cramped, collegiate space: no windows, no glamour. My office and Wendy Bartlett's—the women's coach—were originally a hardball court that couldn't be converted to the softball dimensions because then there would have been no hallway to leave the facility. There are racquets piled in giant logjams. A smattering of random trophies, hats, and videotapes crowds the thin white shelves that encircle the room at eye level. A couple of framed articles on the team and a few plaques are on the walls. A small refrigerator bears a note from the 2005–06 team. I never lock the office, I never worry about whose bag or shoes are heaped in unruly clumps. Throughout the day, the players come in, plop down in the big black leather chair next to my desk, and talk. After breakfast, before lunch, after class, before lab—they come to my office. I sip a Diet Coke and we talk.

At the start of the season I let the players set the terms of engagement, but I still force them into a regular routine of keeping in touch. Once we have a rhythm, I can then speed it up if I see that I'm not getting through to a certain guy. Each week I eat dinner with every player—my rule is at least once a week, either alone or in a small group. Not once in their thirteen hundred days as a Trinity student does twenty hours go by for a player without some form of communication from me. I am always in touch. I take their temperature, so I know what's up. They know I care. Young people have a heavily compressed sense of time—a month in college is like a year in the real world—so my efforts feel significant to them. Their parents like it, too. They are thousands of miles away, and most go years without seeing their boys.

At the holidays, I invite all my players to stay with me at my family's celebrations. Usually a half-dozen guys have nowhere else to go and take me up on my offer. They sleep on my parents' couches, they do dishes, go shopping, and break bread. They become closer to one another and to me, and those bonds—forged by spending ninety-five hours continuously together—are a key way of strengthening the team.

With the time comes love. There is no doubt that love wins. Love can be created only in the loving—love comes from the many acts and deeds of loving. You can say "I love you," and it means something, but it means much more to show it. We were not sent into this world to be alone. We were born to love. If over time my players come to believe that they are at the center of my universe, they will in return feel a commitment to me and to the program. They will be engaged and on their toes. They see that I am not coaching them for selfish reasons. They see me network to help graduates find jobs: making calls, writing reference letters, and getting them interviews. They see me hug alums. They see me go to weddings and funerals. They see me answer the phone again and again on Christmas Day, as dozens of graduates call to give holiday greetings. They see that this is a lifetime relationship, with the Trinity segment just a miniscule part of the journey. On the gym at West Point is a plaque with a quote from General MacArthur: "On the friendly fields of strife are sown the seeds that on later fields will bear the fruit of victory." This is a lifetime process, this is about *later fields*, not simply about winning dual matches.

This is not a suffocating, helicoptering style. I am not trying to be their best friend or their father. I'm their coach. It's not about me: I do not Twitter or Facebook. I don't go to their dorm rooms or fraternities. I calibrate it carefully. Bobby Bayliss, the squash and tennis coach at Navy when I started at Army, told me repeatedly that you could always take a wall down, but it was very hard to put a wall back up. The boys know about my life. I am always up-front about Matthew, for instance, or when a marriage is breaking up. But I make sure there's a balance. Everyone has a nickname but me. I'm Coach, not Paul.

Early on in my coaching career I learned the cost of not putting in enough time with each player. Danny Hammond was one of the greatest racquet players in Army's history. In squash, Hammond ambushed the legendary Mike Desaulniers and became the only player to take a game off Desaulniers during his college career. Hammond went on to win first team All American recognition by virtue of being ranked tenth in the nation—the only Army player to be a first-team All American during my nine seasons.

On the tennis team, Hammond went 16–3 at number 1 his senior year. (He was six feet six and had a blistering serve.) But unbeknownst to me, he was seriously struggling with his academics. Late in the season the commandant told me that Danny could not go to the NCAA tournament. When I told Danny, he gave me a malevolent stare and stormed out of my office, yelling, "You didn't fight for me, you let me down," and slammed the door. My face turned red, as if the door had smacked it.

The only thing left on the regular season schedule was the annual Army-Navy dual match. All week Danny had shown a disputatious animation. Down at Navy, it was a very hot, stifling day, with no breeze coming off the Chesapeake. In front of three thousand middies, Danny went out and tanked the first set 6–0. Just gave up. Everyone was sweating through their sneakers, leaving footprints on the court, everyone except Danny. It was embarrassing to see him do this at all, but it was especially bad because it was the Navy dual match, the most important day of the year, an event that most kids remember for the rest of their lives. I was dumbfounded. After the first set, I called him over to the picket fence. "Is this what you want your legacy to be, to tank your last college match?"

He flashed his teeth at me. His eyes widened, as if he had swallowed an earthquake. "Screw you," he said. "You didn't fight for me; why should I fight for you?"

I snapped. I reached over the fence and grabbed him by the shirt. "You're fucking crazy. Stop this, right now. You sonuvabitch." He snapped out of it. I let go of his shirt and he walked back onto the court. He won the next two sets at love, 6–0, 6–0. It was an absurd scoreline.

We didn't talk on the bus ride home.* If this had happened thirty years later, I would have rightly been fired on the spot. I made a mistake that day. Once you lose control, once you cede the honor and goodwill that innately come with your title, you leave everything up

---

* Years later we bumped into each other and rekindled our friendship, and I was able to help him get a job coaching at Bowdoin, where he did terrific work.

to chance. Intimidation is never a long-term solution. I should have caught his academic problems early on, worked with him to keep his eligibility. I should have known he was besieged by work. I should never have let it get to the point where, to get back at me, an Army player wanted to tank a match against Navy.

Serendipitously, people drift into the Trinity program to fill out various support networks so that I'm not carrying the whole leadership burden. The whole college is very supportive. The president, Jimmy Jones, has one photograph behind his desk: Gustav after winning the Atlas Lives match in 2006. With his dogs, he comes to most of our home dual matches. Rick Hazelton, the longtime Trinity athletic director, was an anchor. Most squash programs just don't have the overt and active support of both its president and AD.

By pure fluke, James Montano is our assistant coach. Montano grew up in a half-dozen states and in Germany, and after graduating from the University of Connecticut in 1995, he found a job at UConn in the development office. He loved to joke that he was so clueless that when he went for his interview, he asked, "What do you make here, what do you *develop*?" In 1998 James took a similar position in Trinity's development office. One day, two students came in looking for a work-study job. They were twins, Guarav and Rohan Juneja, freshmen on the Trinity squash team. James had played some squash in Germany, and the combination of knowing the sport and having an international perspective led to a firm friendship with the Juneja brothers. That winter he occasionally stopped by squash practices; he segued into the role of unofficial advisor to the Juneja boys and then to the other overseas players; he started coming to more and more practices and home dual matches and then to away dual matches. After a couple of years, James quit the development position to take a job elsewhere, but he managed to arrange his new schedule to be at practice every afternoon because of his love and commitment for the team. Having been in the military (he graduated from Valley Forge Military Academy and was later in the marines), James led with a fierce, tough-guy attitude, pumping the boys up, motivating, pushing. He habitually quoted from the film *300* ("What is your profession?"), making the boys feel like the underdog, the outsider, the minority—little Trinity against the big, moneyed Ivy League schools. "In the end," King Leonidas says in *300*, "a Spartan's true strength is the warrior next to him." James helps build up an esprit de corps that is critical in tight dual matches.

Belinda Terry is the team mother. She and her husband, Luke (who is on the Trinity board of trustees), were living in London when the Trinity women's squash team, over on a training tour, asked for help in getting new uniforms. Belinda agreed—she had played in a squash dual match while at George Washington years before—and then did so for the men, too. When she and Luke moved back to southern Connecticut, she stopped by the courts while Luke was up for a meeting. She realized that none of the overseas boys had a mother to come cheer for them or to bring them homemade cookies. Now living about an hour away, she operates a second home for the team. She and Luke host an annual Labor Day barbecue for the team and its alums. She boards players during holidays. She does their laundry. They come and rake leaves in the fall. She makes thick rugby shirts in Trinity's colors and at least one T-shirt a year. (Her favorite is one that had the flags of all the nations represented by Trinity players with "C'mon" in each language.) She produces hats, banners, and sweatshirts. At dual matches, when she's not texting updates, she's loudly cheering. Once a coach seated in front of her, turned around, looked at Belinda, then at the Trinity player on the court, then at Belinda again and blurted out, "Who are you?"

"I'm his mom," she replied.

With Mom came Boss. One day in 2004, Colleen Stewart, the access control manager in Trinity's Building and Grounds Department, saw a student walk into her office looking for a job. Stewart employed a dozen kids to walk around the campus reprogramming the security codes on doors. The student was Simba Muhwati. He needed money and had seen a classmate fiddling at a door and asked him what he was doing. Colleen hired him—she was keen to find more staff, as it was not a glamorous job, and although it was open to all students, very few seemed to want to do it and sometimes she had to hire outsiders. Simba liked hanging out in Colleen's office. Other kids from the team started working for access control, and soon Colleen had drifted into operating a squash team support group. Almost every overseas player works for Colleen, who is dubbed Boss. Despite the moniker, what makes her so appealing to the boys is her accessibility. She's young, in her midtwenties, and has married an Irish soccer player she had met at Central Connecticut State University: she knows firsthand what it was like for a foreign athlete to adapt to college life in America. She also relates to them because she understands the value of hard work— her father managed the central energy plant at Trinity. She's also very practical and helps the boys by advising them on how to open a bank account or get a cell phone or a driver's license. They loiter around her office for hours. She comes to every home dual match and most away ones. She comes to the season-ending banquet. Players give her photographs, shirts, and team hats—there's a competition to see who could deliver a new team hat to her desk first. She keeps all but one of the hats in her car—"I have only one head," she says.

We also have a professional photographer on staff. Dick Druckman, a Trinity alum, retired after three-plus decades as a senior vice-president at Bristol-Myers Squibb and started a sports photography business just before I arrived at Trinity. He covers every Olympics and dozens of professional events each month. He comes to most of our dual matches and every year hosts the team at his studio in Princeton, giving us pizza and handing out framed copies of some of his iconic images: Wayne Gretzky's final faceoff in the NHL and Muhammad Ali pointing to the camera at a baseball game.

When I was coaching at Williams twenty years ago, we hosted the national intercollegiate individual tournament. During the weekend, I had a critical meeting I could not miss, so I quickly asked Dave Fish if he could coach one of my players, Rob Hallagan, during his match. Fish was a legend, a veteran Harvard coach who had won six straight national titles. I thought, *This is great. My guy's going to love this.*

I came back after the match. Hallagan had lost badly and was upset. He said that Fish had told him some strange things between games, things that didn't make sense. It was as if Fish was speaking another language. Simply putting the best coach in the country in front of a player didn't work. He had to know the player, what made him tick, what motivated him, what bothered him. A coach had to speak each guy's personal vocabulary.

A few years ago the women's soccer coach at Trinity asked me to come give a talk before an important home match. He had heard I gave inspirational speeches for my teams and knew about my undefeated streak. He wanted to pump up his team. He brought the team to my squash bleachers. I had never met any of them before and all I knew was that they were undefeated and picked to win the league. They were all dressed to play—shin guards, cleats, and ponytails taut, ready to go. For five minutes I was a fire-and-brimstone preacher: "Play like this is the last game of your career. Play like a comet, burn out rather than fade away. Leave no gas in the tank." I was really carrying them along. It was a win-one-for-the-Gipper moment. They were completely entranced and roared out of the room.

They played their worst game of the season and got crushed 7–0.

"For what is genius, I ask you, but the capacity to be obsessed?" This Steven Millhauser quotation struck home when I first read it. If you had to hit the ball a hundred thousand times before you were the best in the world, then you had to sacrifice something. I was obsessed with being a good squash coach, and I sacrificed my relationship with Matthew to make it happen. What I did with my Trinity team—compulsively putting in the time, showing love, creating a caring, supportive environment—I sadly didn't do for my Matthew.

He was born in 1976. His mother and I were high school sweethearts; we got married the summer after I graduated from college. The day he was born, I was in New Haven, coaching the Army gymnastics team at the Easterns. My father called me at the Holiday Inn early one morning. He said, "Hi, Dad."

"Hi, Dad."

"No, hi *Dad*," he said again.

"What do you mean?"

"She had the baby. It is a boy."

I remember leaving the hotel to go to the meet. It was a gorgeous spring day, and as I walked along on York Street, I thought, *My God, I have a son. My life has changed.* As I went into the gym, I also thought, *Oh, it's my father, not my wife, telling me the news. I wasn't at the hospital. I wasn't even in town. That's not good. I hope she's okay.*

As our firstborn, Matthew was a beloved baby and adored as a toddler. But we had two more children—another boy, Scott, when Matthew was four, and a girl, Kristen, when he was seven—and he had to share our attention.

My wife and I grew apart. She became preoccupied with her brother, who was dying of leukemia, and I threw myself into coaching. I worked eighty-hour weeks, a noble thing at West Point. One year I left Christmas night to go on a recruiting trip. I was up before five every morning for reveille. At 5:30 a.m. I would lead a company of 240 men on a three-mile run. Until the halfway turnaround point, they all ran behind me. We turned and everyone raced back to the parade ground. The track team boys always came in first, but I made sure I wasn't beaten by any of the squash or tennis players. Then at lunchtime, some of the other young guys on campus—professors, PE teachers—and I went out on long, loping runs, ten- or twelve-mile jaunts through the leafy back roads and trails at the base. Sometimes we'd jog past Michie Stadium or head toward Camp Buckner, a training center southwest of the campus. In good weather, I also led the squash team on an afternoon jog.

Three runs in a day. I loved running. For many years, I used to jog alone from our hotel to the gymnasium on the day of an away dual match—I did this in a bunch of cities, arriving in a lather of sweat just as my assistant coaches pulled up in the van. I did three marathons. I did one ultra marathon in December 1989. Five of us got up at three in the morning and, trailed by an army jeep, ran out the West Point gates. Nine hours later, we jogged into Giants Stadium in the Meadowlands, where the Army-Navy football game was being played for the first time. The Corps, well aware of our effort to run the fifty-five miles from campus to game, went nuts when we entered the stadium. I'll never forget the thousands of gray-jacketed men waving flags and yelling at the top of their lungs. It was also the last time I ran fifty-five miles. We had forgotten to bring anything more than some sweats, and after sitting in a gelid stadium for three hours, we were frozen stiff and could barely move when we tried to walk out. And Army notoriously lost on a last-second field goal. The lesson: don't run fifty-five miles in December.

West Point was uncomplicated. That was the military way: Black and white. Yes or no. Every Sunday we went to chapel and recited the Cadet Prayer. "Make us to choose the harder right instead of the easier wrong," the prayer went, "and never to be content with a half truth when the whole truth can be won." I had grown up bypassed by the social and cultural tumult of the sixties. I was more a product of the fifties. I was still so young and naïve and innocent to the ways of life.

But children were not black and white. Half truths were the norm, not whole truths. Matthew was mischievous. He had a sheer animal energy. I found that I had no time for ferreting out the nuances behind his behavior. He would throw rocks into the Hudson, even after we told him to stop in case he hit the fishermen along the shoreline. He delighted in orchestrating his trucks and trains into massive crashes that blocked doorways. He was insatiable for attention, and when it didn't come, he would get frustrated and act out. One time I found him on the quad, attacking a statue of George S. Patton with a tennis racquet. I was furious that he would so publicly dishonor the Academy and grounded him for a month. I was always concerned about what people would think. I worried that his misbehavior showed I was a bad leader. If he acted out in public, I would wrench his arm and pull him aside, furiously imploring him to stop, or else. He often came to squash practice but would wander away when it was clear I didn't have time to play with him. It was a tradition for coaches to host their players on the night of the Super Bowl, so instead of sitting on the couch with Matthew and watching the game, the cadets monopolized his father that night each year.

We lived on Biddle Loop in a small row of houses high on a hill overlooking the Hudson. It was known as the Loop, a sort of legends row for coaches: Joe Palone, the soccer coach for twenty-nine years (four Army teams made it to the NCAA semis); Jack Riley, the ice-hockey coach for thirty-six years, who had led the United States to a gold medal in the 1960 Olympic Games; and Leroy Alitz, the wrestling coach (in twenty-three years he taught thirty thousand men to wrestle). Bobby Knight had just moved away. The only other young neighbor was Mike Krzyzewski, who had arrived at West Point a few months after I did to coach the basketball team. As two coaches with young families, we immediately bonded. But the older coaches were wise. Leaving the gym one day, Palone pulled me aside and said, "Don't break Matthew's spirit. Let him run. Children are like horses. You've got to give him some room." I wished I had listened to him, but I was young and confident that I knew how to raise children.

As he neared his teenage years, Matthew developed fickle tastes. He got into edgy hip-hop music. He was creative. He smiled a lot. He loved team sports and was always the loudest, most vociferous guy on the field. And he was good. He played tennis and football equally well.

But there were signs he was not on the right track, or a track I understood. He was very emotional and could cry at the drop of a hat. He was also very shy. At fast-food restaurants, he would grab his younger brother, Scott, and insist that Scott order for him at the counter. He was often very timid. My vision of Matthew was that he would dash to the edge of the diving board and then screech to a halt—to check if there was water in the pool.

Matthew would often show a false bravado and speak in a loud voice, but he usually backed down when confronted. Perhaps the tough talk was simply a way to get my attention in a world full of marching, chanting cadets. In sixth grade he got in the car once smelling of cigarette smoke. At first, he denied he had smoked, saying that he was just with some kids who were. When I stared at him for a while without talking, he admitted he had taken a few puffs. I told him about a relative who died of lung cancer. He said he would never do it again.

I left West Point in 1985, my wife and I separated and divorced, and I led an itinerant life: three years at Apawamis in Rye, New York; two years at Williams College; two years at the Baltimore Country Club; a year at a health club in Seattle; and a year at the Princeton Club in New York. While I was in Baltimore, Matthew came to live with me. He had all but been expelled from two schools up in Williamstown. I saw his face in the bus as it pulled up and thought, "Okay, I can handle this." He stepped off the bus with a bright purple Mohawk. In the numinous light of the bus station, I embraced him, thinking, *I don't think I can.*

He went to the local public school, his fourth school in three years, still in ninth grade. He was a great athlete. He played both varsity football and tennis. But all was not good. He verbally attacked classmates who stared at his tattoos—one was of an Aztec sun on his arm—or hair. After school, he sometimes came to the pro shop at the club and would hang around while I strung racquets. But it was reminiscent of his coming to practice at Army a decade before: I was too busy to pay attention to him. I was driven to achieve my work goals and Matthew was again sharing my time with too many other people. I couldn't break the West Point pattern where my work came first. He would wander off. He sometimes wouldn't go home. Once he took the groundskeeper's golf cart and drove it into a pond below the club's steep sledding hill. Another time, he and the son of a member got into an earsplitting argument in front of dozens of other members. I later learned he was smoking pot at the time, on the weekends and then during the week. I was completely oblivious to the signs, evident in hindsight, that my son was doing drugs. I didn't have the tools, the maturity, the experience, or the energy to manage an unruly, upset child as a single parent. The groundings and scoldings were unsuccessful.

Matthew was a lion roaring—he was my lion—and instead of facing his issues head-on, I ignored them, retreated from them, tried to explain them away.

I sent him back to Williamstown. I knew I was letting him down. I wished my ex-wife and I could have worked together on this, to try to solve the problem together rather than sending it away. But we were no longer an intact family and didn't have the emotional bandwidth to sustain the effort. Once I had taken a weekend off and driven up from Baltimore. After the seven-hour drive, I arrived ten minutes late to pick up Matthew, Scott, and Kristen for the weekend. There was a note on the door: "You are late. I've taken them away."

My parents agreed to take Matthew in. They were in their sixties, and now their retired, suburban life included a pot-smoking, tattooed, angry seventeen-year-old. They were loving and supportive. He behaved pretty well with them, and my sister, Michelle, who lived nearby, put in a lot of time with him. Then pretty much without notice, I was able to regain custody of Matthew, Scott, and Kristen. At this point, I was working at the Princeton Club of New York, living in Pearl River, and getting remarried. The Trinity job opened up and I lunged at it; it would offer us a chance to start anew as a family.

But Matthew spun out of our control. He didn't know how to stop the cycle. I found a small bag of pot in a jacket pocket. He said that he had smoked only a couple of times before, that it was a friend's. As the days went on, I found bags of pot in his room. His teachers called about his skipping class. The principal said he was getting into fights. He was by now unreachable, physically an adult, and somehow he had learned how to control us. He was a master of manipulation. Every concession I made, he increased the demand. He was emotional and outspoken. He was bright and loved reading the newspaper each morning. His mind was there. But Matthew seemed to feel love only when we lurched toward him out of fear of some self-destructive behavior. Then we were in his grasp. I played in to this because I felt so guilty about my obsession with work. I knew I had let him down in the past and now wanted to make up for it.

Matthew was elusive. He missed curfew. He missed appointments. Much of the time, we simply did not know where he was. When he was home, he hibernated in his room, door shut. Like Minerva's owl, he would disappear after dusk.

One night he didn't come home at all. I lay in bed till about three, when I gave up pretending I could sleep. I drank my Diet Coke in the kitchen and waited until dawn before I started calling around. I called his friends. Nothing. I called his therapist, who said not to worry, that Matthew was working it out. I called emergency rooms. I called police stations. Scott and Kristen were scared, shakily eating their toast, dark rings under their eyes.

He came home that afternoon and didn't say a word, but went straight to his room. After sleeping for about eighteen hours, he woke up and came into the kitchen. "Don't worry," he said. "I learned my lesson." *What lesson was that?* I asked myself as he left for school.

Later that day, I found a Ziploc bag of pot when I was putting the coats away. Yellow and blue made green. It was senior spring for him and he was just a quarter credit from getting his high school diploma. It would have been an incredible achievement after all he had done and gone through, his circuitous journey becoming straight at a finish line. But it was not to be. I didn't want to expose his sister and brother to drugs, to make them think it was normal to break rules, pollute their bodies, disobey their parents. I couldn't insulate them from the storm that Matthew carried around with him.

I kicked him out of the house. I went up to Matthew's room. He was sitting on his bed, looking at a comic book. I said, "Matthew, it's over."

I was surprised at how inane I sounded, but then it suddenly felt like we were breaking up. A divorce. I looked around the room, avoiding his eyes. I saw his closet overflowing with a bramble of boots and shirts and jackets. Nothing on the hangers. I was glad he was lounging on the bed, two-dimensional, flat, his brooding bulk not upright and confronting me. "You are old enough to know the difference between good and bad. I have said that this has to be a drug-free house. Your little sister is only thirteen. It's not fair to her." I wanted an apology.

He shut his eyes. I didn't mean to be cruel. I didn't want to accuse him of failure, to make him bear a burden.

"Fine," he said in a sarcastic voice, his body utterly still.

This goaded me. My rage bubbled up. I stepped into the room and said, in a thick voice: "You have to move out."

Wordlessly, he got up. I stepped aside. He walked downstairs, grabbed his blue rain jacket and opened the front door in one fluid motion. He kept going, not turning around, as if he had planned the exit, as if he had expected this for years. He didn't pack. He didn't go through his gear or grab anything. He just walked out without a glance behind.

In the rain, I walked coatless, hoping he would turn around. If he did, I would have let him come back, embraced him, forgiven, given him shelter from the storm. I had created this mess and he was bearing the brunt of it.

He kept on walking down Firetown Road. The odd thing was that it was busy that afternoon. Cars were flying down the road, windshield wipers going, brake lights flashing. and Matthew walking alone. He grew smaller as the distance engulfed him in the blur of rain, leaves, tarmac, and gray sky.

He reached Route 10, took a right, and went out of my life. He had nothing. No money. Eighteen years old. No clothes except what was on his back. Nowhere to go, and yet he still left.

When I started as a squash coach, I knew nothing about the need to put in time and love. I knew nothing about squash, either. In the summer of 1976, Ron Holmberg, the tennis coach at Army, retired. Holmberg was a Goliath on campus, even though he had been there just since 1970. On the court, he had beaten Rod Laver in the junior finals at Wimbledon, played in the Davis Cup, and was in the top ten nationally. His teams were good. He had a tennis racquet model with his name on it. Everyone at West Point knew Holmberg.

At the time I was an assistant gymnastics coach, and I applied for the position. I had come to West Point in the summer of 1974, fresh from Springfield College. I had meet Colonel Johnson, the head gymnastics coach, two years earlier at a training session at West Point when I went out for the U.S. Olympic team. He had said, "You know, when you finish at Springfield, maybe you could come coach with me here." I didn't make the Olympic team, but I found myself a job.

In 1974, the gymnastics assistant coach position was designated for an enlisted man, and therefore, on my first day at West Point, Colonel Anderson, the officer in charge of the physical education department, informed me that instead of going to work with Colonel Johnson, I was headed to Fort Dix in New Jersey for basic training. It was a nine-week ordeal I'll never forget: five-in-the-morning wakeups, a shaved head, dog tags, rifle disassembling, thousands and thousands of push-ups. I had a crusty drill sergeant who had done two tours of duty in Vietnam and held no truck with a college boy like me. We bivouacked in the woods in midwinter. We did gas warfare training, which meant taking off your gas mask in a room full of tear gas and yelling out your name, rank, and serial number—it felt like a million ants crawling up your nose.

Private First Class Paul Dominick Anthony Assaiante returned to West Point a different person. I loved the team and the physical skills that gymnastics had taught me—a party trick of mine was walking a long distance just on my hands, with my feet high in the air—but I decided to quit coaching after getting hurt. It was a Saturday in December 1975. I was in the gym, training a few cadets. I did my usual floor routine. I finished my final double back flip, but as I went into the second flip, I bailed out early. For a second I thought, *Oh, this is nothing. I'm okay*, as I tried to quickly rationalize what had happened. But I lay on the mat and could not feel my entire body. I was paralyzed.

Ned Crossley, the head coach, called for an ambulance. As I lay on the mat, I floated in and out of consciousness. An open-faced young EMT came and pricked my foot with a needle. This was the Babinski test, to see if I had feeling in my feet. I croaked out a dry-mouthed yes even though it was not true. The ambulance drove me the hospital as

I winced in pain. The X-ray revealed that I had badly bruised three vertebrae but that the paralysis would be temporary, just a result of the swelling of the spinal cord. It took a whole day to get feeling back and a week before I could walk comfortably. The doctors said I could compete in gymnastics again, but I was too frightened to attempt the dangerous moves necessary to coach the way I wanted. I spent hours in spotting belts and cables trying to regain the courage I needed, but it was gone.

Tennis seemed a better outlet for me. It was safer, more social, less narcissistic, and easier to learn than gymnastics. The proprioception—the sense of where my body was in space—I had developed in the gym allowed me to know where my racquet needed to be. Ground strokes came to me quickly. I never developed that sort of instinctual hand-eye coordination that guys who grew up playing had, and my game was based on determination and drive, not deftness of touch. Of course, being who I was, I started to obsess about tennis. I played several hours a day, seven days a week, often with officers or junior varsity players. I read every book I could find. This was at the end of the wooden racquet era: tight shorts, socks pulled up high on the ankles, nylon stringing that you could use to spin the serve: rough or smooth.

Getting pretty decent, I entered some tournaments. I won the Orange County and Rockland County championships. I earned a regional ranking after reaching the later rounds of big events. I once played a match at the Port Washington Tennis Academy on Long Island against a local high school hotshot. A lefty, he was able to swing his serve so wide it would smack into the screens before I could touch it. I had heard he was pretty arrogant, but he wasn't with me, probably because I wasn't good enough to get his attention (he beat me 6–4, 6–3). A couple of months later I saw his name in the paper: John McEnroe had made it to the semifinals of Wimbledon.

It was around this time that Holmberg retired. I wanted to become a head coach rather than an assistant, and I liked tennis, so I applied for his job. It was a grueling process, as they offered the job to seven other finalists, all of whom turned it down once they learned that the coach would be a member of the Physical Education Department. That meant leading the daily 5:30 a.m. reveille run—reveille was rain or shine, every day West Point was in session— teaching gymnastics, wrestling, and other programs six days a week and no summers off. They offered me the job because I seemed to be the only person in the country interested in it.

When I got the phone call, Colonel Anderson and I met for an hour in his office. He outlined the job description. As tennis coach, I was also now the head squash coach. "Squash?" I asked. "What is that?" He did not smile or even grin. He escorted me over to the second floor of Cadet Gymnasium and showed me West Point's squash facility: twenty old squash courts queued up along a crepuscular hallway. Every court had a smear of marks along the walls where thousands of carbon-based balls had slammed.

At age twenty-seven, I was now the U.S. Military Academy's coach of a sport I had never heard of. Had Holmberg done this, too? I never knew it existed. I didn't know how to score, what the rules were, what techniques and strategies players used. I didn't know any of its history. I didn't know where to recruit players or buy equipment. It was entirely new. I only knew squash the vegetable and I didn't like it.

I brought in the returning upperclassmen. By then I had learned that in the previous season Army had come in eighth in the nation (one ahead of Trinity, it turned out) with a 10–6 record. Six lettermen walked into my office, all crew cuts, strong legs, and earnest faces. I introduced myself and, with brutal honesty, said I knew nothing about their game. They said, "No problem, Coach," and escorted me out onto the court—at first they had thought I must have been joking, but within seconds it was painfully clear I was serious. They taught me the basics and explained the rules. I blindly stumbled into an essential fact of living: you earn credibility if you don't pretend to be someone you aren't.

Worried about handing the reins of a varsity program to a young novice, Army appointed Lieutenant Colonel J. H. Bradley to be the nominal head coach; I was his interim assistant. Bradley, a personable career officer, didn't know much about coaching, but he had played some squash before. He was generous with his time in teaching me how to play. I remembered his hitting boasts, an advanced drop shot where the ball ricochets off three walls. I could never reach his boasts. He would say, "You're fast. Why don't you run and get that ball?" I would say, "I would, but I have no idea where the hell to go."

Over the next days, I soaked up what I could about the history of Army squash. I learned that the courts had been built sometime in the 1930s. Superintendent Maxwell Taylor, an avid squash player, started a varsity team in 1946 and hired Leif Nordlie to coach it. Like me, Nordlie was from the Bronx. He had taught himself both tennis and squash and gotten jobs at a couple of country clubs around the New York area. He was a good player and had reached the finals of the professional nationals (now called the Tournament of Champions). The team was not bad. In sixteen seasons, Nordlie had just one losing record, and fourteen times had three loses or less; in 1952, they came in second in the nation with a 10–1 record and wins over Yale, Dartmouth, Amherst, Trinity, Williams, and Princeton. In 1949, a cadet named Charlie Oliver reached the finals of the intercollegiates.

In 1963, Bill Cullen, a top amateur tennis player, replaced Nordlie. Cullen had played varsity basketball at Wake Forest; that top-twenty team won the ACC title. He was a good squash coach. In 1964, Army held three match points in a 5–4 loss to Harvard. In 1965, Walter Oehrlein ran through a rash of tiebreakers to win the intercollegiate title. The next day, the superintendent announced the victory over the loudspeaker at dinner and all twenty-five hundred cadets gave him a standing ovation. Cullen left in 1970 for Swarthmore, Ron Holmberg arrived and maintained the tradition of excellence—twice the team was in the top five.

My first dual match with Army was against Harvard up in Cambridge. We lost 9–0 and every match was 3–0. I always adored how the *Harvard Crimson* reported on the dual match. They wrote that it was like "nine hydrogen bombs lined up against an equal number of water pistols." In the end, that first season we went 5–6. I was thrilled we had not lost too much ground, but the losing record was not great, nor was our loss to Navy. If we had beaten our archrival, we could have lost our other ten dual matches 9–0 and the Army brass would have been pleased. In fact, Oehrlein later told me that the key thing for his career at West Point, much more important than his extraordinary intercollegiate title, was that Army beat Navy all three years he was on the varsity.

The rivalry was breathtakingly intense, with months of buildup and pep rallies and lectures. There was talk of playing for your country, of honoring your beloved academy. In each of the three athletic seasons, all the Army and Navy teams played the same weekend. If the matches were in Annapolis, the entire academy emptied to go down. If you were a member of a winning team, your life dramatically changed in the short term—seating regulations for meals were relaxed, etc.— and in the long term, you were someone who had beaten Navy.

Navy had thirty-six courts scattered around four gyms. Their coach was Art Potter, who had led the team to the national title in 1957, 1959, and 1967—the only years a non–Ivy League squad was crowned national champion until Trinity won in 1999. Potter pushed the envelope. At every home match, he brought in the entire brigade of Midshipmen—forty-five hundred men in dress whites—to chant, sing, and cheer. Stacking the lineup was an annual charge against his teams. Some years it was said he would blithely place his number 9 player at number 2. In 1959, based on such accusations, Yale dropped Navy from its schedule, a protest that lasted seventeen years.

My first dual match in Annapolis was Potter's last, and he was keen to go out with a final win over Army. We arrived the day before and had a hit on Navy's courts. The next morning when we came back in for our dual match, we found that the doors had been opened and the walls and floor were slippery with condensation from the humid Chesapeake. We later learned that Potter had his middies practice all week on slippery courts. We slithered to a 9–0 loss.

Still, we came in eighth in the nation (out of twenty-two varsities) because of our daunting schedule—we played all the top teams, including all the Ivy League squads, which dominated college squash. I worked very hard, putting in a tremendous amount of time to get up to speed. I read squash books. I asked my players for tips. I went to teaching clinics. But in a way, I never lost that feeling I had that afternoon with the commandant, gazing at the row of squash courts in the old gym: the feeling that I was an outsider, that I was a guy with a vowel at the end of his name in a WASPy sport, that I was too young (I grew a mustache to look older than my players), that I was a latecomer to the game.

Every couple of months the entire time I was a coach at Army, I dreamed that I was coaching the match against Navy, and a general would walk down the bleachers and onto the court and stop the match. With a microphone, he'd tell the crowd, "This man is an imposter." Usually I woke from the dream and could not go back to sleep, afraid that the dream would return. Once in real life I went down to a country club in Virginia to give an exhibition. I wanted to look like a real player, with an armful of fresh racquets as I strode into the club. I called our racquet company and had them overnight a half-dozen new ones to me. They arrived still in their plastic wrapping, and I shoved them into my bag. When I got to the courts, I proudly walked out with five of the new racquets under my arm, feeling great. I took a racquet out of the wrapping and went out to warm up like the big-time pro I was. My opponent hit a ball to me, and I swung at it but oddly didn't make contact. I glanced down. The racquet was unstrung.

It was not just squash. While tennis was more familiar to me, I didn't feel entirely comfortable with that sport, either. In 1981, Colonel Jim Peterson asked me if I wanted to put together a book about tennis. I asked a dozen friends in the tennis world—Vic Braden, Fred Stolle, and a gaggle of fellow college coaches—and cobbled together a collection of essays and photographs for *Championship Tennis by the Experts*. The book did fine: I think at least seven people read it. But I was still an outsider. At my first tennis practice at Army, I stood in the wrong position by the net and one player returned a serve right into my temple. I went down in an instant, and for a second, I thought I was back on the gymnastics mat with another career-threatening injury.

Squash at Army presented one major problem: Only once in my nine seasons at West Point did I have a freshman who had played squash before. Almost all of them had never even heard of the game. None of the other top squash programs, not even Navy, faced such a situation. It was a miracle that I could field at team at all, let alone produce two All Americans: Dan Hammond, a first-teamer in 1979, and Dan Kellas, a second-teamer in 1983. Moreover, the team stayed good. In fact, I am more proud of one statistic than any other in my career: in my twenty-eight years of college squash coaching, every single team of mine, including the nine at Army, has been ranked in the top ten in the nation at the end of the season.

At West Point I started to become a real coach. I recruited most of my squash team from my tennis team. Some did it to stay in shape or to develop their racquet skills. Others did it because it allowed them to eat at the training tables reserved for varsity athletes, thus avoiding some of the mealtime hazing that all the other plebes endured. And some others did it simply because as a plebe their only other option for the winter was intramural boxing. Fear is a wonderful motivator.

Having to teach the game to pure novices each year forced me to learn the game—to figure out strategy, tactics, and technique—from the bottom up and, just as important, to learn how to impart the information. It also gave me a sense of the long view, that this was a four-year process, and this in turn taught me that coaching was really a lifetime process, that I was not just teaching them a new game but leading them to new values, new attitudes, new horizons. Each fall I told my players that I did not know more about squash than they did. They appreciated my honesty. I said I could not help that much with the technical side. I was a gymnast. I knew about movement, about the body in space, about strength, agility, flexibility. I told them, "Here is what I can do. I can whittle it down to the essence. I can make you fit and I can help you attain a flow. I can make you a better athlete and a better competitor and hopefully a better person."

But mostly I worked on what was between their ears. I knew that in order to take these converted tennis players anywhere, I had to learn what truly made them tick. I learned by watching body language. I could tell what they were feeling and thinking about from how they moved on court. I didn't need to know the score. I could tell from their facial expressions, their shoulders, their posture, what they needed to hear in between games. You could especially see it in the introductory handshake at the start of the dual match. The way a person was carrying himself told the coach and the opponent what he was feeling emotionally and psychologically. The one thing I knew was that a player has to keep his head up. It was what my grandmother always said: Keep your head up; walk like a proud stallion. I found that this was also good advice going into a squash match. You might not feel good, but don't let your opponent know that.

For *Championship Tennis by the Experts*, I interviewed Billie Jean King and asked her for some important coaching tips. She said, "Number one, never let a player be late to anything. Number two, body language will tell you all you ever need to know. The body can't lie." I think of her second piece of advice about ten times a day—whenever a player walks into my office.

In year two, Colonel Bradley, my nominal overseer, disappeared, reassigned to some other corner of the West Point bureaucracy. We switched to a new ball, the 70+, which was slower than the old Cragin-Simplex hardball. The game was still in our North American eighteen-and-a-half-foot-wide court, but the new ball brought it closer to the international softball game that was played everywhere else in the world. I started to get the hang of squash, and our team record improved, first to twelve victories that season, then fifteen, and then eighteen, the most wins in Army history. (It helped that I scheduled as many dual matches as I could, as that was the only real way our neophytes could improve: by seeing different styles and playing against guys other than the dozen Army teammates who knew just as little as they did. Unlike players in many college towns, we had no one in the surrounding community to spar with.) I slowly integrated into the squash community. I started playing tournaments and recorded my top pro North American singles ranking of nineteen. In 1979, I was elected secretary of the collegiate association. I twice ran the individual nationals at West Point; at the first one, in 1978, we were able to inaugurate a new glass-back show court paid for and named after an alum, Russ Ball.

In 1980 and 1981, we reached our highest rank, six in the nation. Our 1980 season, when we went 18–5, was especially exciting as we had our one real shot at beating Navy. In the dual match, held at West Point, we were up 4–3 and leading in both of the final matches. The crowd of cadets was screaming—the loudest, shrillest noise I have ever heard. Eventually it came down to our number 5 player, a junior named Russ Berkoff. It was in this match that I learned the lesson of loving my players.

Russ had been my only bona fide squash recruit at West Point. He had grown up in Buffalo and learned squash at the Jewish Center, where his father, Saul, worked. Berkoff was pretty good. He won the Buffalo C championship as a fifteen-year-old, capturing a pressure-filled final 15–13 in the fifth. The same year he made it to the second round of the under-sixteen nationals before losing to Mark Talbott. Two years later he again made it to the second round of the nationals, this time the under-eighteens, before again losing to a future Hall of Famer, John Nimick. Russ even played on the Buffalo team that competed in the old national team tournament at the adult nationals in 1977, going down valiantly to the eventual winners, Mexico City. Russ had true squash credentials.

What's more, he applied to only three colleges—Navy, Air Force, and West Point—and his first choice was West Point. I felt incredibly lucky to have him. Once he arrived, though, we butted heads. He thought I was cocky. I thought he was immature and not contributing to the team off the court. He struggled academically and was getting up in the middle of the night to study. I was not attentive enough and wouldn't give him the space necessary to balance his squash and his studies. Eventually, he quit the team. I managed to persuade him back for our Navy match. It was at home and I thought with Russ on board we might have a chance to pip the Midshipmen.

At the start, Russ played beautifully. His parents and his girlfriend had driven down from Buffalo and he seemed inured to the noise and pressure. He went up 2–0, and when he got to 14–6, Bobby Bayliss, the Navy coach who had succeeded Art Potter, came over to me and shook my hand. "Great job, Paul. Congratulations, the better team won today," he said. "You guys were too good for us today. I can't bear to watch any more of this." He walked out of the gym and got into his van.

Forty-five minutes later, I came out to the van and said, "Bobby, you've got to come back in. It's in the fifth game." Russ had squandered the eight match points and was about to lose.

A few minutes later it was official. Army had again lost to Navy. I pulled Russ into my office and yelled at him. I let all my frustrations out. "We were this close," I said angrily. Russ was equally upset, with me and with himself,

It was a horrible mistake. Coming this close to beating Navy— losing eight match points—was a catastrophic burden to place on a twenty-year-old, and I should have been comforting, not accusatory. He played on the team senior year, but I had lost any chance to redeem myself after the incident in my office and we maintained a strictly business relationship. After he graduated, we lost touch. I later learned Russ Berkoff spent two decades in the Special Forces in the Middle East and Asia, showing he could respond under pressure, *real* pressure. Much of coaching is knowing when to say something and when to keep silent. After the loss to Navy in 1980, I never again talked to a player immediately after a match he lost because he would be too worked up to hear anything. It was best to let the emotions settle.

The next day I wrote a long letter to Bayliss. I complimented him on his team's hard work and courage. It was, I think, a kind of expiation, of apologizing to Russ. Bayliss, meanwhile, wrote me a letter expressing his deep respect for our team, for Russ's good sportsmanship, and suggesting that it was better to be lucky than good. Our two letters passed each other and arrived at West Point and Annapolis on the same day.

Nonetheless, the Navy loss hung as a specter for me. For years, I thought about it, going over every interaction with Russ, replaying everything I did wrong, knowing for sure that the reason Russ had not clinched one of those match points in the third game was because I had not gotten to know him. I hadn't provided a loving environment. I hadn't put the time in.

Years later, when I became the coach at Williams, our first dual match was against Navy. Our team was much, much better, but given my goose-egg record against Navy I thought, *Well, here's my chance to blow it again.* We won 9–0. It was a very small satisfaction—there were a dozen people in the gallery, about 990 fewer than our dual matches at Army—but satisfaction nonetheless. Still, I never forgot Russ Berkoff.

Vikram Malhotra was from Mumbai. He was as heralded a recruit as we could get from India. Just before he got to Hartford, he captained the Indian national junior team to a fourth-place finish at the world junior championships in Zurich, Switzerland. He made it to the quarters of the individual tournament as well, losing 9–7, 9–7, 9–7 to the eventual champion in a very exciting contest. And he had won the under-eleven, -thirteen, -fifteen, -seventeen, and -nineteen national titles, becoming the first person to sweep the junior titles in India.

A descendant of John Coltrane in spirit, Vikram could move the ball according to the prescribed traditions, and then he could beautifully improvise, sending out an arpeggio of unexpected, unreturnable shots. He had flair. He could alternate between soft, skyscraping lobs, medium-pace crosscourts, and the occasional volley crushed into the front-wall nick. He had a beautiful sense of deception and was able to wrong-foot anyone. Each winter he had trained in Cairo with the Egyptian national coach, Amir Wagih. In Wagih's stable were the two great thoroughbreds of twenty-first century squash, Amr Shabana and Ramy Ashour, winners of a combined five world championships. Shabana and Ashour played aggressive, attacking squash, and Vikram ended up absorbing that mentality.

In some ways, he was a typical Indian squash kid. He started to play at age nine when his father, a textile exporter, took him to his club and gave him a lesson. Within a few years, he had to choose between cricket and squash. He was good at cricket, an opening batter, new-ball bowler, captain of his school XI. But he selected squash because he wanted to be on the national stage, king of a sport, and it was almost impossible to do that in cricket, with millions of boys playing.

He got good at squash, training at the Otters Club, but had a dev-astating early tournament loss to someone he had beaten in practice, someone who had gone out and played a bunch of tournaments and suddenly was toughened up. He wept after the match. At the cere-mony concluding the tournament, his father pointed out the trophies. "Do you want one of those?" he asked.

"Yes," Vikram said.

"Then start training."

Vikram ended up at number 8 on the Trinity ladder. It was not surprising. He had the classic freshman-year experience. He started too low on the ladder—I didn't want to batter the egos of the guys high on the ladder by having him start at the top—and he did not have enough time to climb up. Compounding the issue was that he severely twinged his hamstring early in January and it took weeks to recover. He was not good at challenges and lost a couple, including one to our number 7, Andres Vargas, in a match I thought he would surely win. He also had a whirlwind time in January. He arrived on campus one afternoon, after forty hours of travel (Mumbai to Dubai to JFK), and the next morning he returned to JFK on a training trip to Colombia. Moreover, he struggled to get up to speed academically at the same time he was thrown into a varsity sport. Like many of the Indian recruits, he took a long while to adjust to life in Hartford, the classes, the homework, the routines. He had never been to the States before matriculating and was a bit homesick. He spent hours each day on his cell phone, talking to his father. He also fell behind in his classes. When I saw this happening, I jumped in immediately. I was not going to have another Russ Berkoff or Danny Hammond situation.

Vikram was introverted, and for all his barrel-chested, quicksilver flamboyance on court—the earring in each ear—he was sensitive and finicky but also very sweet and kind-hearted. He was a congenital gear-head and wanted the latest and best stuff. (He owned more cricket equipment than some cricket pros.) He wanted his headband to match his shoes. He wanted a particular racquet with a particular stringing tension. (Most guys were thrilled to get a racquet restrung and couldn't care less about the tension.) Sometimes he coasted—like many supremely talented people, he couldn't always find relevance in practice.

At number 8, though, he was vastly more skilled than anyone he played. He didn't lose a game all season. Even against Princeton, he was dominant. On Valentine's Day, he played against Santiago Imberton. Vikram poleaxed him, losing just fourteen points.

Today, as we gaze at the lineup, Vikram is our only automatic point, we think. But Santiago, a tall basher from El Salvador, had caused us fits year after year. He was a bit of an unorthodox player, an attacker who hit unusual shots—he was as apt to scythe a reverse (a shot that put the ball dangerously out in the middle of the court, useful mostly for its surprise factor, since no one usually hit it) or a skid boast (an unorthodox lob) as he was to drive the ball. Most distinctively, he had a magnificent hold, one of the best in the collegiate ranks: he could dangle his racquet above the ball, waiting until the last possible moment before flicking it.

Today, Vikram struggles slightly in the first game, unable to clinch game point, and then he imperiously strokes two consecutive drop shots, *bam, bam*, as if to say, *Well, I've let this foolishness go on long enough and now I am going to end the game.*

After the first game, I counsel him not to let up. But he does. He is feeling some of the pressure. The crowd is hectoring just feet away, screaming about his shoes, his earrings, and his hair. He starts to fool around. He hits a reverse serve, highly risky in a sport where you only get one serve, not two. Santiago goes up 7–3 and then 8–7. Vikram starts attacking only when it is his serve, and he methodically tiptoes back into it. Serving at 7–8, he has a long rally. With brio, Vikram does a magical thing, something no number 8 player pulls off: He holds his racquet as if he is going to hit a drop and then at the last second wrists a hard, high drive. Santiago is frozen and can't touch it. The shot says, "So you think you can hold the ball? I can do it better than you." He wins the next two points in the tiebreaker.

Now I am worried about a letdown. I saw them all the time. When you were very good, you often played teams that were not. I told my players when we were about to face a much weaker opponent, "Show this man respect. He's got on his college uniform. He has been practicing all fall, too. He's been lifting weights and doing sprints. He came here today to play. Show respect by trying your hardest. Play eight gut-busting points at the beginning, all high and wide, no shots. No balls below the cut line. Long points. He's going to come into the match trying to stay out on court as long as possible—you know, the whole 'I paid my entry fee, I want my money's worth' attitude. Show him that staying on court is going to kill him. When he is winded, chop him." Once, a few years ago, Shaun Johnstone was up 9–0, 9–0, 8–0. He was playing Dan Petrie, an excellent player from Brown. Petrie had grown up in Cincinnati and was well coached, a nice, hard-working kid, and one of the top Americans in collegiate squash. At 8–0, Shaun dove twice for balls. Shaun always dove—his nickname was Stones, but this stone moved more like a Super Ball. It was nice to see him diving when he was ahead so much. He wanted to win every match with three doughnuts. That was respect.

I remembered seeing Lou Holtz's Arkansas football team up by a huge amount after a first half. When they kicked off to start the second half, they tried an onside kick. The message was clear: Never let up, never give an inch. Someday the tables will be reversed and you'll want the same respect.

Part of the issue is about numbers. The score is just one measurement of success, and I spend much of my time trying to inculcate an indifference to the score. The score is just one story. You can't ignore it, but you should care more about how you're playing and what the next point is going to be about and how you feel. You should play the same regardless of the score.

In the third game, Vikram runs out the string. He squeezes off winners at will. He is playing one point at a time, which is hard to do when you are either winning easily or losing badly. His win knots the dual match score at Trinity 2, Princeton 2.

CHAPTER FIVE

Learning to Lose: Randy

Ben Hogan knew how to lose. He knew how to recover from setbacks. He grew up poor in Fort Worth. As a boy, he found his father after he had committed suicide. Hogan won thirty professional golf tournaments before capturing his first major—still the record for the most tour wins prior to a first major.

At the 1946 Masters, Hogan finally maneuvered himself into position to win a major. He was eighteen feet from the hole on the seventy-second green. But he three-putted and lost by one stroke. He did it again later that summer, at the 1946 U.S. Open, three-putting the final green to miss a playoff by a stroke.

Somehow he recovered. Later that year Hogan won the 1946 PGA Championship, and in 1948 he captured the U.S. Open and the PGA. In 1949 he suffered a horrific car accident. The doctors told him he'd never walk again, let alone play golf. Sixteen months later, he stood over his second shot, on the eighteenth fairway at Merion Golf Club, in the last round of the 1950 U.S. Open.

He had to make par to get into a play-off. It was the thirty-sixth hole he had played that warm summer day. He was exhausted. He had just bogeyed fifteen and seventeen. Was another late-round collapse in progress? The memories of the three-putts from 1946 were burnt into his mind; the memories of the three Grand Slam victories were there, too. He pulled out a one-iron, the most difficult iron to control. He cracked the ball two hundred feet on a rope, landed it at the front of the tiny, postage-stamp green, and rolled it up close to the pin— a stunning shot. He easily two-putted and forced the play off, which he won.

Hogan striking that one-iron at Merion is one of the most famous photographs in sports. But whenever I see it, I think of those 1946 three-putts.

Sports are about losing. If you add up all the wins and losses in anyone's career, you'll come up with more losses. Even the greatest players, when you toss in all those middle-school meltdowns and minor-league blowouts, don't have winning career records. Failure is inevitable. If you make an out seven out of ten times in baseball, you punch your ticket to Cooperstown. One hundred and twenty-seven players have to lose for the 128th to be crowned U.S. Open champion. Life is about losing. After all, we lose our parents and our friends, and eventually we lose ourselves.

Originally, I wanted this book to be titled *Teaching Your Child to Lose*. How you manage loss is the critical difference between good and bad leadership. Parents and coaches often react the wrong ways, and young people learn more from how we react than from what we say after a loss. The performance might be almost exactly the same in a win as in a loss—the strokes the same, the production the same, the sweat the same—until the very end when the scoreboard reveals a different outcome.

The winner gets satisfaction and moves on. Winners seldom reflect at length upon a win. Why fix what's not broken? Upon winning, kids usually lock the victory in a box. Regardless of whether they win in straight 9–0 games or 10–9 in the fifth, they tend to treat the match the same. That's why a rematch—like today's with Princeton—is so tricky, as some of the winners from the first dual match will not have learned enough from their win.

The loser, on the other hand, has toppled into the abyss of self-examination, swiping the magnifying glass over every play. He has internalized the match and takes it personally. A win produces not enough concern; a loss produces too much. You see this in collegiate tennis, when a player loses a first-set tiebreaker. Instead of thinking, *Okay, I'm close; I just need to adjust a couple of things a little,* the player often is crushed: *Oh, how terrible. I lost a breaker. I'm down a* set. *This is a disaster.* Results are nothing more than progress reports, but a lot of athletes can't read them.

I saw this in Marty Clark. A four-time national champion, he was one of the best U.S. squash players of his generation—a dozen years after he quit the pro tour, his highest world ranking (fifty-nine) was still fourth-best all-time among American men. Extremely bright, he had squeezed everything he could from his limited athletic ability. At the same time, he was a perfectionist and had trouble when things went wrong, and he'd hassle referees and opposing players if he sensed a loss was coming.

In 1996, I was appointed the U.S. national men's coach. I thought it would be a blast to work with the top American players. Instead, I was back juggling egos and would have just a few days a year to correct a decade of bad habits. At a tournament like the 1999 Pan-Am Games in Winnipeg, there were four players on the team, yet only three could play, so I was guaranteed to have 25 percent of my team angry with me on any given day.

At the 1999 Pan-Am Games, Marty melted down after frittering away a 2–1 lead over Graham Ryding, a Canadian player ranked in the top twenty in the world. As he insolently tore into the ref, he was on the verge of being defaulted. Somehow he finished the match, and I quickly guided him into an adjacent badminton court. For twenty minutes we screamed obscenities at each other. I was brutal and frank. I told him he had embarrassed himself, our team, our sport, and our country. He was close to tears; I was shaking with anger.

When we finished, I turned and saw his parents—they had been watching this whole pas de deux from the corner of the court. Afraid they would be upset with how I had just treated their son, I tiptoed past them. Marty's mother grabbed my arm and whispered, "Thank you."

Randy Lim, Trinity's number 5, has the same issue. He doesn't know how to lose.

An axiom among coaches is the notion that you can't coach speed;

it's God given. Randy Lim is fast. He's quick to the ball and quick to recover when he finds himself out of position. He stalks anything loose with a vengeance. In addition, he has incredibly soft hands, a truly tactile feeling for the game. He can hit a drop shot so softly that it seems to have been blown to the front wall rather than hit. He is whippet-thin, no more than five feet seven, with about negative 3 percent body fat. He is a proud man, cocky as a bullfinch. At the start of his swing, he will hook his wrist down—as if he is delicately holding a stinking dead fish. It is an extra motion that suggests, *I have plenty of time. You are not rushing me.*

He was an All-American as a freshman. He is consumed with numbers. He wants to be number 3 on the ladder. He is not. He is number 5 and probably should be number 6. Since he arrived a year and a half ago from Malaysia, he has been slowly recalibrating his self-perception and image.

Swimming was his passion when he was a boy in Penang. He won national junior age-group titles in the butterfly and breaststroke. He loved the freedom he felt in the water. His uncle played squash, and at age twelve Randy hit once a week to keep in shape for swimming. He started to get migraines; water getting trapped in his ear seemed to be the cause. He tried track and field (he would go on to run the eight hundred and fifteen hundred meters in high school) and badminton, perhaps the most popular sport in the country, but at age thirteen he made squash his sport. He wanted to excel, to be the best, so he carried his lifestyle over from swimming and eagerly began a twice-a-day training regimen. After three months, Penang squash officials selected him for their junior squad. He was on the Malaysian team that went to the world junior championships in 2004 and 2006. He was never the best junior in the country in part because he declined to enter the national squash academy in Kuala Lumpur—despite his intensity, he wanted to keep some balance between squash, his studies, and his social life. Also, he suffered a horrific motorcycle accident when he was seventeen. One rainy night a car plowed into him and sent him skidding off his bike; his arm was ripped open and his foot required twenty-five stitches.

After graduating from high school in December 2005, Randy entered a local college and studied engineering. His friends on the junior squad went out to play the pro tour, but Randy's thoughts were on transferring to a U.S. university. His sister had just finished at Arizona State, and his father's brother was in the Special Forces of the U.S. Army and based in Austin. Randy applied to schools with good engineering departments, such as San Jose State and Nebraska. He then emailed with Kimlee Wong, a Malaysian who was two years ahead of him in school, and Kimlee persuaded him to apply to Princeton, where he could study engineering and play squash for a top-caliber team. Princeton deferred him and Bob Callahan, the Tigers coach, thoughtfully passed Randy on to me, suggesting that maybe he could get in to Trinity.

Randy dashed up the ladder upon his arrival in the fall of 2007. He beat almost everyone in challenge matches, getting to number 3. But after winter break, he plummeted to number 7. He had trouble adapting to the team aspect of Trinity Squash, to caring less about his spot on the ladder. He had scoured the Internet before coming to Hartford and tracked down the results of his future teammates. He calculated. He had finished third in a major tournament in Kuala Lumpur; Manek had finished eighth. He could not accept being number 7 on the team, well behind Manek. Kimlee was number 2 at Princeton; Randy was as good as Kimlee, and Trinity had beaten Princeton.

Early in his Trinity career, sometimes his emotions would get the best of him. In a match against Yale, he lost the first game to a guy who was about ten inches taller and a hundred pounds heavier. Randy left the court scowling. "You can't play squash," he blurted out, half to his opponent, half to himself. "You suck." He chucked his racquet along the hallway and refused to go back on court for the second game. "I'm not playing," he told me with an imperious glare.

"What do you mean?" I said.

"This guy sucks."

"You have to go back."

"Cannot," he said. It was a competition to see who could speak in the shortest sentences. That was about the only thing he was winning that day. We talked to him for another minute and persuaded him to go back out. Pissed off, he cleaned up the next three games. The joke went around the team and for months, when anyone didn't want to do something, it was one quick word: "Cannot."

At the intercollegiates that year, he almost gave away a match. He was playing Santiago Imberton in the finals of the consolations. Santiago was someone who, on paper, Randy should have a fairly easy time with. But it was a consolation match, the last of six matches he had played that weekend, and the tail end of a long season, and Randy, it occurred to me, seemed to have little appetite for a hard fight. After losing the first game 9–6, he blatantly tanked the second 9–0. I got up from the bleachers, and after a deep stare into Randy's jaunty brown eyes, I walked away. I was not going to watch him embarrass himself.

The upperclassmen, however, saw this as a sign that I was leaving it up to them. They sat Randy down after the second game and laid into him. He won the third, 9–3. Santiago pushed it to the limit in the fourth and Randy escaped 10–8. One of the guys came to get me, and I came back for the fifth. "Shark, Shark," they yelled after each point. He won the fifth 9–2.

As a sophomore, Randy was in a better space. Although he was not actively practicing, his Buddhist upbringing seemed to have emerged a bit and he was calmer and more mature. He played epic, two-hour challenge matches, not giving an inch. He landed at number 5, which was better for his ego than being number 7. Reverting to his Malaysian junior routine, he started (along with Goose Detter) to put in a morning training session: biking, treadmill, sprints. I watched with interest, wondering if they were overtraining. With college kids, it's always tricky to discern peaking, when players are at their apogee of fitness and energy and enthusiasm. I was worried he might be overdone, but I didn't want to discourage his newfound enthusiasm.

"I come / To answer thy best pleasure; be it to fly, / to swim, to dive into the fire, to ride / on the curled clouds." In *The Tempest*, Ariel is enchanted by the world of imagination and magic. Matthew is enchanted by heroin.

For the first couple of years of Matthew's drug addiction, I didn't know how to lose, either. I was so fearful of heroin, I never could admit he was sick, that he had a disease and that there was no easy cure. I always thought that just one more rehab stint, one more break, and presto, our old Matty would fly back riding on the curled clouds of his vibrant personality. I was embarrassed. It seemed to be entirely my fault. I self-flagellated every morning, going over every conversation I had conducted over Matthew's life. I was a bad father and so I had a son who was doing bad things.

In the days after I kicked him out of our house, sleep was impossible. I lay in bed for hours, picturing him huddled under a tree in a field in the rain. I could visualize success in sports, and I could easily visualize failure with Matthew: violence, pain.

Three weeks later, I heard from him on the phone. "Dad, I'm starving," he said, a quiver in his voice. "I need food."

My anger melted in a second. This was a benison: I thought everything was finished and gone and he was alive. I dashed to my car and met him, on a street corner in Hartford. It was clear he was in a bad way. When he got into the car, he unzipped his teeth and gave me a huge smile, but he looked thoroughly exhausted.

I made him homeless, but in a different way, and with a purpose: A squash friend I knew in the state government was able to push the right paperwork and officially Matthew Paul Assaiante, now age nineteen, was homeless. With that, he was eligible to enter a state-run rehab facility—we could not afford a private treatment center. We found him a bed at a small center in New London, Connecticut. I drove him down on a bleak late-November day. I was not convinced he was a hard-core addict and needed to be institutionalized and the whole way down; he was trying to get me to turn around. "Dad, this is the wrong decision," he said, crying, our car parked on Broad Street. He was nineteen years old and going to a state rehab center. I had no choice, I felt. I couldn't take care of him and I knew the street couldn't, either.

I drove back to Hartford and went that night to the Hartford city hall to receive an award—Hartford Man of the Year—from the Hartford Chamber of Commerce. "You realize that this is a lie," I said to the crowd of nearly four hundred people seated at the formal dinner. "We are here in jacket and ties, yet we have people who are suffering just a few hundred yards from here. I just took my son this afternoon to rehab. We are not making any difference. We are not getting our hands dirty."

For about ten seconds it was deathly quiet. Then the crowd rose and gave me a rousing, standing ovation. They just wanted me out of the room. I wanted to leave, too. I had berated the crowd when really I was just berating myself. I had not wanted to get my hands dirty all these years with Matthew, and now it was too late.

About twice a week I drove down to New London and took Matthew out to the mall. I bought him cigarettes and a burrito at Taco Bell. He was miserable.

"Dad, can Julio come to the mall?" he asked when we talked to arrange our next meeting.

"Sure, Matthew, that's cool," I said, not sure I wanted to meet his friends. Julio was in his forties. Hands weathered with wrinkles like an elephant. Decayed brown teeth. He was a hardened addict. The people running the program were recovering addicts. The atmosphere was thin and insubstantial. It seemed that at any minute, the façade would fall and Julio or Jonah or Frankie would start shooting up. I saw that instead of putting the fear of God in him, rehab was making his drug habit seem normal. These guys had been doing heroin, cocaine, meth, drinking a quart of vodka a day.

In the end, you are who you surround yourself with, and this scene became Matthew's society; the using, the recovering, and the lapsing. Before, he had been a teenager, experimenting; now, I later saw, a couple of weeks in New London and he had graduated into the adult world of addiction.

One night the phone rang. "Can you pick me up?" It was Matthew. "I've gotten thrown out."

"Why?" I was shaking with anxiety. What next?

"I got in a fight."

"What happened?"

"Someone stole my sweatshirt. I thought it was Julio, and well, we got in a fight."

When I picked him up on Bank Street in New London, it was close to midnight. He got in the car. He had a deep trough of purple below his eye.

If not rehab, then integration. I got him a two-bedroom apartment in Simsbury, a car, and a job at a masonry company. At first this seemed like the solution; a new life in a new town. Matthew was out on his own, nineteen, living like an adult, nothing to rebel against. We had dinner once a week. Everyone at work liked him.

The masonry job didn't last more than two months. (I found out later they fired him.) He got work as a dishwasher at the restaurant where my second wife was maître d'. Then he didn't show up one morning. No one at his apartment building knew anything. There were still some things in his place; dirty clothes in trash bags, a couple of CDs on a bureau. In the fridge, I found nothing but a half-empty carton of orange juice. In the cabinets there were no bowls or plates, just a giant box of raisin bran.

I didn't hear from him for two years.

As this was all happening, the Trinity Squash dynasty was beginning.

In October 1994, I applied for the squash and tennis job at Trinity. I had applied in 1990, when I was leaving Williams, but withdrew at the last minute. One of the members of the 1994 search committee had been on the earlier committee. He told me that he was unhappy about offering me the job, because he thought I would just turn it down like I did in 1990. I told him that coaching was my passion and that I was coming to Trinity—either I was going to be on the sidelines, handing out balls, or in the coach's office. It was a bit like when Frank Wolcott tried to cut me from the Springfield gymnastics team. I knew it was the right place for me and I had to have it.

Trinity had always had a strong squad. It built courts in 1929, the first non–Ivy League university to do so, launched a club team in the thirties, hosted the first intercollegiates in 1932, and in 1941 hired their first coach. Roy Dath had started coaching there in 1958 and for twenty years ran a solid second-tier program; his final record was exactly five hundred wins. After he left, Trinity ran through seven coaches in sixteen years, a revolving door that included some top-ten finishes and some good players, such as Don Mills, who became a great coach in Cincinnati; George Kellner, a renowned arbitrage businessman in New York; Mark Lewis, who once reached the finals of the U.S. nationals. In the mid-1980s, behind the play of Bill Doyle, the team achieved its best results, coming in third in the nation in 1984 and second in 1985. Nonetheless, the greatest squash player in Trinity's history played a just single match for the Bantams. Mark Talbott, the number-one-ranked American junior in 1979, spent most of his freshman fall semester at Trinity and played in the Harvard dual match, getting crushed by Michael Desaulniers. In December he quit the team to backpack around Africa. He later came back and turned pro, won over a hundred tournaments, and was elected to the U.S. Squash Hall of Fame.

When I arrived in the fall of 1994, Trinity boasted a solid nucleus of returning lettermen from a team that had gone 10–4 the previous season under John Anz. (An alum, Anz was leaving to go into commercial real estate in New Haven.) Five of the top nine were seniors; everyone was American. The facility, the Kellner Squash Center, was excellent. There was a block of the five original 1929 hardball courts, nicknamed the Dungeon, along with an adjacent facility of eight softball courts that Gordie Anderson, the country's top squash court builder, had installed. Rising behind the new courts was a carpeted, pyramidal amphitheater that allowed for more than five hundred spectators who could watch a couple of matches at once.

Softball was the international version of squash, with a slower ball and a wider court, and by the early nineties it was obvious that the United States, despite having played our hardball version for over a century, was going to switch to softball. In 1992, on the advice of Anderson and Gerald Hansen (a Trinity alum and head of alumni affairs at the college), Rick Hazelton, the Trinity athletic director, had anticipated the switch to softball. He built ten new courts: three were softball, seven hardball. The new courts were cleverly constructed with no weight-bearing walls, so it would relatively painless for Trinity to convert them to softball dimensions, which they did quickly in the fall of 1994, when men's squash made the switch. I got the job at Trinity, despite my journeyman resume, because the Princeton Club of New York randomly had a softball court (which was very unusual in 1994) and so I was able to portray myself as ahead of the curve, knowledgable about softball and able to hit the ground running.

Trinity was one of the few collegiate squash programs with softball courts. Other schools felt it would be too much to our advantage to play our dual matches there, and for two seasons we were forced to host dual matches in the Dungeon. Softball in a hardball court was horrible: the court was not wide enough for effective crosscourts, and the tin, two inches lower, made it easy for anyone to short-circuit a rally by drop-shotting, regardless of whether an opening was there or not. (In 2002, we took the old hardball courts, which had not been substantially renovated since they had been built nearly seventy years before, and made two three-wall glass courts. The Dungeon became the Palace. Now we had ten courts and one of the better squash facilities in the country.)

In our first season, I told the kids that if we won ten games in our dual match against Harvard—the clear favorite to win the nationals— I would shave my head. We lost 9–0 and grabbed just six games, so I did not lose my hair. We got to number six in the country our second season and I did the same thing, offered up my scalp if the team won ten games against Harvard. This time it was closer, with a 7–2 loss that brought our total to nine games.

Once upon a time, this would have been enough. All I had to do was get a few prep-schoolers from the Main Line or Greenwich or Brooklyn Heights, boys who had been playing for a half-dozen years in the usual club training grounds, throw in a couple of random recruits from the tennis team, and I would have a good program. No one took it very seriously: my first goal at Trinity was to hear the squash ball being hit in a court—just once, I begged—between the end of the season in March and the start of the next one in September.

That didn't happen until I had a fateful meeting in the early spring of 1996. The president of college, Evan Dobelle, called me into his office. It was one of those days when the wind had died down and there seemed to be a tinge of extra sunshine on the sidewalks. I barely knew Dobelle, having met him only a couple of times since he had come to Trinity the previous summer. I was nervous—Dobelle was one of those guys who commanded complete attention when he was in a room. (He'd had a senior position in the Jimmy Carter White House.) My stomach was in knots. What had I done wrong?

"What will it take to be a top squash program?" he asked. Before I answered, he told me about attending a meeting with Ivy League presidents and leaving with a question about Trinity athletics: What if we had a sport in which we could compete with the Ivies? "Not be national champions, Paul, but just contend and maybe knock one of them off once in a while."

"Well, we would need international kids, guys from the top squash nations overseas," I told him, explaining that the best squash in the world was being played not here but overseas, in Europe, the Middle East, and Asia. But getting those kids was suddenly easier. American squash had just converted to the international standard. Recruiting overseas guys used to be a pain, as players were reluctant to learn a new version of squash, our hardball game. Now, they could come right in. I was babbling.

"Oh, that's great," Dobelle replied. "This'll fold nicely into our new diversity effort. But these boys will have to get in on their own. We can't compromise our admission standards. As for money, we've no scholarships. They'll have to qualify for financial aid like anyone else." I said fine. He signaled that this was the end of the meeting.

No more than two minutes had passed. As I opened the door and turned to say goodbye, Dobelle got up from his desk and said, "Don't blow this."

I went back to my office and thought, *Okay, what do I do?* I was blindsided. After working at three colleges, I thought I knew how academia worked: There would be a committee, a survey, a task force, budgeting analysis, memoranda, a report. People had visions and dreams at universities, but the arcane bureaucracy smothered them. Instead, Dobelle had executed a complete end around the process. A two-minute meeting and now a revolution.

The first step was unknown. This was before the Internet and email had been thoroughly established, and it was much harder to track players. It seemed daunting: I needed guys who had taken the SAT or the TOEFL (Test of English as a Foreign Language, an English proficiency exam) and were good students; guys who would not get homesick; and guys who were great players and yet would give up their dreams of becoming a top-ranked pro. Who would fit that bill?

At the time I was also the U.S. men's coach, so I had established relationships with some coaches overseas and was about to start calling around when my phone rang. It was Bill Doyle, my old friend from my Apawamis days and now the Harvard coach. Incredibly, he had a player he wanted to suggest, an English schoolboy named Marcus Cowie. Harvard just deferred him. Within ten minutes of leaving Dobelle's office, I had our man.

I rung up David Pearson, the English men's national coach. I had met DP at a college coaches' clinic at Princeton the year before. (We were all trying to get up to speed on softball and Bob Callahan arranged for some mentoring by Pearson.) I told Pearson what had happened, that Trinity had given me the green light to recruit some top kids. Pearson, agreeing with Doyle, said, "Call Cowie. He's very, very good."

The following morning, I called the Cowies' home in Norfolk.

The phone was busy. (This was 1996, when not many English homes had voice mail or call waiting.) I called a half hour later. It was busy. I called a half hour after that. It was busy. I called Pearson back to confirm he had given me the right number. I then called Marcus every half hour all day. Finally, at five p.m. (eleven at night in the United Kingdom) the telephone rang through. My heart leapt. I thought it would never happen.

"Hullo," said a weary voice.

"Yes, I am Paul Assaiante. I'm the squash coach at Trinity College in the States, I'm—"

"Yes," the voice said—it was Alex Cowie, his mother. "You are the tenth coach to call today. Here's Marcus."

Marcus got on the phone. I gave him an improvised pitch about Trinity squash, how we were trying to build up the program (I did not tell him that this effort had been going on for just a few hours) and how we would like to bring him to Hartford for a look. Soon afterward, Marcus came to the States (paying for his own ticket) to visit a half-dozen colleges. The other coaches did the usual stuff with him: touring the campus, seeing the courts, talking with an admissions officer, spending a night in a dorm—staid, formal, and bland. I thought, *Well, let's make this like a basketball program and recruit in a big-time way.* I arranged for a short meeting between Marcus and Dobelle. I drove with him up to Boston and we bought tickets to a Red Sox game. Fenway, unlike most American ballparks, closely resembles many soccer and cricket grounds in England, a cozy, idiosyncratic bandbox, plunked in the middle of a neighborhood. Marcus felt right at home. When he returned to England, I had two alums call Marcus: Luke Terry, who was running Credit Suisse in London, and the CEO of Gillette in London. Marcus was sold.

I soon discovered that there was no free lunch. In our first big home dual match, against Princeton, Marcus paraded around the court as he lost to the squat Peter Yik, complaining about a leg injury and clearly annoyed that some short, unknown North American (Yik was born and raised in Newfoundland and had spent his high school years in Vancouver) was beating him. Marcus's style on court, it turned out, was flamboyant. He hit the ball with venom. He loved to shake his fist after his opponent hit a ball out of bounds. He pushed and bumped and collided. He exploded at the referee. He was a yakker. He muttered to opponents, quietly blasting them with a flurry of curses, put-downs, and mocking praise. He played to the gallery, waving his arms, cracking bilious jokes, throwing his hands up after a bad call to get a reaction. Marcus believed that squash was personal, that it was an elemental, mano a mano combat and he should do anything to avoid losing.

He was an absolute delight off the court. He had a cutting wit—he favored broad, blindingly funny jokes—and an effervescent person- ality. He was lively and social, happy-go-lucky and fearless. On his recruiting visit, he had walked out of the Trinity gates and strolled around the adjacent neighborhoods, not something that most students would do on a lark.

In his first season, Marcus reached the finals of the intercollegiates, the end-of-the-year individual tournament for the country's top sixty- four players. It was at Dartmouth. He was playing Daniel Ezra, from Harvard. Ezra, a hardworking lefty with redwood-burl thighs, had played regularly against Marcus in England, and they had a tense but respectful rivalry. Ezra's parents had moved from Bombay to London when he was thirteen years old to improve his squash game. Following in the footsteps of his brother Adrian, who had won three intercolle- giate titles for Harvard in the early nineties, Daniel Ezra had reached the finals as a freshman and won it as a sophomore. He was picked to win it again.

Marcus and Ezra had split their matches during the season. Now at the finals, Ezra pulled ahead. He won the first game. In the begin- ning of the second, Marcus banged his hip in an awkward collision with Ezra. During the injury time-out, he said that he wanted to stop. I said, "You can't pull out. You're the first Trinity player in history to make the finals. I don't care if you drag that leg around the court, you're not quitting."

It was the wrong approach. Marcus now coursed with a manic intensity: diving, scratching, and questioning referee decisions. The panache of the great junior god was gone, replaced by an elemental rage. In competition athletes often become blind. The performance is no longer on a stage but in a furious, dark closet of adrenaline and aggression. Players lose a sense of a wider reality. In some sports, especially the ultracontact ones like wrestling, football, and lacrosse, the sound-and-fury approach is not entirely inappropriate. But in the one-on-one sports, the successful athlete usually manages to hold on to the greater world. The harder you try in squash or swimming, the slower you move. But somehow Marcus, in his rage, kept moving and kept winning.

I couldn't believe what was happening. I had always dreamed of coaching a player to a national championship, yet now I wanted to crawl under a rock. Ezra looked bewildered under the crush of all the yelling and pushing, and Marcus won in four games.

During his trophy acceptance speech, he told everyone how happy he was and how I was a father figure to him. A fan from another school came up to me and said, "If this indeed is your son, it's time to spank him."

I was so shocked, I didn't say a word.

"You need to change his diaper," he added, and walked away.

The measure of a coach is not what your players accomplish on the court but how far you take them off the court. My test is not how many titles you win but what your players are doing in twenty or thirty years: Are they happy? Are they doing good? Are they doing well?

In my twenty-eight years as a college coach, I have had just three men win the intercollegiates. That is fine with me. Since Marcus, I have not been particularly concerned with that. I want them to be winners in life, not just college squash, and putting too much weight on a player's winning an individual honor inevitably creates an imbalance in the team's psyche. Because I enjoyed him as a person and because I wanted to win, I ignored Marcus's bad on-court behavior. I deluded myself to believe being a great coach was about winning a big title. If I had been tougher on him early on, if I had ridden him hard, he would have been a better sportsman and would probably have achieved more on court. I needed to say something to him after his first match—after his first day of practice, really—but instead, I let him get away with it. It was a little like Matthew; I thought that if I ignored the problem, it would go away.

At the end of his sophomore season, Marcus won his second straight intercollegiate. He was out of shape and we were not sure he could stand the schedule, which at the time had both the semis and finals on Sunday—a brutal way to end a tournament. The match was played with fifteen-point, point-a-rally scoring. (College squash switched in 2001 to nine-point, hi-ho scoring.) Marcus was up 2–1 and 13–5 in the fourth, just two points away from his second title. He was again playing Ezra. Despite his lead, Marcus was dead in the water. In a few minutes it was 13–12. Marcus shanked a return of serve and the ball crazily shot to the front wall, a rug-burner. It landed a piano-string width above the tin: 14–12. On the next rally, Marcus took Ezra's return of serve and hit a bad shot out in the middle. In the same motion, he keeled over and collapsed against the side wall. Ezra, not seeing that Marcus was splayed flat on his back, leapt up to the front of the court, took a mammoth swing at the sitter, and tinned it. Game, match, and championship to Marcus.

We had to help Marcus off the court. It was a courageous effort but unnecessary. If he had trained, he would have never found himself in such a position. The desire to be a champion was, for Marcus, gone. When he first started to play squash, he thought that the point was to improve his technique, to learn how to hit the ball the perfect width and length. Like most sports, like life itself, the desire became the point. He loved the compulsion. He loved hitting the same shot again and again. He loved the almost hypnotic rituals, the concussive sound of the ball hitting the wall, the kinesthetic thrill of reaching a short drop shot and snapping it back. He loved the sore glutes. Most of all, every imperfect shot only strengthened the centrifugal spiral of wanting to do it better.

Then he learned the point was not finding perfect length but wanting perfect length, and after a year at Trinity, after winning the intercollegiates, he learned that he didn't want it anymore. He had grown up in a pressure cooker. His mother, Alex Cowie, was a legendary athlete in Great Britain. She played at Wimbledon seven times. Within three years of entering a squash court—her first time was during a rain delay at a tennis tournament—she had become one of the best women players in the world. She coached the English national women's team for fifteen years, leading them to four world team titles. She was a delightful, quirky woman. After Christmas of Marcus's freshman year, we took the Trinity team to her club, Barnham Broom in Norwich. When we walked into the club, she was smoking a cigarette while giving a lesson on court. She ran our practices each day. One morning, the boys came in a little lethargic and sleepy. After ten minutes of watching them do serving drills, she brought them into one court, declared, "This is rubbish," and canceled practice for the rest of the day.

From an early age, Alex and others had pointed Marcus toward becoming a top-flight professional squash player. Many observers felt that he had the potential not just to be a top-ten player—the usual limit of prognostication—but that he could be a world number one. He was the Great Hope, the Del Harris of his generation, a big, tall, strong player destined for greatness. (Harris won a record four Drysdale Cups, the British Junior Open under-nineteen title.) Marcus won the 1995 European junior championships in Tel Aviv, and in January 1996, he lost in the finals of the British Junior Open after being up 2–1 on Ahmed Faizy of Egypt. He had then taken a year off after high school to train full-time with his brother Stuart and Cassie Jackman, a top female pro who also worked under Alex Cowie at Barnham Broom. His world ranking when he got to Trinity was 103. Yet throughout it all, he had never taken full ownership of his squash career.

College life, after his self-denying, monastic apprenticeship as a child prodigy, was too full of temptation. He was an insatiable sponge and sucked up all there was to offer on a wealthy American college campus in the nineties, including all the destructive things. He adored Michael Jackson, slapping a giant poster of him on his dorm wall. At Trinity, Marcus was the King of Pop. With his tall build, blond hair, and exotic accent, he was a rock star on campus, easily the most well-known Trinity student, with women hanging on him at parties like starfish. He moved off campus and had a circle of hard-partying friends.

He became a Ruthian figure. He sometimes went out the night before an away dual match on the opponent's campus, reveling in the limelight, the whispering—"There's Cowie, he's Trinity's number one"—the bravado of the country's best college player out at three in the morning.

He spent his junior fall in Morocco and came back in January 2000 completely out of shape. That was not a real problem in the short term. The mind, not the body, was the final arbiter in a squash match, and if he willed himself, he could beat most guys. His incredible racquet skills were an unshakable core of his game, enabling him to pin his opponent in the four corners. A dead man's fingernails keep growing. But later in matches his skills would break down under the strain of relentless pressure; against the very best his training had to be there in reserve, and it was not.

Still, he had a superb record his last two years. He lost just one challenge match—the only one in four years—and it was to Thad Roberts, a wonderful American who played no higher than number 14 on the ladder. Marcus notched sixty-four career wins, a remarkable statistic; it was the highest ever at Trinity at the time. (Now it's third all-time.) In dual matches he lost a couple of times, which is to be expected when you're playing the best player at each college. It was his play in the intercollegiates that exposed his declining game. In his junior year, he lost in the quarterfinals to Tim Wyant. A strong U.S. player who played number 3 at Harvard, Wyant was a Cincinnati kid with great leadership skills. (He and his three siblings all captained their college squash team, and he went on to run the Bronx's urban youth enrichment program, CitySquash.) He was good enough to make the U.S. team and attempt the pro tour after college, and athletic enough to start on the Crimson varsity soccer team. But still, Marcus should have handled him without too much trouble. Instead, he was flat and tentative, and Wyant, slithering like a motorcycle through traffic, got to every ball. Marcus seemed not to care. The day before, he had narrowly won a match in five, playing a far lesser player, and the rumor had floated around the courts that he had been losing points on purpose, that he was just fiddling. He could not do that to a player like Wyant, who beat him in four, winning the last game 15–7.

Marcus and I were bunking together at a hotel in Philadelphia. When I got back to our room two hours after the Wyant match, it smelled of tobacco smoke. When I found Marcus, I told him he was off the team, he was out of the hotel, and that he had to make his own way home to Hartford. At the team banquet the next week, Marcus got up at his table and spoke to everyone, tears running down his cheeks. "I've embarrassed the team," he said. Marcus had the all-star disease: too much too soon. He had been a great young player, but as he became an adult he had not matured.

He begged to be allowed to play his senior year and the team agreed. His mother moved over from Norfolk for the last month of the season. (According to college squash rules rules, a parent cannot be an official coach, so we unfortunately could not let Alex coach at matches.) Even with Alex in town, Marcus was less of a presence than ever. He was disconnected from the team, and his colleagues were disenchanted with his lack of leadership. He didn't show up for some of the captains' practices in the fall and even midseason he was absent or late. When he did practice, he played at full throttle—I've never had a better practice player than Marcus—but he was also hampered by a groin injury.

We won all of our dual matches, but that was because we were simply much more talented. If we had been pressed, we would have collapsed. Against Harvard at home his senior year, Marcus had pulled the stunt of partying all night and never getting to bed. (This was something of a tradition in certain adult squash circles: guys showing up in the locker room for a match still dressed in their tuxedos.) Marcus lost the first game of his match badly. He went to the bathroom, threw up, and returned to win the next three games.

In his intercollegiates, he reached the final to play Peter Yik. The tournament was at Trinity, and it was an opportunity for Marcus to go out on top. Yik had won the title the previous year and had been a veritable backboard all season, getting everything back. Marcus went up 13–1 in the first game, sprinting angrily around the court looking like an obstreperous commuter dashing for the subway. He lost the game in overtime and then disappeared. Yik took the next two 15–1, 15–4. Around the bleachers were a lot of Princeton guys and a lot of cheering: Yik was a good kid and won the annual sportsmanship award that year. I searched for the Trinity guys, but very few teammates were watching the match. Most had pointedly retreated to my office and were watching a squash video. When Marcus came off court, there was no one from the team to greet him.

My failure with Marcus Cowie stuck with me for years. Again and again, I kicked myself for not attacking the problem right away. I let Marcus down by not being there to help him modify his behavior. More to the point, if I had recruited him a decade later, I would have worked much harder to connect with him and force him to run to his roars rather than passively allow him to wander away.

Luckily, there were signs of success at the same time as I was making a hash of Marcus's issues. At the February 1998 nationals, when Zafi Levy lost the 4–4 match against Harvard's Tim Wyant, no one thought it was a big deal. At the time it was not seen as a historic dual match or the answer to a trivia question. The Harvard team believed they were just asserting their traditional prerogative as national champions. This was their thirtieth official national title (more than all other schools combined) and their fifth straight. It was a given: Harvard was number one in squash.

The pinnacle of sportsmanship was the handshake at the end of a match. After our gut-wrenching loss, everyone reluctantly gathered in the Zanfrini fencing room next to the courts for the presentation of the trophies to the winning team. Harvard and Trinity lined up, and the president of the association, Bob Callahan of Princeton, began to give out the winning team's trophies. (There were none for the other finalists.) Bob announced both the Trinity and Harvard number 10 players' names. Treating this just like the prematch introductions, our number 10, Rick Sheldon, strode out and shook the hand of the opposing number 10, silently congratulating him on the win.

It was a wordless sermon. This had never happened before at the postgame awards ceremony. Rick was from Minnesota, and he was instinctively good-natured. The rest of our team followed suit. One by one they shook the hands of their conquerors.

It turned out to be the last time we would lose a dual match. The handshakes were the beginning of the streak.

Today, Randy Lim faces David Canner of Princeton. Like Peter Sopher, Canner came from Washington. Pigeon-toed, he sometimes is awkward out on court, tightly wound and grim faced. But he also attacks from all parts of the court with a low, hard drive reminiscent of Michael Ferreira. He is smart and tough to beat.

Randy rushes out to a quick first-game victory, 9–2. Randy is confident again. He is a great front-runner. He had easily overcome Canner when they were juniors, but Canner had surprisingly hammered him in three games just eight days ago, 9–3, 10–9, 10–9. It was a shocking defeat. It hit Randy like a punch to the solar plexus, and he had trained hard all week. He also watched the video and saw that Canner was pushing him to the back, that he needed to move forward. Now, with the lead, he is lollipopping around the court, bouncing and hopping with exuberance.

The second game is massive. If Randy can get a 2–0 lead, it's going to be an awfully steep climb back for Canner: very rarely can a player at this level swim up from the chilly depths of a 0–2 deficit. Randy is adroitly keeping the ball on Canner's forehand, an unusual game plan—most players' backhands are weaker—but it is working, as Canner often opens out on the forehand and hits a flat, loose ball. Randy, with a crisp efficiency, jumps to 5–0 and exchanges points until it's 8–3, and he's one point away from 2–0.

Canner saves a game point with a blistering shot out of nowhere. The Princeton crowd, sensing a reprieve, cheers loudly, chanting Canner's name and excoriating Randy. The noise shocks Randy. He has a five-point cushion, but as Canner chips away, he remembers last week, when he had squandered a humongous lead in the second game. He promises himself he won't do it again. Canner wins another point. The dread sets in. Randy has done the squash equivalent of putting the stopper in, turning on the sink faucet, and walking out of the room; it will be a few minutes, but inevitably the water will flood into the hallway. Canner creeps back to 8 all. Randy nervously chubs a ball into the middle of the court and Canner puts it away. At 9–8, Canner smacks a backhand into the nick. The score is 1–1.

Randy walks off the court with a deflated, beleaguered look. He says he is exhausted, tired beyond belief, and the pressure not to lose is draining his energy. He is out of sorts. He's wearing just one wristband, on his nonplaying arm. It is very common that once a player has a big lead and lets it slip away, he becomes disorganized and disheartened.

Randy abandons his game plan. Balls are flying to Canner's backhand. Randy shoots off the serve, even though Canner has time to anticipate the shot and gobbles every single one up. The last thing he wants to do is draw Canner forward unnecessarily. The third game is ragged. The fourth isn't close.

Princeton is now up 3–2 and needs just two more wins to take the dual match and the national championship.

CHAPTER SIX

Confidence: Gustav

Gustav Detter—known as Goose—loses the first two games 9–5, 9–5, to Kimlee Wong, a Princeton senior. I had told my players before the match to send a message early on—punch their opponent metaphorically in the nose. Instead, it has been Kimlee doing all the punching.

This is an unbelievable situation. They have known each other for years. Goose's national coach in Sweden, John Milton, had coached Kimlee in England while Kimlee had attended Wycliffe College. (Kimlee had grown up in Malaysia but attended Wycliffe, a prep school in the Cotswolds with a good squash programs; he took a year off after graduating from Wycliffe to play the pro tour.) Two seasons before, Goose and Kimlee had played twice: Kimlee won the first time 3–1, but at the nationals a few weeks later Goose had come back from a 2–1 deficit to win in five, total match time: two hours, ten minutes. Last year they again faced each other twice: both were 3–0 thrashings in favor of Goose. He had discovered that after about an hour of hard, lung-squeezing, leg-sapping play, Kimlee would slowly fold. It had to do with his body type, that physically he would hit a wall. Their junior year scores reflected the hard first game and then a collapse: 9–5, 9–2, 9–1, and 9–7, 9–4, 9–2. Just eight days ago when we played Princeton on Valentine's Day, Goose had again dismissed him in three, 9–6, 9–4, 9–4.

Like Vikram at number 8, Goose at number 2 is considered a safe bet to win today. But the tough-first-game formula is not working. Goose is torpid, moving like a sick turtle. At 3–3 in the first, Goose tins three straight shots. Kimlee has disrupted his rhythm. My ignoring Goose's game plan—I barely discussed tactics with him all week— has put him at risk. Callahan came up with the perfect strategy. He taught Kimlee to slow things down and not allow Goose to push the pace. At times, Goose likes to amp it up and play in a Mike Tyson–like frenzy, always going for the ferocious winner. To counter that, Kimlee is hitting slow, soft balls. With exacting precision, he is dinking some straight drops to Goose's forehand and then lobbing to his backhand; Goose, like most lefties, does not have a magnificent high backhand volley. At the first opening, Kimlee is going for the kill. By the end of the first game, Goose has begun to play Kimlee's style and, of course, isn't playing it anywhere near as well as Kimlee can. The second game starts out wonderfully. Goose dashes out to a 3–0 lead. A skein of unforced errors brings it to 3–3. For the next fifteen minutes the score seesaws to 5–5, with multiple lets and changes of serve. Although Kimlee comes out of the stalemate and wins the game, he has had to expend an enormous amount of energy. Callahan's strategy is working but at a cost: The game takes about twenty-three minutes. With Goose playing so poorly, it should have been quicker. This could come back to haunt Kimlee. Maybe he's punched out. He's up 2–0 but perhaps Goose has a chance.

In large part, the reason I am not wholly pessimistic is that three years before, Goose Detter had pulled off the most miraculous escape in college squash history. It was February 2006 in Hartford, Trinity versus Princeton. We had anticipated another well-coached Bob Callahan team, but we still expected to win handily. Instead, we found ourselves in a 4–4 dogfight.

We were doomed. In the final match, we were sending out Goose, a sandy-haired freshman from Sweden. Princeton offered senior Yasser El Halaby, Hesham's older brother, who was en route to winning the intercollegiates for the fourth time. Our guy was still figuring out where his dorm was; their guy was laying claim to the title of best collegiate player in history. It was an atrocious mismatch.

Outside Pakistan—really, the Khan clan in Peshawar and their wondrous patriarch Hashim—Egypt was the preeminent squash country in the world. Egyptians won the British Open, the Wimbledon of squash, in each of the first five decades after the tournament was founded in 1930. They played beautifully, with looping swings and cold-blooded calm under pressure. In the 1990s, after an uncharacteristic dormancy, Egyptian squash revived under the fierce brow of Ahmed Barada, who won major tournaments and reached number two in the world. Cairo's leading daily newspaper, *Al-Ahram*, sponsored a glass-court tournament, picturesquely staged in front of the Pyramids of Giza. Squash became, after soccer, the most popular sport in Egypt. Barada wearied of the national attention and quit suddenly in 2000, and a massive fleet of youngsters sailed in behind him: Amr Shabana won the world championship four times; Ramy Ashour captured the world juniors twice and reached number one in the world by age twenty; Karim Darwish got to number one; and at the top-level tournaments Egypt was always the most well-represented nation.

Another swashbuckler was Yasser El Halaby. He was a first-rate player (he had won the under-seventeens at the British Junior Open), but was considered not as promising as Shabana or Ashour. One day a family friend of the El Halaby's walked into Bob Callahan's office and said, "I have this kid you should recruit."

"Who do you have in mind?" he asked. Callahan was skeptical. Like me, he got this kind of pitch regularly.

"Yasser El Halaby."

Callahan's jaw dropped. The friend helped facilitate it with Princeton's admissions department, and Callahan told no one except his wife and Neil Pomphrey, his assistant coach, keeping it a secret for many months. We were all stunned when we finally heard the news.

His start was rough. It was less than a year after 9/11 and he had trouble getting a visa. He arrived just as classes started, and he was the only Egyptian student on campus. Still, he turned out to be pretty dominant. He lost four times in dual matches, but won the intercollegiates singles as a freshman, as a sophomore, and then again as a junior. No one in the history of men's intercollegiate squash had ever come into his senior year with a chance to win a fourth title.

In the 2006 match, Yasser won the warm-up. He cracked the ball around the court, while Goose nervously stabbed short rails, poking at the ball as if he were at an ATM reaching for his money. The warm-up was a psychologically rich ecosystem. Players often ignored the mantra of observing their opponent, watching his shots, and judging his abilities. Instead, they would try to slash the ball past each other so it trickled to the back wall. This advertised strength and skill.

Not that Yasser needed to. The dual-match score was 4–4 before the warm-up began. Shaun Johnstone, our number 2, had gone down to Maurico Sanchez in a marathon five-gamer. Because all the other matches that day were quick 3–0 affairs (three of which ended in a 9–0 third game), everyone else was finished. Normally, the number 1 guys went on court with a couple of other matches still in progress and the outcome of the dual match still in doubt. This time, it set up perfectly for Callahan: 4 all, with his Michael Jordan getting the ball. The stage was set for Yasser to bring it home.

I ran into Callahan outside my office. We started chitchatting. It was casual, like we were two friends bumping into each other in the park. We talked like the match was over. It never occurred to me that Goose could win.

"Listen, you did a wonderful job," I said. "Well done. Great coaching. Your kids were great. Congratulations." It was like the time Bobby Bayliss shook my hand during the Russ Berkoff match.

We stood there for a minute or two more, talking about the season, and then both of us said at the same time, "Well, we should go watch the match."

At the start, Goose was tense and didn't playing well. He desperately wanted to beat Princeton. He had applied for an early decision to Princeton and they had rejected him. It was like a fourth-round draft choice trying to prove something to a team that passed over him.

Ice hockey was his original sport. Goose had grown up in the southern Swedish city of Malmo. His father had played professionally as a defenseman in Sweden and even skated once in an exhibition tilt at Madison Square Garden against an NHL all-star team that included Bobby Hull; Goose's older brother played for the Swedish junior national hockey team. When he was twelve, Goose picked up squash and discarded hockey. Within a few months, he reached the finals of the under-thirteen Swedish nationals. He went on to win all the other junior divisions and play on the national team in the world championships.

One night he had a dream about going to college in America. A few weeks later, at a tournament in England, he met Bob Callahan. He went home, looked at Princeton's website, and decided to apply. It was an anomalous decision. None of his friends in Sweden were going to the States for college. In squash, not a single Swedish player had ever been an All American.

Princeton did not accept Goose, despite Callahan's urgings and his good grades. (It was in part because of a bad TOEFL score; his English was not that good.) Callahan, ever generous even with his rivals, called me and said, "I've got a great kid, Gustav Detter. Didn't get in here. Maybe you can get him into Trinity."* I worked with Goose and had him retake the TOEFL—he eventually took it four times—and he got in.

James Montano, our assistant coach, picked him up at the airport in August 2005. Goose stared at James's big national championship ring and listened as he told him about the history of the program. Goose didn't know how he would fit in. His style, very different from that of the attacking Asians on our team, was more like that of a prototypical grinder from Europe. He played as if it were 1986. Back then, attrition ruled in the international softball game. Players trained to a height of gut-sucking fitness. They played five-minute points, hour-long games: outlast rather than outwit. In the 1990s, this changed. The advent of lighter, larger racquets, the limits of fitness, the change to fifteen-point, point-a-rally scoring for pros (which was eventually reduced to eleven points), and the coming of a new generation of shotmakers such as Barada and Canada's Jonathon Power quelled the grinders.

---

* Callahan was always a helpful friend. In the early nineties, he had called me about a job opening at the Princeton Club of New York, enabling me to move back east from a failing club in Seattle.

The news had not reached Malmo. A southpaw, Goose had a wicked, whipping forehand and a steady backhand, but nothing up front. He couldn't shoot. Instead he took the ball early, volleying and pressing, and most of all, he had great length and width, the core of the game regardless of how many flashy gunslingers rode into town. Offense attracted crowds, but defense won championships.

A very competent player, he managed to sneak up to number 1 on the ladder early that winter, but he was not number 1 material. In fact, Goose would never again play number 1 for Trinity, as a week after this Yasser match he would lose in a challenge. Even at number 2 he would suffer defeat five times his freshman season.

The day before the match, I told Goose that getting on court with Yasser would be like getting into a washing machine for forty-five minutes. Indeed, Yasser spun Goose around in the first two games, winning 9–7 each time. He was in control. There was a little razzle-dazzle and a lot of straight, tight drives. He also tried to end points quickly, shooting off the serve repeatedly. Goose looked skittish, like a stallion in a paddock. After the second game, I pulled him into a stairwell beside the court. The Princeton guys smelled blood. They hopped up and down, slapping Yasser's back.

"You judge a man's character in a time of adversity," I told Goose, about to launch a stirring speech.

He cut me off. "I can beat him," he said, his face glossy with sweat. He had seen that he was close, that Yasser was not that far out of reach, and that there was a chance he could win. Maybe it came in the first game, when he saved a game ball. Maybe it came early in the second game, when he snagged a point after a marathon multiple-miraculous-gets rally. Yasser clearly wasn't running rampant, but I saw no indication that Goose could win.

I nodded my head and said, "Whenever you're ready." And then, desperate to think of something concrete for him to hold on to, I added, "If things speed up, slow them down, and if they slow down, speed them up," in the hopes he could disrupt Yasser's rhythm. In my head I was thinking, *I can beat him*—*yeah, you and the pope.*

A good coach has to be a good liar. When I was coaching at West Point, I met a delightful young man from Rhode Island named JD Cregan who ended up at Trinity He had a wonderful career, and in his senior year he was the number-three seed at the intercollegiates. He drew Dan Kellas, an Army player who was your classic West Pointer: not very skilled or experienced but a grinder who was all heart. Their match was at 8:00 a.m. Looking for something to hang on to, I told Kellas that he was used to being up at that time, and JD, as a normal college student, wasn't. An ambush was possible—though highly unlikely, as JD was so much better a player. Sure enough, at 8:00 a.m., JD came out looking a little sleepy, and Kellas, up since five a.m., won in three: 15–6, 15–11, and 15–14. If they had played one more point, our guy would've had no chance; JD had finally woken up and settled in.

The determining factor was confidence. The wrong shot or the wrong technique or wrong tactic, employed with self-belief and conviction, is better than a textbook game executed tentatively.

A sheep to the slaughter, Goose went back on court for the third game. I walked through the gallery. The yellow and blue walls seemed to oscillate with the roars of the crowd. No one talked to me. It was like a baseball dugout and I was a pitcher throwing a no-hitter that no one wanted to jinx by talking to me. But it was more like I had given up a walk-off grand slam. For a couple of minutes, I hid out in my office, just trying to absorb the fact that we were going to lose, and then I lay down on the back side of the bleachers, staring up at the ceiling. When I got up, I saw Callahan; his thin smile, hiding under his black mustache, was tighter than ever. He gave me a gentle glance that reminded me that without him I wouldn't even have Goose on my team.

The third game looked like a repeat of the first two. Yasser jumped out to a 5–2 lead. Goose battled his way back, reeling off four straight points to go up 7–6. Yasser was shooting off the serve—the match having lasted three-quarters of an hour, he wanted short points now. Yasser got the serve and won two in a row.

It was 8–7, match ball for Yasser. One more Princeton point and our unbeaten streak was finished. I turned to my team and said, "Okay, act like men. Behave appropriately. Congratulate the Princeton guys. There is no shame here."

Meanwhile, at the other end of the bleachers, the Princeton players were having conniptions. They punched one another and gave noogies and high-fives in a wild, mewling horde. Bob Callahan gave a similar speech to them, trying to settle them down—"Don't celebrate too hard. Be gentlemen. Don't storm the court"—but the joy in their eyes was so strong, and they were about to tear onto the court and jump all over Yasser in a screaming, writhing pile. It was going to be awful.

Yasser adjusted his striped headband and served. The rally was short. Nervously, both players flung out shots without firmness. Goose shoveled a backhand drop up to the front wall. Onto it early, Yasser tried to flick a roll corner, but the ball was too close to the side wall for him to get a clean stab at it. He tinned it.

Goose was still alive. Emotionless, he took the ball and quickly served. He won the point, bringing the score to 8 all and sending the game into overtime. Twice they exchanged points—twice Yasser was serving with a chance to make it 9–8 for another match point—but Goose kept locating tiny, aleatory holes of daylight to place the ball. Goose got to 9–8 and went momentarily mad. He fist-pumped, yelled, and hurled his racquet into the corner of the court. It was a delayed reaction, as if the emotion of having saved the match point a couple of minutes before had finally bubbled to the surface. He filched the game 10–8. The crowd screamed, "Goose, Goose, Goose!"

After the game, Yasser pulled off the sneaker on his right foot to change his sock. It turned out that he was injured. There had been a pro tournament in Rochester the weekend before. A bunch of Trinity alums (including Lefika Ragontse and Bernardo Samper) had entered, as well as one of our seniors, Reggie Schonborn. Once in a while I would let the boys play in an off-season pro tournament just to get some experience; many of them didn't want to give up the tour entirely upon coming to college, so I always told them they'd be able to go if it fit into the schedule. But I worried it would drain them and distract them from the true goal—the Trinity team. Luckily, Reggie won only one match, then he lost and came home. Yasser, on the other hand, played four matches in four days, reaching the final before going down in a hard-fought five-gamer against Miguel Rodriguez, an up-and-coming Colombian. Moreover, at the Rochester tournament Yasser had experimented with a custom orthotic shoe insert. When he got home late on Sunday night, his feet were blistered and sore. He didn't practice on Monday or Tuesday. On Wednesday evening, he went on court against Goose. He told Callahan, "I'm going to get this done." But he was in pain and wasn't moving well.

The effort to close it out in the third was deadly, and in the fourth he seemed a bit stiff-legged. He wasn't limping, but he also wasn't moving as fluidly as he normally did. Early on, when Goose lacerated a crosscourt past him to take a 5–1 lead, Yasser let the game go.

This was a mistake. I always tell my players never to give away a game—never give an inch. You might save some physical energy, but you'll be handing over a big hunk of confidence to your opponent. Before the fifth, I told Goose, "Yasser has basically taken a half-game rest in the fourth. He mailed it in. So he's going to come out firing in the fifth. The first two points are going to be the hardest first two points you've ever played in your life. Stand tough. Don't give in."

Both players changed their shirts, donning unmarked white T-shirts for the final game. It was symbolic. This was no longer college versus college but the ultimate distillation: man to man, two guys with sticks and a ball in a small box. I remember seeing Goose's heart visibly thumping against his chest. He was working incredibly hard, and although he felt his power increasing, I wasn't sure he could he sustain it. Did he really believe he could win?

Each of the first two rallies of the fifth game lasted more than sixty strokes. Goose won both points and was up 2–0. Yasser had nothing left in the tank. His feet hurt. The crowd yelled after every Trinity point, and the match ball from the third game lingered in his mind. He was shattered. He tinned a half-dozen balls in the game. At 8–1 in the fifth, I was still nervous. I thought that somehow Yasser would come back. He was the better player. This could not be happening. I thought of one Pan American squash tournament in Brazil in which Tim Wyant was up 2–0, 6–1 in the third against an Argentinean. The altitude and humidity (and pain—he had lost half of a front tooth to an errant swing by his opponent) abruptly closed down his body. Suddenly, Wyant was a puddle. He lost the match without scoring another point. (The last three games were 9–6, 9–0, 9–0.) So I thought somehow this kind of collapse could happen. Yasser could come back.

He didn't. Goose won the last two games 9–2, 9–2. When it was over, when Yasser's final forehand boast tinned, Goose shook Yasser's hand. As Yasser exited the court, Goose hurled the ball into the cheering gallery and did a quick somersault, landing on his knees, his fists by his ears, à la Borg after winning Wimbledon. Captured by Dick Druckman on film, it was to become the signature image of our dynasty.

An hour later, gutted by the effort, Goose vomited into a trash can in my office. We sat in my office until after one in the morning. "I don't want to go home and go to sleep," I said. "I fear that when I wake up, I'll learn that it was all a dream." I checked my email. There were dozens. One was from Tom Wolfe: "If Goose never does another thing in his career at Trinity, his place in squash history is secure and the words 'Goose, Goose, Goose' will echo forever." I went home and Goose and Manek walked back to their dormitory.

The next day, Goose walked into Mather Hall, the main Trinity dining cafeteria. A murmur went around, and suddenly people stood up and started chanting. Soon it was a standing ovation. "Goose, Goose, Goose." The dual match had been on a Wednesday night. On Friday, several players got calls from Trinity women asking if they knew where Gustav was. Later that night, he traveled with an entourage of more than a dozen people slipping in through the back doors of fraternities and holding court, his acolytes in a circle around him three rows deep. He was no longer anonymous. He had shouldered the burden. The next issue of *Squash Magazine* had Goose on the cover, on his knees after winning the fifth game, with the headline ATLAS LIVES.

Nobody handles match-play pressure perfectly. It would be inhuman not to be affected. I do my best to prevent too many meltdowns by creating an environment of equipoise. I never have a team dinner the night before a big dual match. I used to, religiously, until the night before the Harvard dual match in 1999, when Lefika Ragontse innocently asked me, "Why are we celebrating before we've done anything?" The kids are always spastic by then, all over the place emotionally, with jangling nerves and misplaced energy. They need distraction. They need to do their homework and talk to their roommates and meet their girlfriends for a late-night coffee and be a part of the college rather than being isolated and obsessing about the upcoming dual match. Some are too nervous even to sleep. I tell them, "The key night of sleep is not the night before you have to do something but the night before that. It's the second-to-last night that is the most important. So don't worry if you can't fall asleep. You don't need a big sleep. You'll be fine." The mantra—we will be all right—is said a thousand times a season. It starts when the freshmen arrive and we ponder what recruits have matriculated at other schools. It continues when results pour in, when blogs, Twitter posts, Facebook pages, and articles begin to dissect what might happen when our team meets another.

In practices, I try to replicate the physical and mental pressure of a match. Drills: boast-drop-drive drills, lob-drop-drop-lob drills, crosscourt-drive-drive-crosscourt drills—all at match speed. We practice serving and returning serves not in a lazy, goof-around mode but with fierce concentration. We plop three guys in a court and do pressure sessions in which the guy in front is under tremendous attack for three or four straight minutes, able to hit only drives or crosscourts no matter where the ball is. I like situation games or drills that break old habits and established new patterns. I loathe the lackadaisical.

Matches create a concern for the outcome. With a scoreboard come a school newspaper article and a report on the Web. In the players' eyes, practice leads to nothing. I try to make practices more like match play physically to reproduce the mental strain. I reenact the kinetic trauma of a match as much as possible. For many coaches, fitness training takes place elsewhere. That is wrong. You can run on a treadmill until you zoom off in a puddle of sweat; you can fly up the concrete steps of the football stadium until you reach the last row and peek out over town. But on court, deep in the fourth game, the lungs gasp for air, the legs go wobbly, the sweat stings the eyes, the goggles steam up, and the ball shrinks to something as small as a black-eyed pea and as far away as the moon.

When I first arrived at Trinity, I decided that this would be like West Point: my team might not be as experienced or technically adept as Harvard's, but they would be fitter at the end of a match. I make them train on court as much as possible, with a racquet in their hand, so when they feel the propulsive sting toward the end of a long, tough match, they say, *I want this. I have worked to get this. I know I can overcome it. I am not afraid.* I want the burn to come on court in practice so that it always arrives in the same way and they deal with it calmly and play through it. It is sometimes masochistic. They'll be exhausted, splotches of sweat invading their shirt. Their brains, starved for oxygen, will start to panic and drown in their own CO_2. Their bodies will feed on themselves, chewing up their muscles. They need a second set of lungs. It gets to the point where they can hang on for only one more ground stroke before they pass out or throw up, just one more rally before their lungs explode.

Exercise is never a punishment. Like community service, it should be positive. I never make the guys run laps or do push-ups as a penalty. I don't want them to associate heaving lungs and failing legs with fear or disappointment or failure. Exercise buys you fitness, which buys you fifth-game victories. In the long run, exercise is for life. Who at the age of fifty thinks, *I think I will go for a run today because I feel like I need to be punished?*

After the second game against Kimlee today, Goose comes off the court and I know what's going on. He is frozen and confused. The pressure has sapped his energy; the running has sapped his brain. His eyes are fibrillating as he blinks away the thought of losing. He has grown up tremendously during his four years at Trinity. He is about to graduate with a 3.93 average, having majored in economics with a minor in Chinese. He has a girlfriend from Connecticut. He is our Doug Flutie, a short, clean-cut, likable kid who once pulled off a miracle. But with all the growth, he is no longer innocent. One miracle is asking a lot; a second miracle is absurd. Down 2–0 to Yasser, he had a naïve confidence he could come back. Today he believes he's going to lose.

A player's style is dictated by his personality as much as by his physical strengths and talents. It is as idiosyncratic as a fingerprint. Goose was conservative. He was clueless some of the time. After the Atlas Lives match, the guys talked about how he was now a big man on campus, how if he wanted to meet women, now was the time. They told him, "Any girl you've been waiting to hit on, well, now's your chance."

He said, "Why would I want to hit a girl?"

He was shy. However much he appeared to revel in the adulation of the women at the fraternity parties, he was uneasy. The cafeteria scene after the Atlas Lives match embarrassed him so much that he left without eating.

No matter what level of accomplishment a person reaches, everyone wants approval. The key is to use the "but" technique. I start off every coaching interlude with a positive remark and then interject a "but" to add a modification. This works but the opposite does not.

Today with Goose, I bypass the positive and go straight to the negative. I yell for about thirty seconds, high volume, a couple of F-bombs, intense. "This is about fighting. This is about showing me what you've got. You are going to have to do this on sheer guts. You are playing like Kimlee. But Kimlee isn't my player. I don't coach Kimlee. I only coach Gustav. Be Gustav. You can accept defeat. But Parth won't let you accept it. Vargas won't let you accept it. They're dying out there on the other courts. You can't let them down. You've got to prolong the points, extend each point as long as you can. Win each point three times. This is Heartbreak Hill. You've reached the twenty-mile mark of the marathon. Guys who hit the wall, no matter how hard they've trained, they will accept quitting. Not with us. Not now, not ever."

I find it helpful to do this, to get in their grill and yell. There are times when being unruffled and patient—my standard game-day mode—isn't the best way forward. I usually try to get them to laugh, like I did with Simba last year when I explained about the *Lion King* or with Pat Molloy in 2004 when I cracked a joke about Chinese food. I open up some space for the pressure to leach away. But once in a while, I get on someone. If you do it too often, you anesthetize them to the tirade and it becomes meaningless. But if it is rare, it works.

I am not sure if it has worked with Goose. He seems as if I have slapped him. He doesn't say a word—Scandinavian inscrutability. I tell him what I always tell players when they are down 2–0: "You and your opponent will finish the match at the same time; the goal is to make him travel farther and endure more pressure and hardship along the way."

"Squash is like sex," I say, giving him one of my hoary lines, trying to end with something positive. "The object is to make it last as long as possible." He laughs and leaves me with a smile. He goes back onto the court and shuts the glass door.

The door shutting reminds me of the 2005 nationals. We were playing Harvard in the finals, up at Harvard. Bernardo Samper, in his final dual match, lost the first two games to Sid Suchde. He was too emotional, the opposite of Goose here. The crowd was yelling for its hometown hero, just like today's crowd. I quieted Samper down. I told him he was the better player. He took a deep, slow breath and got up. He looked at me and I knew he was calm again. When he went on the court, he turned and shut the door delicately, as if it meant the world. He went on to win in five.

Today it takes about twenty more minutes for Goose's body to catch up to his mind. He's down 4–1. I shift in my seat, regretting that I had yelled. I should have kidded him—about Fabio, for instance—made light of something, more funny jokes about sex. Now he's 4–1 down in the third, a long, long way from home.

Until this moment, the Princeton players have dominated the tunnel. Because there are no glass walls, the tiny, four-inch window in the door to both of the old courts is a prime spot to watch the matches. Teammates can watch through it so they can give better advice between games. Moreover, their encouragement, despite the thrum of voices in the gallery, can be heard by the players on court. It's almost like a secret pipe that can funnel a friendly, positive voice into the court that no one but the two players can hear. When Kimlee goes up 4–1 in the third, the few Princeton players in the tunnel flood out. They don't want to miss the moment of sweet victory. They want to be upstairs in the gallery, among their classmates, rather than in the claustrophobic tunnel. Once they leave, our team claims a small but psychologically powerful bit of territory.

Goose and Kimlee trade points for about five minutes. Then they have a short point. Goose wins it with a sweet bit of legerdemain, appearing to prepare a long drive and at the last minute flicking the ball high and crosscourt. Kimlee, normally jackrabbit quick, doesn't have his first-game speed anymore and in desperation he smacks it off the back wall, resulting in a sitter that Goose dinks for a short drop. Kimlee has such a vast distance to cover now that he barely gets there and hits a rail right next to his body. Goose is ready for it—automatic stroke. Goose gives me a cool, subdued nod as he heads to the server's box. I know instantly the message. It is Samper shutting the door delicately. Goose is telling me that he will win.

It's incongruous: He's down 2–0, 4–1 and just five points away from defeat, and he's certain he's going to win? But he is right. Kimlee is tiring. This point is the first indication. It is so subtle that only a few people see it. Squash is like that. Squash is a game of territory. With the plain, niveous walls, it's like boxing, with sticks. Unlike almost every other racquet sport, there is no net separating you from your opponent. You brush his arm, you push off his back, you smell his sweat, you hear him suck in his breath, and you count his heartbeats. In this intimacy, you can absorb your opponent's anger or fear—squash is the Stockholm syndrome at 125 miles per hour—or you can press your confidence onto his deflating ego. If you exude self-assurance, your opponent will begin to question himself: *Why is he hitting freely when he should be nervous? He's not playing well, yet he's smiling? What have I done wrong?* Most of all, you can tell when you've found an infinitesimal crack in the façade.

Goose audaciously starts to hammer away. As in all beautiful games, there is no clock in squash, and Goose makes each point last forever. He scuttles after every shot by Kimlee and drives it, relentlessly, to the back wall. He cushions drop shots, not to win the point outright, but to push Kimlee forward. He backs Kimlee out on any loose balls, claiming more and more territory. His dirty-blond hair, bottled up in a yellow bandana, flops on every lunge. Kimlee, in turn, begins to bend over in between points, trying to catch his breath. He cleans his goggles. He wipes his right hand on the wall, sometimes leaning in until his head rests against his hand. Goose is playing physically. He is about the same height as Kimlee but much bigger. They have a couple of collisions in the early part of the game and Kimlee starts to massage his shoulder and his hip. The referee, Hunt Richardson, even gives Goose a conduct warning for unnecessary contact.

Unlike most young players, Goose is no longer panicking in the face of his dwindling time on the court. He looks the same as he did an hour before. He is calm, collected, and breathing easily. I realize that Goose has climbed into the center of the storm. He is quiet inside, while the entire building is rocking, buffeted in the winds of this historic match. He works hard but without fear. Instead of feeling deflated, Goose is confident.

Three rallies—three scoring points to Goose. In the space of a minute, he has completely changed the match. He ties up the score. Kimlee goes up 6–5, three points away from victory. But he is clearly fatiguing. Goose hits a soft, high, well-placed crosscourt and Kimlee stabs at it, his feet out of position, his racquet late. It doesn't even make it to the front wall. Kimlee will never get so close again. Goose wins 9–6. The first half of the game, to 4–1, took twenty minutes, the second half, a punitive eight minutes.

In the fourth, Kimlee tries to reestablish his physical presence, to command the center of the court, to cut off Goose, to stop the advance, to make retreat the only option. But Goose, wearing a new shirt, comes out firing. He knows that often you are down 2–0 and you win the third, and then the other guy comes back out having caught his breath and wins the match 3–1.

Not today. Indefatigable, Goose keeps digging out balls from impossible angles and keeps making Kimlee play another shot. He flicks a crosscourt drop off every one of Kimlee's serves to his backhand, not trying to win the point, but simply to move him up. He goes up 3–0 then withstands a ten-minute stalemate, with the score changing only once, to 3–1. It was classic, tension-filled, serve-to-score hi-ho squash: the scoreboard frozen, the boys' tactics being employed, reconsidered, discarded. Just as in the third game, Goose wins the battle and never looks back, grabbing the rest of the points with ease. The levee is breached. Goose has broken him.

I tell him after the fourth not to relax. He should be pissed off that he has found himself in this position, tied after a hundred minutes of play. After a hundred minutes, he should be in the shower with a win.

In the fifth, Kimlee is nervous. He fist-pumps after winning the opening rally—fist-pumping at 0–0? Then he starts cramping. The game is just three minutes old and he's exhausted. Goose comes over, the concerned friend, not the bitter rival. Kimlee stretches against the floor and the wall. After a two-minute delay, he wins the next point. Again, a celebration. It is 1–0 in Goose's favor. Goose wins the serve back. Kimlee appears beaten. His head droops down. At 2–0, Goose smashes three straight balls from the front of the court to the back.

Kimlee backhands the first two off the back wall; he can't reach the third. Goose goes up 5–0. Kimlee pulls it back to 5–3, but off a deep lob Goose cranks a decidedly risky volley drop shot for a winner. He's got Kimlee on the ropes and they both know it. If this were Frazier versus Ali in Manila, it would be the end of the fourteenth round and Eddie Futch would be stepping into the ring to stop it.

This time when he wins, when he pulls off another incredible comeback against Princeton, Goose doesn't fall to his knees and raise his arms. He lies down on the court, supine, like a corpse, only his racquet twitching. Atlas Lives, no doubt, but Atlas is exhausted.

CHAPTER SEVEN

Control: Andres

We are now tied with Princeton 3–3, going into the final cycle. It is half past five in the afternoon: four and a half hours have passed since we had introductions. Very few team sporting events last this long, and the players, the coaches, and the crowd are drained. The incredible drama has dashed any hope of an exit before dusk.

Even after what happened eight days ago, no one has expected this much excitement in the dual match. For one thing, three of the six results from the Valentine's Day meeting are reversed, which is a pretty large swing. Moreover, of the six matches played so far, only one has finished in the minimum of three games; two have gone to four, and half of them have gone to five. This is unusually close. Five-game matches are statistically uncommon in top-flight college squash. On average, two or three of the nine matches will go the distance at any dual match. On Valentine's Day, for instance, Trinity versus Princeton produced three matches that lasted five games. In the three other dual matches this Sunday among the other top-eight teams, kids played a total of twenty-seven individual matches; just four were five-gamers.

Little do any of us know that all three of the remaining matches will go to five games, and it will be another two and a half hours before the result gets decided.*

---

* Even our number 10 match goes to five. In collegiate squash, you play ten matches, even though only the top nine count. It's a relic of an earlier era, when transportation was an issue and sometimes guys made it to their dual match and sometimes not. So we always play the tenth match and each player goes at it fullspeed. Today, Charlie Tashjian, our senior cocaptain from Greenwich, takes on Jesus Peña from Mexico. It is a classic match, indistinguishable from any of the other nine. They have played each other before in the juniors and know each other's games. Charlie plays the best squash of his life. The packed

Andres Vargas had a warm, droll personality leavened with a dry Colombian wit. He was a sophomore. For a not-so-imposing person, he spoke with a surprisingly rich bass of a voice. He won matches not because of superior talent but because of fitness and mental toughness. He was El Gato Grande, the big cat, a play on his short stature (five feet nine) and his feline grace on court.

At thirteen he started squash at Pueblo Viejo Country Club in Bogotá. He won two national junior titles in a row. About 15 percent of his all-boys Catholic high school left the country for college, but Andres was not planning to be one of them until he ran into Bernardo Samper, a Bantam from Bogotá who had thrived in Hartford. Andres shot me an email and I called him a couple of hours later, and he was hooked. He spent a couple of months brushing up his English for the TOEFL by watching movie franchises like *The Lord of the Rings* and *Harry Potter.*

When he landed at JFK in late August, Andres was supposed to meet up with Randy Lim so they could take a car to the campus together. This oddly modern moment—two teenagers trying to find each other in a busy foreign airport, neither having any idea what the other looked like—cemented a friendship. (They met up without a hitch.) When they got to campus, they discovered their rooms were on the same floor of the same dorm and they became best friends.

In his freshman year, Andres lost to David Canner in the Princeton dual match 3–2, but then he beat him 3–1 at the nationals. He was a second-team All American. He was very good. He had a strong inner focus and was a good leader, someone who led entirely by example. He worked hard, a first-one-in, last-one-out mentality at practice. He spent the summer in a traveling summer squash camp, coaching American juniors in Spain, Germany, and Holland. He was primed for a great sophomore year.

---

gallery gets into it, matching the cheers from the other courts. Peña wins it in five close games.

Instead he had a topsy-turvy season. He loved hosting us in Colombia after New Year's, but he had a physical breakdown soon after. His freshman year, everything was so new and exciting, but in his sophomore winter, the New England climate took a toll. The lack of sun and warmth sent his body into hibernation. Squash no longer greatly interested him. It might have been a mild case of seasonal affective disorder. He had mostly snapped out of it by mid-February, but it lingered. This was a classic sophomore experience. The novelty of freshman year had worn off and it was too far from the finish line of senior year.

Today, I wonder if he has fully recovered. He is taking on Kelly Shannon, a freshman from Calgary. Like many freshman, Kelly got injured mid-season (so many of them have never pushed their bodies this hard before), though his was a freak mishap: after the first snowfall of the winter, he slipped coming down steps outside his college and pulled a muscle in his back. He took six weeks off. Eight days ago, Kelly played in his first match since the accident, and an epic match with Andres. It was a contrast in styles: Andres, the steady, conservative retriever, the absorber of punishment—imagine Bjorn Borg—versus Kelly, a McEnroe-like magician who attacked all the time. Kelly let a 2–1 lead slip away and Andres won in five. It was a peculiar scoreline: 9–2, 2–9, 2–9, 9–5, 9–3. Basically every game was a blowout. Andres's victory had sealed the Trinity win at 5–3; his teammates had swarmed his court and mobbed him afterward. It was the highlight of his Trinity career to that point.

Now Andres feels he must be the hero again. He stretches and limbers up, but still feels tight. He walks around the top of the three galleries, getting a glimpse of the matches, but that doesn't settle him down. He goes outside Jadwin and in the chilly gray afternoon listens on his iPod to the Al Pacino pregame speech from *Any Given Sunday*. He had played it the week before and the speech had pumped him up—*"one inch at a time."* Today, he has too many thoughts racing from synapse to synapse, and Pacino's rasping, yelling voice just makes him more nervous.

The first two games are close, but Andres pulls them both out. His face is straight, emotionless. This is good. He's going to clinch in three and we'll be on the road to victory.

That is how little control I have over this dual match. As with everything today, it seems I am dead wrong.

Coaching is about giving up control. A good coach is akin to a referee: unnoticeable at most points of the match, flitting past the action like a butterfly, alighting on a problem for a second and then moving on. But many younger coaches, with their boundless energy and driving ambition, dwell on every issue, thinking they can control everything—to such an extent that they draw the attention and focus back to themselves. Many use guilt as the teaching tool, making their players feel awful if they let down their coach. A coach needs to put the players first. The athlete wins or loses, not the coach. There is no way to generate resentment more quickly than to make the athletes think that they are doing this for you. Putting the players first also intrinsically means tailoring to the individual player rather than imposing a team-wide system. But young coaches love systems. They love being called a genius. They love being known as the guy who slept in his office after an all-nighter studying film. In most major sports, the television cameras do it all wrong. They invasively jump to the coach after every important play, even though it's the players who should get the attention. There is an easy test to see what kind of coach someone is. Most coaches, when you ask them when their next match is, say something like, "Oh, I play at ten tomorrow," and I bite my tongue. It's a red flag. I know *I* am not playing; *we* are playing.

Every season after New Year's, we have a fortnight training session. Classes don't start until after the Martin Luther King Jr. holiday, so I have the guys' undivided attention. We sometimes go on trips around the country or overseas, and this year we went to Colombia for a week. It was a good sojourn. As a team, we had never gone to South America before. We stayed as guests of the families of Bernardo Samper, Andres Vargas, Daniel Echevarria, and Miguel Rodriguez (a top-thirty pro who was a friend of the program even though he didn't go to Trinity). We explored the fascinating city of Bogotá, celebrated Baset's birthday, and benefited from training for a week at eighty-three hundred feet. The altitude killed us.

Most athletes, when working out in Bogotá, run up Cerro de Monserrate, a small mountain outside town. Rodriguez scooted up in thirty-one minutes; Reggie Schonborn and Goose Detter did it in thirty-nine; most guys squeaked in under an hour. I walked up in ninety minutes. My knees were killing me. Only the knowledge that the boys were waiting up at the summit kept me going. In the end, the team scampered down the last stretch and walked up with me, spiritually carrying me to the summit. We all took the gondola down.

We also came back with a new code word, a new mantra: *once*, the Spanish word for eleven. *Once* (pronounced "on-say") was the code word, but right after we got back from Colombia, we also came up with a new purpose. Simba's father had died of a heart attack just after we landed. Simba flew home—his first trip back to Zimbabwe since coming to Trinity—and stayed in Harare for nearly two weeks. When he returned, we dedicated the season to his father's memory, and at the end of every team huddle, we shouted "SIMBA!"

For the other week before classes started, we stayed in Hartford. Very few students were on campus, and we had no impending dual matches to prepare for, so it was the one uninterrupted, focused stretch of time I had to really teach.

Quakers have a theory about faith called continuing revelation. They believe that there is no final dogma, no conclusive, hard-and-fast truth. Instead, there is more to learn. Quakers test what they know against new experiences and information. If you think you know it all, you are doomed to be let down, as anyone who has endured an earthquake or tsunami can tell you. God's love is infinite and so you can discover something new as you go through your day. (I also liked to tell players what the burlesque performer Gypsy Rose Lee said: that God is love—but get it in writing.) For Friends, life is an ongoing process of questioning and searching, learning and relearning. The most important word in the dictionary is *why*.

Modeling the right behavior is a central component of how to coach properly. I show my guys how I believe in continuing revelation by bringing in outside coaches and players to work with us. It teaches them that I'm not tied to my ways. The team—the development of my players—comes before my ego. I'm trying to learn. I'm asking questions. I want them to see that just because I'm fifty-six and have gray hair doesn't mean I have all the answers. All I do is just unbox the balls and roll them out on the court. *I am going to walk with you*, this says. *I am going to seek with you.*

One of my first overseas recruits, Rohan Bhappu, was a Zoroastrian. On his recruiting visit to Trinity, we spent a long time at lunch talking about the tenets of his religion. His mother summed it up: "Good thoughts, good words, good deeds." A decade later, when my father died, I called Bhappu to go over the phrasing, for I had pondered it again and again and wanted to use it as the basis for my eulogy at my father's funeral.

I also bring in other coaches because my players get used to me. They roll their eyes whenever they hear, "When I was at West Point . . ." Familiarity breeds disinterest.

When I was at West Point—well, I started the whole process of learning when I was hired as the squash coach in 1976. I knew nothing about squash, so my second thought upon getting the job (the first thought was, *What's squash?*) was to seek a mentor. I needed some tutelage. I needed a coach. I called up Dave Fish, the squash and tennis coach at Harvard, whom I once met for about ten seconds at a tennis tournament. Fish was a respected figure in both games, although he was just two years older than me and had just succeeded Harvard icon Jack Barnaby. I drove up to Cambridge, and he allowed me to follow him around for a day and learn how he ran drills. I've never forgotten his generosity.

Sometimes I bring in Mike Way, an Englishman who's a former Canadian national coach. With a buzz cut and pale skin, he has the cadaverous look of so many squashmen after decades of working inside a fluorescent-lit box. Mike makes a deep impression on the guys in part because he has credibility and a proven track record and in part because his ego is clearly no longer in the lead like a young coach's usually is. He has confidence in what he does, but he recognizes that there's more than one way to hit a volley or crack a drop shot. Elite athletes are elite because they know the game well. You can't be rigid and doctrinaire with them. Almost all innovation originally comes from the players—they figure something out and eventually the coaches learn it.

Mike loves to tell the story of how he got started working with Jonathon Power, the former world champion. Around 1994 he took up coaching a Canadian teenager with potential named Graham Ryding. Soon after they started, Ryding's PSA ranking soared. One day Ryding had a friendly match with a kid named Jonathon Power. After they finished, Way huddled with Ryding, discussing the match. Power approached them. "Do you notice something about my game?" he asked.

Way said, "Yes, I do," and offered a few tips. Power asked him if they could have a lesson together. The next week, Way took Power into the court. He said, "Let's work on your forehand drop shot."

"Which one?" Power asked.

"Which one?"

"Yeah, which one? I have six."

"Six?"

"Sure," Power said, and ran through them, demonstrating the tiny differences in his stroke.

Way told this story to show not only how immensely talented Power was, not only to demonstrate how Power, like most top players, had an abiding fascination with his sport and all its obscure details, but also as an example of how Power taught Way about the game. The teacher became the student. We can all learn. No one is in control.

Then Way lowered the boom: "Well, in the end, he actually had only four drop shots."

Curt and sometimes crass, Mike holds players in the palm of his hand. He gives analysis without candy coating. He says what he thinks and he thinks clearly. You can tell when someone knows what he's talking about because he can make it simple and concrete. If it's complex, if he plunges off on meandering tangents and salts his oracular pronouncements with "of course" and "obviously" and "frankly," then he doesn't really know what he's talking about.

Like me, Mike tries not to play with his players. Competition is for other teams, not the coach. For seven summers, I was the head coach of a World Team Tennis squad, the Hartford FoxForce. Invented by Billie Jean King in 1974, World Team Tennis is a lighthearted, fan-friendly pro circuit. When the Hartford team was launched in 1999, Billie Jean asked me to coach the team. (I was a good choice in their eyes: not expensive and yet well connected in Hartford.) World Team Tennis was a fascinating change from college sports. With tennis pros, I was dealing with people who often had gone through even less emotional development—they had been cosseted since they were eleven or twelve—but had way more power (read: money, fame) than my college players. My first season was a rough one. I didn't know exactly how much coaching I should do, as all of my players, like Mardy Fish and Monica Seles, were already so accomplished and already had full-time paid coaches. When I asked Billie Jean what advice she had, she simply said: "These are great players but they still want approval. They are still as insecure as anyone else."

At one practice, I was hitting with a young South African woman with a bright future. We started playing points, slow and easy, but I was hitting the ball well and really pinning her in the back of the court, coming in behind my low, skidding approach shots and angling my volleys away for winners. The points had a nice, flowing rhythm.

After we finished the practice, she came to net and swore at me. She said she had never been treated so poorly, that I was trying to upstage her. She did not want her coach to challenge her. We were not even keeping track of the points—there was no score. Yet I had challenged her. Our relationship deteriorated and by the end of the season she wouldn't talk to me.

That was the last time I got on court with my players to play. I would still feed them balls or demonstrate a shot, but I never played points again. I had competed a bit with my players at West Point. After all, we were all learning the game and we were about the same age. It created confusion. It brought down walls that need to be up. A coach is a coach, not a player.

Eventually it came to be that even if I'd had an urge to get on court, I couldn't. After all the running and jumping and landing and sprinting in gymnastics, squash, and tennis, my knees and back wore out. Between 1998 and 2005, I had eight surgeries, five on my knees and three on my back. After that, there was no way I could compete with the boys, and whenever we played, they played customer squash, keeping the ball in play and patronizing me with comments like "You've got good hands, Coach."

In April 2005 I also had a mild stroke. I was separated from my second wife, living in a friend's house and feeling sorry for myself. In the evening while watching television on a couch, I kept dropping the remote control. When I got up, I felt like I was drunk, even though I hadn't drunk anything. I staggered to the bathroom to brush my teeth before going to bed and couldn't hold the toothbrush. I went to sleep thinking that I'd be fine in the morning, and in my state of depression I thought that if I didn't wake up, I didn't care. In the morning, I couldn't use my left hand and slurred my words when I spoke. I drove to my doctor and told him what was happening. He said I should get some tests.

"Great," I told him. "It's a Friday, though, and I've got a dual match tomorrow at Wheaton. Why don't we do the tests on Monday?"

He smiled. "There's an ambulance idling outside, waiting to take you to the hospital," he said. "You've had a stroke."

At the hospital, the doctors kept bringing in residents to see me. They said, "See that? That is a guy who is not supposed to be in here— too healthy, too athletic, too young and strong." It was just my luck. Now I'm the off-court sage rather than the on-court battering ram.

Just like I no longer play with the boys, it is critical to control your own emotions. You have to learn to count to ten. I've seen this in several situations. At West Point there was a 50 percent attrition rate for students over the four years of the undergraduate program. Because it was such a macho setting, quitting was viewed as a sign of weakness. But the Academy, let alone a career in the military, was not for everyone, and this created a high degree of inner conflict for many of the students there. More than one of my players flunked out on purpose—failing academically was a more acceptable way to exit than to quit.

The crucial point came at the end of sophomore year. A West Point cadet could leave the academy at any time before his junior year began without incurring a military commitment. One sophomore player, Jon Bell, told me on the day of our last match of the season that he was resigning at the end of the school year. Bell, a young African American from Dallas, had been well coached before coming to West Point. He was not inclined to listen to me. In fact, he had scratched PYG on his racquet to remind himself, *Play Your Game* rather than listen to the coach.

When Bell told me he was resigning, I felt like two years of hard, tense work was down the drain. But I bit my tongue and said nothing negative. I just gave him encouragement to do what he felt he had to do. It was best to swallow my pride. Some matters are out of your control. Don't fight it.

At the team banquet after the season, I stood up and in front of the team told him how lucky we'd been to have him on the team for two years and wished him luck. The next day, he came to my office and said he had never known I cared that much for him; he'd never known it really was about him, not about my program or me. He withdrew his resignation and graduated on time.

Another time at West Point, we had renovated the squash courts and added a glass-back show court, and out of laziness, I didn't put back up the various team photographs and plaques that had detailed Army's illustrious squash history. Walter Oehrlein visited one weekend and later sent me a kindly written note asking where his 1965 intercollegiate trophy was. I took his letter as a personal affront, as if he were

challenging my abilities as a coach. It was silly. He was just quering
about Army's history, but I was insecure about my ability to coach
squash. I wrote a long, vitriolic reply. Somehow the day ran out and I
had to leave before I put the letter in an envelope and mailed it. When
I came in to work the next morning, having slept on the matter, I realized Walter was not attacking me. I never mailed the letter.

This experienced echoed one at Trinity. One of my seniors lost
a late-season challenge match for the number 9 spot on the ladder.
I had refereed the last two games, as there was a lot of yelling and
pushing. At the end of the match, in front of the team, he stormed
off the court, screaming, "You hosed me, Coach." When I got back
to my office, I found a pile of uniforms and racquets—he had quit the
team. My reaction was fury: How could I allow such insubordination,
especially by a senior? Then I mentally went through his long journey:
how his father had built a squash court at their house, the pressure he
had felt for a decade now. I sent him an email pretending I had not
seen the pile in my office. I scolded him for his behavior. I added that
it was a wrenching match but that I expected him to finish his historic
career (he went 34–0 in his four years) as a great sportsman. The next
day, he came to my office, gave me a hug, scooped up his things, and
went out to practice.

Another thing about coaching is to be yourself. If you work with
elite players, you can never pretend to be something you aren't. You
can't fake it. While I was coaching at West Point, Army's basketball
coach was Mike Krzyzewski. One winter I asked Mike if I could watch
one of his basketball practices so I could pick up some ideas for my
squash team. Toward the end of the practice, he exploded and went
through a tirade, screaming and gesticulating at his players. Mike was
normally a quiet, introspective person—though I knew he burned
with great passion about his team—so I was surprised by the level of
his emotion. He then ended the practice, sending all his guys to the
showers.

Later that day I walked over to his house—he lived down the street
and my children used to beat up his children—and hesitatingly asked

him what set him off. He smiled and said, in a calm voice, that it had been an orchestrated attempt to get the team's attention and that he had planned the tirade weeks before.

So I decided to do the same thing a few days before the Navy match. I had the team running sprints. They were not giving it their all and so I called them in. In a flash, I picked up a specially selected wooden racquet that was already slightly cracked. I barked at them and in a great show of emotion smashed the racquet on the ground. The racquet artfully shattered into three or four pieces. There was silence, then laughter. The team found this very funny. They knew I could not be serious. One of the guys patted me on the back, and they chortled and went back to finish their sprints.

In the end, coaching simply means keeping track of everyone. Once I took the Army tennis team to Texas for a spring break trip. We based ourselves in Irving and drove out one morning three hours to Waco for a match against Baylor. After our match—we got spanked 7–0—we left Waco, stopping at a lonely gas station outside town. Everyone piled out and went the bathroom or grabbed a snack in the tiny shop there. We got back in the van and drove the three hours back to Irving. When we got to the hotel, we realized we had left one of our players at the Waco gas station. I drove the three hours back to the gas station. He was sitting on the ground in the shade of the awning. He had no money (having left his wallet in the van), no idea who to call (this was well before cell phones) and was desperately hoping that someone would come back for him.

That was when I realized that much of coaching is just getting the people to the right place at the right time. Everything else is a bonus. Of course, you have to have the car in the first place. One year I took the team to Hanover to play Dartmouth. That night, they asked me to borrow the van to go down the road from the hotel to get some snacks. I gave them the key and went to bed. In the morning, we got into the van and drove off and I noticed that the odometer had four hundred new miles on it—they had snuck off to Montreal.

I threw all the lessons I learned about control and coaching out the window when dealing with my son Matthew. It was as if my patrimony, rather than all the wisdom and experience I had gained from my coaching years, would be nothing. I offered Matthew nothing. Nothing but absence, nothing but ego, nothing but pride. I didn't count to ten. I didn't even count to one. I wasn't counting. I didn't show him love. I let his problems deepen. I wasn't there to help him at every fork in the road.

His two-year disappearance was a terrible time. At first I was worried about the fact that I didn't know where my son was. Then I was scared, then apathetic. I just had to wait. I had made him wait, all those evenings when I was coaching. Now I would wait.

What could I do? There was no evidence of foul play. Matthew was just too big—by now six feet one and two hundred pounds—to be abducted. He had run away and we couldn't follow.

One morning in 1998, I was in my office and the phone was ringing off the hook, as usual: coaches, players, recruits, an assistant in the athletic department, a parent.

"Dad, it's Matt."

I sat in silence. It was like hearing the voice of a beloved great-uncle who had died. Finally, I realized I had to say something, "Matthew, where are you?"

"I'm in jail. In Waterbury. Can you come bail me out?"

An hour later I walked into the Waterbury County Jail. We hugged. I led him out to the car. He told me about the charges—drug possession, disorderly conduct—about being clean and getting set up. He looked like someone else's son. His hair was in cornrows. He had more tattoos, including a giant one that snaked up his arm, an elaborate design of fish biting fish, with water, flowers, and flames. He was much older.

We went back to his house in an old section of Waterbury. The screen door lay flattened, half crushed, on its side. Inside, the mortar along the ceiling was grouted with sunlight. Two pit bulls barked.

The kitchen table glistened with a greasy, black sheen. Matthew's girlfriend, Karen, was there. "Mateo," she said dully, from the bedroom when he walked in, barely greeting her boyfriend who had just spent the night in jail. Her two kids were watching a television in another room, sitting on the floor, which was more comfortable than sitting on the plastic-sheathed couch.

We went out to lunch at a diner. Karen was a stripper. Her stage name was Bobbi. She worked at a club near the diner. Matthew had gone there one night and fallen in love with her. He had come back, night after night, not sure if she was just talking to him for the tips. She called him Mateo. She was from Puerto Rico.

I bought him a car and gave him some money to buy food for Karen's two children. He got a job as a bar back at a restaurant in Waterbury. A few weeks later, it was Christmas, and Matthew, Karen, and her two children came down to my parents' house in Pearl River. My parents treated the two kids like they were grandchildren, giving them presents, taking them for little outings. They even drove up to Waterbury a couple of times that winter to take the whole family out to dinner.

Another phone call, another police station. "Dad, I'm in Bridgeport." He had gotten caught dealing heroin. I got him into the Salvation Army rehab place in Bridgeport, which was a pretty decent center. (I was becoming an expert on Connecticut's rehab facilities.) Once a week I went to Bridgeport to take him out to lunch. We walked through town to a Friendly's on Main Street. It was just a couple of blocks away, a five-minute walk that took us nearly half an hour. Matthew knew everyone. Guys sauntered up and said hello, fist-punched, hugged with their arms banging chests. These were his dealers, his social network, his life. Each time, Matthew said, "This is my father. This is the guy I've been telling you about. He's my hero."

I bristled at this. *I am no hero. I am standing here with my son who has insanely difficult problems.* I felt I was floating around in a William S. Burroughs novel. I didn't know Matthew.

Ex-addicts ran the center and they knew the manipulative behavior that Matthew and other users would employ. After a month, he got thrown out for stealing. A few days later, Kristen, Matthew, and I drove up to Warwick, New York, to celebrate Scott's wedding. Matthew was in the backseat, throwing up the whole way. It was a stomach virus, he said. He had chills. His joints ached. He had a fever. His blue T-shirt was mottled with sweat. We turned off the Thruway and stopped at a 7-Eleven for a Diet Coke. "Dad, you need to know something," he said, our hands on the door handles. "I've been using."

"Using?"

"Brown sugar, Dad. Heroin. I've been shooting up. I'm going through withdrawal."

Scott was furious at Matthew for showing up in such a state. Kristen cried most of the way back. We all stared straight ahead, the crush of wheels on snow the only sound. We could not even get our act together to pretend for Scott's wife, Lisa, and her family and friends that we were a real family. It was a watershed moment. It was clear that Matthew was no longer the brother or son that we knew. His illness had taken over.

In 1998 the U.S. Olympic Committee gave me a Coach of the Year award. I was being honored for my quarter century of work with young people. It was incredibly inspiring. On the plane to Houston to accept the award with my father, I read *Tuesdays with Morrie*. As the plane landed, I was weeping, so moved was I by the power of the story and by my own failings with Matthew. It was a case of the cobbler being the worst-shod person in the village. Here I was, perhaps at the pinnacle of my professional career, surrounded by athletes and coaches from around the world, meeting Muhammad Ali, and I was deeply miserable. "I've done a better job with my players than with Matthew," I told my father.

"That's because it's easier," he replied. "They go home."

Understanding the overseas players' effects on me and the team proved to be my biggest challenge. It was the hardest thing I had to handle as a coach. I had to figure out what I could control and what I had to not worry about.

The first of my trials with overseas players came to a sad ending. Soon after we lost that last match to Harvard, Zafi Levy told me that he wanted to transfer. It was the right decision. I called my old friend Dave Johnson at Williams and that fall Zafi moved up to Williamstown. He thrived there and was an All American each season. After a break trading at Lehman Brothers, he returned to Williams in 2002 to succeed Johnson as head coach. Since then he has done a wonderful job and has been a personable colleague.

In his wake came the class of 2002, the first extraordinary recruiting class. We landed Noah Wimmer, the number three U.S. junior and a personal favorite of mine. He was quick on the court and gregarious off the court. But even more important, that year we cracked the Indian continent. India and Pakistan had a wealth of squash excellence and players who were highly motivated educationally, but it was not easy to break into their communities and lure players to Hartford. Besides the cultural differences and geographic distance—which meant their juniors never traveled to the States for our big junior tournaments—they had also never heard of Trinity. They knew of the Ivy League schools, of Harvard, Yale, Princeton, but not Trinity. So it was a struggle.

The first Indian I landed was Rohan Bhappu, an elegant, smooth player with a creative mind. After that, I recruited the Juneja twins, Rohan and Guarav, who had played for India in the 1998 World Juniors at Princeton just weeks before they arrived in Hartford. At the last minute, I got Akhil Behl, the Indian national champion.

Lefika Ragontse was the player with the most improbable journey to Hartford. He grew up in a diamond mining camp in the Kalahari desert in northern Botswana. The camp had a single open-air squash court. He parlayed his squash ability into stints at a boarding school in South Africa and a training sojourn in Toronto. I met him in the steam room at Apawamis during the qualifying for a pro tournament. In 1998, Lefika's sister had suddenly died, and the scrawny

Batswanan changed the direction of his life and applied to one U.S. college: Trinity.

For many of my overseas players, that kind of complete coincidence was typical. Unlike many Americans, they had not spent years obsessing about college, researching, investigating, plotting. Almost all were planning to go to the local university in their city, and they came to Trinity because of the squash, not knowing anything more about the college. Many of them applied only to Trinity.

As with Lefika, I met Bernardo Samper in a steam room. It was during the 1999 Pan American Games in Winnipeg. I was there coaching the U.S. team; Samper was on the Colombian squad. In the steamy fog, we chatted about college squash and Trinity. He said he had no interest. I said fine, but as I was leaving the locker room, I dropped my business card in his squash bag. A few months later, he discovered the card—like most kids, his bag was a jumbled mess—and sent me an email.

Michael Ferreira had blindly applied to Harvard, mostly on the basis of its hallowed name. He had not studied for the SAT (he was too busy with A levels and his squash), and he scored too low to get in to Harvard. When I heard he was interested in coming to the States for college, I immediately called him. I called on his birthday (the twenty-second of December), then on Christmas and on New Year's Eve. I always went through the parents—they had to be comfortable—and spent hours talking to them about our program and about the United States, as their son had never been to the States before. I even chatted a lot with Ferreira's sisters. It was through the whole family that the decision got made. On the plane ride over from London, Ferreira watched *American Pie II* and thought that would be what college was like in the States.

The next year I was recruiting Reggie Schonborn, the national junior champion of South Africa. An Afrikaner living in the city of Bloemfontein, he was applying to a couple of South African universities when a friend of his named Nadeem Osman, who was a freshman on our team, suggested he apply to Trinity. We emailed a couple of times and then I called. After I'd had a long talk with his parents, Reggie got on the phone. Laconic, he seemed hesitant, like he was hiding something. He mumbled about maybe applying elsewhere. He was referring to the University of Cape Town, but I suddenly thought, *Oh, the Harvard coach, must have gotten to him.*

So I said, "Well, it sounds like you are more keen on Harvard."

"Harvard?" Reggie asked.

"Yes, sure, Harvard is fine for you. You've got good grades, good scores." And I went on for a while about how great Boston was before hanging up, thinking I had lost him to Harvard.

Reggie got off the phone and turned to his expectant parents. "He said something about me going to Harvard," he said. "What is this Harvard? Why is he pawning me off on some dodgy, crap school I've never heard of?"

The hype arrived with our new 1997–98 recruits. Doing a feature on us for the first time, *Squash Magazine* ran a cover story about the recruiting class. Preseason rankings came out and Trinity was number one. We had lost just two of our top nine, we had the two-time intercollegiate champion in Marcus Cowie, and we had six recruits, all of whom might have played number 1 on any other squad.

I took the ranking list and posted it on my office door. Above it, I wrote, "Prove it. You've done nothing yet."

We went and steamrolled the country. Marcus played number 1, Behl number 2, Preston Quick number 3, and Lefika, who everyone thought might play number 1, found himself at number 4. We ran out twenty men against Yale and won all twenty matches. In early February, we dismantled Harvard 8–1, in Cambridge, the first time they had lost at home in a decade (ninety-one straight dual matches). In all but 7 of the 124 individual matches that season, we won the match 3–0. At the nationals, held at Harvard, we blew out Princeton in the semis 9–0 and then vivisected Harvard 8–1 in the finals. It was the first time a non–Ivy League school had won the national title since Navy captured it in 1967. Sitting next to me on the bleachers at the Murr Center watching us clinch the dual match was Zafi Levy. The Williams van had left—he was so intent on watching that he couldn't leave.

It was an intoxicating time. We met with the Connecticut governor, John Rowland, in his office, as he proclaimed it Trinity Squash Day in the state. The city put up a highway sign along Interstate 84 proclaiming that we were national champions.

But all the attention came with a dose of humility. A Trinity alum who was an owner of the Boston Red Sox invited the entire team to a game in the owner's box at Fenway Park, and I threw out the ceremonial first pitch. It was a disaster. I was a bit nervous—you had no idea how big the Green Monster is until you stood below it, nor how noisy forty thousand New Englanders can be. It was a chilly night. The ball was new and slick. The public address announcer told the crowd that I was the coach of the national championship squash team.

As I turned around to wave at the team up in the owner's box and my daughter and dozens of her friends in the bleachers, I caught a glimpse of the JumboTron screen. There I was, thirty feet tall. I froze up. My hands were like fists of ice. When it came time to throw the pitch, I was so tight that the ball fluttered like a wounded pigeon and bounced on the way to Jason Varitek, the Red Sox catcher. Everyone said I should practice throwing. I said, "I've been a professional athlete. I can throw a baseball sixty feet." It turned out I needed to practice.

Coming off the field, I heard an adenoidal snarl from the seats. "Nice throw, Coach," a fan yelled to me in a pitch-perfect South End accent. "By the way, what the hell's squash?"

In the beginning, I was stunned by how difficult it was to integrate the overseas and American boys. There was a social divide. Almost all the Americans were in Alpha Delt (eight of the top nine of my first team in 1995 were AD brothers) and the overseas guys never joined a fraternity. Many of the foreigners were remarkably different from the American kids—in looks, in tastes, in interests—and accepting them took a level of sophistication, empathy, and maturity that some prep-school Americans just didn't have.

Moreover, the overseas guys were taking spots on the ladder. In the old days, a player enjoyed an inevitable rise up the ladder through his four years. Recruiting changed that, and quite a few of the Americans on the team reacted negatively. It was a new paradigm being thrust upon them that no one, in the seventy years of intercollegiate squash, had ever seen before. A guy like Noah Wimmer, the best American recruit in 1998, might arrive heralded as one of the top U.S. juniors, and never play in a major varsity match because of all the overseas players.

We saw it right away a few weeks after we landed Marcus Cowie; he suggested I contact a fellow Englishman, an old friend of his named Steve Ayling, who might be interested in joining the team. Marcus had told us how good Steve was, yet after he joined the team he promptly lost challenge matches to the top four guys below Marcus. He looked fabulous on court—he pulverized the ball—but he couldn't beat anyone. As we reached the nationals, I met with the four seniors on the team and told them I felt we should just move him to number 2. They all agreed. Ayling was definitely the second-best player on paper. Perhaps it was just taking a while for him to adjust to college life. We parceled out the underclassmen, and each of the seniors was supposed to speak with a certain number of them to pave the way for my announcement the next day. One of the seniors forgot to tell his designated players. At practice the next day, there were a couple of dropped jaws among the Americans when I said I was bucking the challenge system and leapfrogging Ayling to number 2. Then Ayling ended up losing in the dual match. He ran into financial difficulties and couldn't come back after the spring semester. He was the only recruit I've ever had who failed to graduate.

Duncan Pearson epitomized the transition. A Chestnut Hill Academy grad, Pearson came up from Philadelphia to Hartford in the fall of 1997 as one of the top juniors in the country. He had great expectations, in part because he boasted an unmatchable pedigree, as his great-uncle and great-great-uncle were Stan Pearson Jr. and Stan Pearson Sr., who combined had won a total of seven national singles championships. Pearson found himself at number 5 on the ladder—until Loua Coetzee arrived from South Africa. So he played number 6 on the second-best team in the country. In both dual matches against Harvard, he lost in tiebreakers in the fifth game.

In his sophomore year, he came back to campus with high hopes. He thought that with graduations, the transfer of Zafi Levy, and the experience he had gleaned as a freshman, he'd move up. Instead he witnessed the arrival of our incredible recruiting class and was bumped down to number 10 or number 11 for the rest of his career.

The team was winning national championships, which was great. A ring was a ring. But because he was so low on the ladder, Pearson never again played a competitive squash match. It was not because he was a weak player. In fact, because of all the talented recruits and the tension of intrateam challenge matches, Pearson actually improved tremendously in college. It was just that he had no place to show that. In dual matches, he played only against weaker schools, and all his matches were inevitably 3–0 laughers. And since he was number 10 or number 11, he was not invited to the intercollegiates (the sixty-four players had to come from the top nine), even though he was assuredly one of the best thirty players in the nation.

Still, he good-naturedly stuck to the team, and in his senior year he was cocaptain. The night before the finals of the 2001 nationals, I told Nadeem Osman, our regular number 10, that I was putting Pearson in at number 10 to reward him for his four years of service to the team. Since the nationals were at Yale, Pearson, like all of us, had gone back to Hartford from New Haven to sleep on campus and I just barely managed to track him down to tell him to bring his gear for Sunday. He won his match against Harvard and was one of the ten guys awarded the Potter Trophy for playing on the national championship team. A few weeks later, Pearson's younger brother Eric was visiting. The cup was lying on a couch and Eric sat on it, violently smushing it. The cup, already an eloquent symbol of all that was good and not so good about Pearson's collegiate career, was now square rather than round. He liked it more that way.

In practical terms, I needed the bombsquaders to push overseas guys, to nip at their heels to make the top nine. I needed fierce challenge matches. The bombsquaders translated college squash for the overseas guys. Intercollegiate squash had thrived for four generations in the United States. The bombsquaders explained the history, the geography, the nomenclature, the people of the American squash community. I also needed bombsquaders to keep our team fresh. Squash was brutally exhausting to the body. Physically, it was as draining as a cross-country skiing race or a day on the Tour de France. I wanted to keep our top nine injury free, rested, and match hardened but not exhausted. We often had to play two matches in a weekend—we'd go to Williamstown and play Williams and a visiting Vassar squad the next day. Having very good players who could jump in was critical. In the end, the impact I could have on my number 22 player was as large as the impact I could have with the number 1 player and I tried to treat the bombsquaders well. Usually one of our cocaptains came out of that cohort.

As time went on, everyone became used to the system and understood their roles coming in; even if a player had been great as a junior, he knew that it was unlikely he'd be at the top of the Trinity ladder. The social divisions fell away. Some of the Americans did not join a fraternity in large part because the squash team became an ad hoc house, with its own rituals, nicknames, jokes, and deep friendships. Guys began to go on holidays together: perhaps that all began when Duncan Pearson invited Loua Coetzee on a spring-break road trip to the Florida Keys. The overseas guys began to blend in on campus as Trinity's international diversity push yielded more and more foreign students—early on they stuck out a lot.

Handling my overseas players' egos required a completely different set of skills. They grew up in countries where squash was a popular sport. Having survived a sustained culling process, they were the best in their nation. They'd been coddled by their families, their friends, their teachers, their coaches, their clubs, and their governments. Everyone stroked their egos. They played for their country at the Commonwealth Games or the World Juniors. They were in the newspapers and on the evening news. At tournaments they got byes in the first round, and over the weekend they saw their names inexorably inch to the right of the draw sheet. Galleries filled behind them when they played. They got free racquets and their bureaus were larded with trophies.

But they were still hard-nosed street fighters. Squash was not an end in itself; it was a means to something else (money, an education). When they cared about something, they fought for it. They came out firing on the first ball they saw and they didn't let up until the post-match handshake.

College squash ironically meant they were giving up a dream. Many players had hoped to go pro, and coming to Trinity was a concession that perhaps they were not that good. Very few players managed to go to college and then join the pro tour. That was changing somewhat. Julian Illingworth, a Portland, Oregon, kid, had played at Yale until graduating in 2006. He was pretty good—he started his record streak of six straight U.S. national adult titles as a Yale junior—but he never won a national intercollegiate title and in fact reached the finals only once. Within three years after graduation he had reached twenty-eighth in the world, the highest ranking any American man had ever achieved. The standard in college squash was improving and Illingworth's game didn't deteriorate while he was at Yale, which it would have done a decade before. But the distractions of college—classes, parties, clubs, fraternities—meant that he hadn't been through the two-a-day, monastic training routine that most nineteen-year-old pros endured.

I had to deal with a surprising amount of homesickness. The overseas boys had to adapt to new food, new climate, new customs, new language, new friends; to classes in English, tough coursework, late nights in the library. Even the squash was a change. Courts were different, as most of them grew up on concrete or paneled courts, while we played in maple courts. The temperature was different—not as hot and humid on court. They had to get used to wearing protective goggles, an American tradition that had not yet extended overseas. They usually had to switch racquets if they wanted to borrow the free ones I got. Squash players, like most very good athletes, employed voodoo, superstition, cryptoscience, and obsession when dealing with their racquets, and being forced to a new racquet was, for some, the equivalent of an old blacksmith being forced to use a new bellows and tongs.

They also saw a stunning display of xenophobia and racism. At away matches, opposing fans swore at our players. They screamed "white nigger" at Shaun Johnstone, a Caucasian man who, like his parents, was born and raised in Zimbabwe; Shaun responded by flipping them the middle finger. (We severely chastened Shaun for this the next day. Besides being unsportsmanlike and stooping to their level, it showed a lack of focus.) They yelled "Bastard Ass-fuck" at Baset Ashfaq. They shouted sexual vulgarities at the mother of one of our players, a woman who was going through a bitter divorce. They shouted "towel head" at Rohan Juneja, who played wearing his traditional Sikh turban. In some matches involving our subcontinental Asian players, the crowds yelled "Go back to India and bomb Pakistan" or "terrorist" or "You're Al Qaeda" or something about Osama bin Laden. At Williams one year they held up signs that read THEY MIGHT BE NATIONAL CHAMPS, BUT THEY CAN'T SPEAK ENGLISH and WATCH WILLIAMS PLAY TRINITY AND TEACH THEM HOW TO READ.

At one match, a fan screamed, "Trinity's full of douchebags."

I turned around and said evenly, "You're not showing a lot of class."

The fan responded, "Trinity's coach is a douchebag."

My players shrugged it off more often than not, considering it the price they paid for a great collegiate experience.

The bond *between* overseas guys was not seamless. It was a global group. In the past fifteen seasons, we've had players from the United States, Canada, Mexico, Bermuda, Jamaica, El Salvador, Colombia, Uruguay, Brazil, Switzerland, England, Sweden, India, Pakistan, Malaysia, Singapore, Zimbabwe, Botswana, and South Africa. Some years, each of our nine players was from a different country. Some were hidebound rivals—Pakistanis and Indians—and we had to over-come cultural stereotypes as much within our cohort of foreigners as between them and the Americans.

Some of the old-school squash mandarins bemoaned the influx of overseas guys. They accused us of bringing in professionals (when many players at other schools had also taken time off after high school to test the pro tour). They gossiped about how the players were poor students (when in fact the squash team's GPA was higher than the campus average and some years we had the highest GPA of any Trinity sports team) or how they didn't graduate (when in fact all but a single recruit, Steve Ayling, has graduated from Trinity). I received vitriolic emails, angry phone calls, and more than one vinegary harangue at a squash tournament. In March 2004, the *Harvard Crimson* ran a widely referenced article titled "The Evil Empire of College Squash" and claimed that we had four athletic scholarships on the team. (We never had scholarships.)

The most self-serving claim was the most false. Harvard's article suggested that overseas kids were hogging spots on college varsities, a gentle amnesia blinding them to the fact that there have always been overseas guys on top teams. Harvard's 1951 team, the first Crimson team to win a national title since the thirties, featured not only a bevy of St. Grottlesex products but Johangir Mugaseth from India. Three of the top nine on Dartmouth's 1991 team, ranked fifth in the nation, were from overseas. That same year, when Harvard was ranked number one, its top nine included players from India, Israel, and Canada. Moreover, twenty overseas men have won the individual championship since 1931.

In reality, our players were not mercenaries. They became a vibrant part of the Trinity campus. They joined clubs, ran the student government, held work-study jobs, and partied at the fraternities. They wrote theses. Over half of the overseas guys took a semester abroad, usually in places where it was difficult to play much squash. Moreover, the guys stayed in the States after graduation. More than two dozen of my players became teaching pros at country clubs. A few gave the pro tour a shot. A few also joined the doubles tour, which is based solely in the United States and Canada. Many took jobs on Wall Street. Only about 20 percent of the overseas guys even went back home within five years of graduation. They were not ringers who performed their jobs and departed for home.

We had raised the standard of intercollegiate squash, and we did it legally, ethically, and appropriately. At the beginning of the 2008–09 season, we had a way to prove it. On the first day of November, the day of our first official practice, a sixty-page memorandum landed on the desk of Trinity president Jimmy Jones. It was an anonymously written report on Trinity's squash recruiting, an obvious product of Internet research. There were claims that we had violated a whole host of NCAA and New England Small College Athletic Conference rules. (Even though squash was not an official NCAA sport, everyone in the game followed NCAA rules.) President Jones, a man who had a high standard of ethics, took the matter very seriously. It was an anonymous report—he could have buried it. Instead, he hired lawyers in Indianapolis who regularly dealt with NCAA investigations. The lawyers interviewed each of our players and coaches; my interview lasted more than three hours. The process was grueling and dangerously dispiriting: all season the suggestion that we had done something illegal hung over our heads. Some of the examples of our alleged violations were so off base it was silly—the compiler of the report had trolled around the Internet, bottom-feeding on gossip and coincidences. One example was the accusation that Andres Vargas had played in a pro tournament in Bogotá as a freshman. I asked Andres if he had left campus in October without my knowing it, flown to Colombia, and played in a pro tournament. He laughed, it was so absurd. It turned out that there was another player in Colombia with the same name.

In February the verdict came back: every single charge except a minor one was completely unsubstantiated. The one fault was that we were not following NCAA rules about gap years: in essence, we should have been reducing eligibility for each year beyond one that a student takes off after high school graduation if he accepts any level of squash income, even if it doesn't cover his expenses. The lawyers demonstrated that ours was beyond reproach. In fact, they showed that other college squash programs were in direct violation not only of this rule but many others as well.

It turned out that we were running a clean program, well within NCAA and NESCAC guidelines.

Although it was stressful at the time, the relief we felt at the conclusion was very deep. I knew we ran a legitimate program, but no one else knew for sure until we endured an NCAA-style investigation. It had been an unnerving time. I had always lived by the mantra, "What's the worst that can happen?" In this case, I didn't have an answer.

All the *mishegas* struck me very hard. I wanted approval more than success. I left West Point in part because I wanted to be a winning coach, and then once I was a winning coach, I found that I craved not the title or the ring but the cheers of supporters. I found it very upsetting to be criticized on the Internet or to find out that someone disapproved of my Trinity program. At squash clubs I sometimes overheard gossip by players that would leave me in tears. Some people viewed Trinity as a den of iniquity stocked with villainous, unsportsmanlike foreigners, guys who had played on the pro tour and were miles away from the amateur ideal. One parent had waved an American flag after Tim Wyant disposed of Marcus Cowie at his junior intercollegiates and then got in Marcus's face and jawed at him. I would have given up the streak rather than have friends and colleagues think poorly of me. One day in Ecuador I was talking to Richard Chin, a player on the U.S. team. He looked at me absolutely dumbfounded and said, "Assy, I am surprised that you didn't realize that this was in the cards. Heavy the head that wears the crown. You need to recognize that this is always going to be there. You've changed U.S. squash—but don't expect everyone to cheer for you."

Years after the Atlas Lives match, I got a long, kind email from Yasser El Halaby. He told me something very wise and very true that his father used to say: successful people have to pay a success tax.

Today Andres is up 2–0, but there are signs he is not in the catbird seat. He has been running too much, his silky elegance destroyed by too much effort. After the second game, James says to him, "You have to bring it home. We're down. It's all you."

For some guys, this is just the right sort of message, the little extra puff of wind that fills the sails and pushes the boat home. For Andres, it capsizes him. He hears Princeton's roars from next door. It does sound bad. I think of that great passage from the end of Raymond Chandler's *The Long Goodbye*: "It all depends on where you sit and what your own private score is." Even though he is up 2–0, Andres suddenly thinks he's in trouble.

Andres knows only one speed—all out—and he's unable to manage it when he runs into this strong wind of pressure. His swing shortens. It gets so compact he could play in a telephone booth. He has lost his feline fluidity. He plays with a wary deliberation, like a beginner. He is thinking too much. He is hearing too much. He starts to hear the fizzing, bubbling crowd. They whisper gibberish just before he serves. When he makes a mistake, they howl with glee. Only during a long rally can he escape the crowd.

On top of it all, he is is wolfing down power gels. He slurped down a package of the sticky goo before his match. After the first game, he ate another. Now he is fully wired on caffeine and sugar. In the third, he hits a wall. His tank has run dry. He tries to bend his body to his will, but it is unwilling.

At the same time, Kelly is playing extremely well. He had not practiced all week. Callahan sat him out for the Friday match against Penn, but he had endured a long four-game loss against Rochester's Joe Chapman in the semis on Saturday. Miraculously, despite a total lack of match fitness, Kelly is hanging around. He is attacking with his volley—a brilliant move; again, Callahan has outcoached me—rushing Andres, who wants nothing more than long, slow points. Kelly is getting stronger rather than weaker as the match wears on.

In the next three games, Kelly wins twenty-seven points, Andres just nine. Kelly, having watched video, seems to know what Andres is going to do and is volleying everything with precision. For Andres, it is almost hypnotic—Kelly could do it in his sleep. Andres remembers a match in Peru when he was down 2–0 to a lesser local player and the gallery was going berserk, but somehow he gathered himself up and pulled it out in the fifth. Here the fifth game slips away in a hurry.

Andres comes off court like a ghost. James hands him a Gatorade and he can barely hold it, his hand is shaking so much. A glistening film of sweat coats his arms. He looks like he has just been tossed in a washing machine with rocks.

Princeton now is up 4–3 and needs to just one more victory to win the dual match. Once again, it is coming down to the wire.

CHAPTER EIGHT

Performance: Parth

Playing number 1, number 4, or number 7 for a college squash team is daunting, mentally. After the pregame jitters, the pep talk, the pulsing excitement of the introductions, and the cold-stare handshakes, you do nothing. You sit. An hour and a half goes by, two hours, sometimes more. You referee the first match. You counsel teammates. You marinate in a bouillabaisse of anxiety. The obvious analogy is a relief pitcher in baseball. But a reliever's job is to come in and face three or six batters and shut the door. In college squash, you come in as a starting pitcher—with your team behind.

Supreet's match at number 6 lasts well past a hundred minutes, and then Randy's, at number 5, although just a four-gamer with only one tight game, extends for over eighty minutes. Add in warm-up time, the three or four minutes in between games, a time-out for Supreet's skinned knee, and a stoppage for Hesh's broken racquet, and it is nearly five o'clock, four hours after the start of the dual match, before the number 4 match starts.

Parth Sharma is normally an anchorman at the end of our lineup, but this afternoon he is adrift in the beginning of his match. He has some prolonged, solid rallies and the score is close for much of the game, but it's clear Dave Letourneau, the Princeton number 4, is the better player today. Parth started out slowly last week against Letourneau, when he opened up with a 9–2 clinker, and once again he's off to a bad start. The waiting has hurt him.

Parth is from Jaipur, India. His father, a doctor, played squash, and when Parth was twelve he started playing at their one-court club. Soon he was vastly superior to any other junior in Jaipur. When he was sixteen, his parents sent him to a squash academy in Chennai. He won the Indian national juniors in 2006, was runner-up in 2007, and reached the third round of the world juniors. He was a gamer.

He played at number 5 as a freshman. He split matches with Hesham El Halaby. We saw incredible talent. He had an extended flourish on his backhand, but it was a steady, almost metronomic swing, and he made few errors. We called him Tsunami, for he rolled over opponents. He had no holes in his game, no glaring weak spots, a complete player. He was like gravity—inexorable.

Parth versus Letourneau is a showdown of two sophomores, the only same-class pairing in today's nine-man dual match besides Goose and Kimlee. Letourneau, another Calgary native (he and Kelly Shannon were best friends growing up) and a former Canadian junior champion, also has a well-rounded game, with rocketing drives and delicate drop shots at his disposal. Last year, Manek had lost to him in the regular-season dual match but beat him at the nationals because we had discovered, by watching film, a tiny weakness. Letourneau loved short forehands. At the nationals, Manek kept the ball on Letourneau's backhand side, never hitting it short to Letourneau's forehand. And when the ball was short on the left, Manek looked for the straight drop, Letourneau's usual response. Manek flummoxed him and won in four.

This year Letourneau has closed that window, and Parth, a superb counterpuncher, has to retrieve his way to victory. Last week, he lost the first game because Letourneau cut off and volleyed all the cross-court balls with a clean, short stroke. But after the first game, Parth bounced back to snatch the next three by hitting the ball straight at all times. If he had an opening, he hit it deep to Letourneau's forehand. It was the first time anyone had suggested hitting it to Letourneau's forehand. Parth played classic contrarian squash: Attack the other man's strength. If you survive, he's got nothing left. Well, almost nothing. Letourneau didn't give in easily and pushed it into overtime in the fourth before falling.

This afternoon Letourneau is running roughshod. He has clearly watched some video and seen that he needs to volley Parth's straight drives. He seizes the second game, which is shockingly not as close as the first. Parth, it seems, has no answer for Letourneau's game plan. Letourneau is just better today.

After the game, Parth says, "The fire is not in my heart."

We ignore it. Sometimes it is best to pretend you don't hear things. If you start to address it, then it will be true. Before matches, Parth never doubted his ability, but now that the match has begun, he has lost faith. I tell Parth, "You have to hit some high, wide crosscourts now. You can't be afraid of the crosscourt. You're not playing the way you can. Remember how Peter Nicol looks: composed, tight targets, and unflappable. Play like that."

In the third, Parth is playing better, but the score doesn't reflect that. Letourneau goes up 7–2 and is serving: two little points away from victory. Parth looks up to the crowd, as if for a spark, and then glances away, finding none.

Tied dual match. We're down 2–0 and falling behind in the third. I have seen this before.

Since our streak started in the autumn of 1998, we've escaped with 5–4 wins on seven occasions. One of them came at the 2004 nationals, when Trinity was playing for history. The team had broken a bucketful of records, including winning 107 consecutive times. But no one had ever won the national title 7 times in a row. The record, set by two earlier Harvard dynasties, was 6 consecutive years. It didn't mean much to me, but the kids glommed on to the stat.* To be the

---

* Harvard won the Association Nine-Man Team Trophy from 1968 to 1973 and 1983 to 1988. Before the national team tournament was started in 1989, the intercollegiate national champion was subjectively crowned by determining who had done the best in their regular season. There was also a so-called Four-Man (and later Six-Man) Trophy awarded to schools whose players won the most rounds at the national individual tournament, the intercollegiates, but since it was based entirely on each man's achievement rather than a dual match (and since just six of your nine players represented the school), the trophy was regarded as more of a statistical fluke than a serious method of determining

greatest ever, we had to get to 7. We were playing Harvard, it turned out, in the finals.

The streak had taken on a life of its own. For three years we had played just one relatively close dual match—a 6–3 victory in the finals of the nationals against Princeton. Otherwise, it had been bread sticks and bagels: 8–1 and 9–0 wins. It was getting easy and we were getting soft, riding the sheer talent we had recruited rather than the fitness, skills, and collective strength that we might have produced on campus. The team motto was "Too Strong." It was cocky—true, but a little too cocky. Literally. Around then, the team cheer when we huddled before a dual match evolved into "COCKS!"—a triple-entendre reference to our school mascot, the Bantam.

We beat Harvard 7–2 in the regular season, and it was a very close 7–2. At the nationals in New Haven, most of the fifteen hundred spectators at Payne Whitney were pro-Harvard, despite the Yale location, because everyone loved an underdog. Payne Whitney, the Yale gym, was a Gothic cathedral. It really looked like one. Built during the Depression, it had fifteen courts, balconies that enabled fans to lean almost into the show courts, and hardly an inch of breathing space. It was a stone evocation of squash history: it was the oldest college squash facility still in use in the world.

After three matches, Harvard was ahead 3–0. The losses were shocking. Reggie Schonborn at number 3 had creamed his opponent 9–0, 9–0, 9–3 in our 7–2 win a month before; now he succumbed in three, his first loss ever for Trinity. The Crimson needed to snag only two more matches out of the next six and the streak was over. It was a frothing mob scene. Grown men hugged each other, jumping up and down and running through the gallery whispering in stage voices—not

---

who had the best team in the country. The only asterisk with college squash was that from 1923 through 1936, Harvard never lost a dual match. But those dual matches were unofficial, as intercollegiate team squash was not formally organized until 1942.

"Harvard's going to win" but "Trinity's going to lose, Trinity's going to lose." By osmosis, we had absorbed the negative energy.

I called the team together off to the side of the glass show court. "Can you smell it?" I asked them. They were dead silent.

Michael Ferreira finally said, "Smell what?"

"I can smell fear. We need to find a way to push fear out of the house."

A nervous, collective laugh covered the silence.

"Listen," I continued. "It is a beautiful spring afternoon outside. We're going to eat at this great Chinese restaurant on College Street after the match. They've got the best dim sum. Speaking of China, right now the sun is coming up in Beijing and Shanghai. It comes up every day. A billion people in China are waking up and they are putting on their pants and going to work and none of them give a shit about what happens here."

Somehow, my talking about Chinese food and life outside the squash courts broke the tension. The players saw that this was just a dual match, that life would go on, that they would shower and go out to dinner and go home. This was something to savor, not fear. I told them to mouth the words *I love this* in between points. "Say to yourselves, *I love this game, I love this chance to perform at the highest level. I welcome the pressure. I enjoy this opportunity to show off all my hard-earned skills. I love this moment.*" I was telling them, in other words, to run to the roar.

They went back out and played hard and true. I walked behind the courts and all my players were whispering to me, to their teammates, to themselves, "I love this game." The dual match tightened. American Will Broadbent hammered Bernardo Samper, 9–1, 9–1, 9–2, but Shaun Johnstone at number 8 and Nadeem Osman at number 5 swept their matches to keep us in it.

Just like Parth today, Jacques Swanepoel was down in a huge hole in the 2004 dual match. He had lost the first two games and was behind 6–2 in the third, but he came back to steal it 9–6. I told him when he came off the court, "Are you okay? What are you doing? You look like a deer in headlights. Go out there and hit the ball deep. I don't care if you lose, but at least play. They don't give trophies to statues. They give them to moving players." Jacques won in five.

The two final matches, with Harvard up 4–3, got uncomfortably close. Yvain Badan, nicknamed Swiss, was up 2–1 to Harvard's James Bullock, a senior from Jamaica. Swiss was down in the fourth game 8–6 and laboring. Somehow he climbed back in, saved game ball, and took the fourth 10–8 to win 3–1. If it had gone to five, Swiss would have been cheese.

The last Trinity man, a reliable five-eight whip-crack senior American named Pat Malloy, was playing a very good Canadian kid named Shawn DeLierre. Malloy snatched the first two games. After losing the third game, he came out of the court looking shell-shocked. *Uh-oh, this is suddenly going badly again,* I thought. I asked Pat what his favorite Chinese soup was and he laughed. He toweled off his face and asked me what the dual match score was. He must have known, since the entire crowd in Payne Whitney had descended upon his gallery. Hating to give him the information, thinking it would freeze him, I hesitated.

"Four apiece," I said in a whisper.

"I've been waiting for years for this moment," he said. "Now get the hell out of my way." He went out and won the fourth in a frenetic fashion, reeling off the final seven points in a flurry of shot making.

Afterward, when we got to the Chinese restaurant, I told them about my favorite tennis player of all time. Arthur Ashe, a second lieutenant in the army, had lived in the Bachelor Officer Quarters at West Point for a couple of years in the late 1960s. When he won the 1968 U.S. Open, he returned to a standing ovation in the dining room. Every year before the Navy match he would come back to West Point to speak a few words to the tennis team. He always talked about choking. Arthur's brother John fought as a Marine in Vietnam and knew about things larger than a tennis match. Every year Ashe had said, "Everyone chokes. You choke on the tennis court. You choke on the battlefield. Bullets flying overhead. Explosions. People choke.

When you are choking, move your feet. That is what my brother John said he did in Vietnam. Breathe and move your feet."

To avoid a choke, I told my players, play at 75 percent to counteract the adrenaline. Hit it four feet inside lines. Take a moment. Get into the moment instead of fleeing it. If you are returning serve, you are in charge. You dictate when the point will begin. Never return serve until you are ready. Replenish your lungs. Do not be blinded by the score. Immerse yourself in the scene. Concentrate on what you smell and what you hear. Be entirely present in the moment. Be confident.

You want a strong opponent. You want the ball with the match on the line. You want it to go to the tiebreaker in the fifth. This is what you have worked for. You want to challenge yourself. You want to grow. Be active, not passive. Move your feet. Feel joy in the physical expression of your mind and body. Embrace the purity of the moment and don't think about the future. This is not mindlessness. You are not forgetting all the training, forgetting your expectations, your hours of sweat, your dreams. A match is a celebration of the effort you put in at practice. You are just staying in the moment, not going beyond the court, the ball. Relish the performance. Allow it to come. When you come off the court, I want to have to pry the racquet out of your hand—not because fear has grown into rigor mortis but because you don't want the moment to end.

You have worked hard in practice. You have been effective in practice. You have earned the right to be effective in a match. Think of a match as if you had bought a ticket for it. You want your money's worth. You are putting forth your best effort. You have the knowledge and the skills to succeed. Pretend you are on Broadway, that you are a performer on stage. People take great joy watching you. The audience does not notice little mistakes. Be creative. Be beautiful. Feel good about producing your work of art, your sliced backhand, your forehand that sends the ball skimming just above the line, your wonderfully angled volley. This is your Broadway show. The score is for someone else to follow. You do not hold the clicker that changes the numbers on the scoreboard. You are on the stage performing. Perform.

"Thou are slave to Fate, Chance, kings and desperate men," John Donne wrote about death four hundred years ago. It seemed all four were conspiring to enslave Matthew. I never gave up hope, but I often wished it would end. I wondered if it would be better if Matthew died—then he'd be rid of the incredible pain that was causing and sustaining his addiction. It seemed so unreal at times that I imagined it was a performance, a play. It was the third act, and we were in the audience waiting for the protagonist to die.

The possibility of a violent end was real. "Dad, you've got to save me." It was Matthew on the phone, late one cold evening. "There's a hit on my name, someone is going to kill me. They've burned my car." It was a drug deal gone bad; he owed money. He had a car, on my insurance plan. I picked him up and drove him home. As usual, he talked at eight hundred miles per hour, manic, nonstop. At the time I didn't know it, but it was the drug talking. I never saw the car. For all I know, he sold it and made up the story that it was burned. He was gone by the next weekend.

On a bone-chilling night one November a year later, the Hartford police called. They had a body down at the morgue that resembled Matthew. Would I come in to identify it? As I drove down to the morgue, I was a divided soul. The instinctive part of me was praying it was another thirty-year-old man. The rational part of me was wishing it was Matthew, that his pain would be finally over.

It wasn't him.

I never hid Matthew's story from the boys. I told them about going to the morgue. Before big dual matches, I told them, "That was pressure, going to a morgue to ID your son." In the telling and retelling, I got uncomfortably numb to the horror. Or rather, I would try, in the alchemical way that people often do, to distill the pain into action, into words, into *something*. It was as if with one vein closed off, I pumped adrenaline into all the other ganglia throughout my extended system. I was eager to be different with my players than I was with Matthew. I could not talk with Matthew on the telephone—he was either missing or in jail—so I called my players every day. The circle expanded. Soon I was having one- or two-minute conversations with probably fifty people.

When people went through a tragedy, I jumped at any opportunity to help. When the husband of the administrative assistant in the West Point physical education department was killed in the Pan Am terrorist attack over Lockerbie, I rushed to the airport. I stood with his widow, Nereida Velez, and a couple of family members and watched as a plane arrived from Scotland. His coffin came off the plane, the American flag draped over it. I have never cried so hard.

My best player when I arrived at Trinity was a sophomore named Michael Bittner. Bittner's nickname was Rock. He had been a quarterback in high school in Rochester and brought a heavily muscled gridiron toughness to the squash courts. He donned an American-flag bandanna for each match, and often during the late stages of a close one, he slipped into a gray T-shirt with PITTSFORD FOOTBALL emblazoned on the front. The lasting image of Bittner at Trinity was from his last home dual match, against what was then our archrival, Amherst, who had beat us the previous year. It was extremely close, and Trinity had just clinched the dual match at 5–3. A freshman, Preston Quick, was going on court for his fourth game. He was down 2–1, and Bittner went up to him, jabbed him in the chest with his index finger, and exhorted, "Now this is when you fucking become a man." Preston took his match in five games.

During his senior year, Bittner's father came down with brain cancer. His father had showed up at one dual match after brain surgery, which had left half of his scalp shaved and scarred. In August 1997, his father died at the age of fifty-five. Though Bittner had graduated the previous spring and it was the first week of school the following fall, I drove the entire team in the college van the seven hours to Rochester; we stayed an hour for the service and then drove the seven hours back. There were more than a thousand people at the service. We sat in a pew in the back of the balcony. It got very quiet when Bittner stood up. "I am Michael Bittner," he said, "and my father was my hero." Everyone in our pew started to weep.

In 2003, Brian Marsden, a Trinity tennis player, learned that his father, Brian Sr., had been diagnosed with a brain tumor. The next year, Brian made it into the NCAA Division III national intercollegiate individuals. It was a huge honor for a tennis player, and his father wanted to come watch—it might be his last time to see his son play—but Brian didn't want him to, thinking it might distract him. His mother, Mary, called me to intervene, and Brian and I had a father-to-son-ish conversation in which I told him all about Matthew and me and how he cannot know the emotional loss his father was enduring right now. They were close. They played tennis a lot together—Brian Sr. had been a top-ranked collegiate player, and together one year they had reached the semis of the national father-and-son championships at Longwood. Brian relented and his father was able to watch as Brian reached the semifinals, the best result in Trinity history. The following months were horrible. His father wasted away, losing his hair, losing weight, and suffering terrible pain. At one point, he could no longer speak.

Then in April 2005, the Wednesday after I'd had my stroke, my phone rang. It was four in the morning. Mary, Brian's mother, was calling. "I can't reach Brian," she said. "His father just died."

"It's four in the morning," I said, almost to myself more than to Mary. "Isn't he in his dorm room?"

"I've called and called. I think he's turned off his phone."

"Okay. I'll go wake him up."

I got in my car and drove to campus. My left side was frozen from the stroke, so I could only shift gears, flip turn signals, and turn the steering wheel with my right arm, leg, and hand. I was thinking, *Wow, Brian Sr. was just fifty-four. That's how old I am. And no one would be able to reach my son.*

I went to his dormitory and up to the second floor and knocked on his door. There was no answer. I walked in. The room was dark, but a wan cadmium light floated in from a streetlight. I stepped over scattered shoes and clothes and knelt besides Brian's bed. I lightly touched his shoulder.

"Brian, Brian," I said softly. "It's Coach."

He rolled over and rubbed his eyes. I could see them in the yellow glow.

"Coach?"

"Brian, your father's suffering is over."

"He's dead?"

"He died a couple of minutes ago. Your mother called me. She was calling you, but the phone—your cell phone was off."

"Let's go," Brian said calmly. He got up and told me that they had just talked a few hours ago. Brian's brother had called from home and put the phone to their dad's ear, and Brian had spoken a few quiet words, not knowing that they would be his last words he ever spoke to his father.

In a minute we were in my car heading to Hingham, Massachusetts, a two-hour drive. On the way I tried to keep him going, keep him positive. I got him to his home just after dawn. It was already busy: a half-dozen cars stood in the driveway. I decided I didn't want to come in. It was the time for the family to be together.

"So this is where the great one grew up," I said. He laughed, a real deep laugh. He was going to survive. It was awful to be a sophomore in college and lose a father, but he was going to survive. We got out. I gave him a one-armed hug, gingerly got back in my car, and drove away.

Today Parth Sharma is down 2–0, 7–2 to Dave Letourneau. This is as hopeless a situation as three years before when Goose was down 2–0, 8–6 in the third to Yasser. The odds on who will win can be figured out in a snap: Parth has to take twenty-five points (while serving) to capture the match; Letourneau needs just two. Twenty-five to two is bad odds. And fate is against us. It is February 22, eerily eleven years to the day that we last lost a match. At this very hour. In this very gym. On the very same court.

The beginning of the comeback is so underwhelming that later people incorrectly report the score at Parth's apogee. They miss when it started, because it hadn't. Parth scrambles and scuttles and snags the serve, and then two points to go with it, when Letourneau tins a couple of shots. But Letourneau gets the serve back. It is 7–4 and he's got the serve. Still hopeless.

Then the match turns. They have a long, windmilling, scrambling rally. On a crosscourt forehand drive, Letourneau hits Parth with the ball.

Parth squeals and swears in Hindi. At this level, getting hit with the ball is extremely rare, so rare that professional players don't wear goggles. Parth feels that Letourneau is going for a cheap point: if Parth has not cleared enough room, then his being hit will mean an automatic point—or stroke—for Letourneau. It is a quick, free way to get to 8–4 and a match point. The ball purples Parth's left thigh.

Parth is wrong. Letourneau is a fair and gentle kid—he is known to call his shots out even when he is down match ball. Letourneau isn't going for the free point. What happened is that in the hurly-burly of the rally he didn't sense where Parth was. He just didn't see Parth. It is a mistake.

In an instant, the referee, Meherji Madan, silently runs through the previous two times he's seen this situation. Years ago he handled a match at a pro tournament in Florida. One player had just squandered a half-dozen match points in the fifth, and the game went into a tiebreaker and eventually to double match point at 16–16. During a frenetic rally not unlike the one here with Parth and Letourneau, one player, an Englishman, hit the other, a Belgian. Madan gave the Englishman the point (and thus the match). Afterward, Madan talked to some other referees and came to the judgment that he had made a mistake. He should not have given a point to the Englishman but rather a conduct warning for unsafe play: if you don't know where the other player is, don't hit the ball. A few years later, Madan saw the same thing happen in a world juniors match in Zurich and issued a conduct warning rather than a stroke.

Today, Madan quickly gives Letourneau a conduct warning for unsafe play. If he had held up and not swung at the ball, Madan would have given him the stroke.

Winners internalize events to their benefit. Parth, instead of getting angry at the alleged slight, channels it positively. He thinks Letourneau's desperate—even though he's up 2–0, 7–4. Letourneau is a bit banged up from his semifinal match the day before—he had played a tight four-gamer against Rochester's Matt Domenick. I begin to think, *Well, maybe there is hope.*

Up from Parth's gut bursts a splash of fire. He wins a point with a volcanic drive. He tugs his shirt up on his left shoulder, as if his shirt is constricting him. It is a good sign—he's working again. Letourneau wins back the serve: a third opportunity at getting to match ball, but then inexplicably slips after serving and Parth gets the serve back. Letourneau is clearly perplexed. His eyes dart around the court. It's as if he is a marathoner coming into the stadium, twenty-six miles done, at a steady seven-minute pace. Now just the final loop around the track. He is in the tunnel and sees a bit of light at the other end and starts sprinting at a five-minute pace. But the light at the end of the tunnel is actually an oncoming train.

Wham! Letourneau cracks two consecutive tins on low-percentage shots, desperate to get the serve back. It is 7–7 then 8–7. Parth intercepts a crosscourt and whips a forehand out of Letourneau's reach to take the game.

Parth comes off the court all fired up. A group of us, led by the other Indians, gather around him, starting to feed him advice. He stops us short. *"Mai usko chodunga nahi,"* he says in Hindi. It means, "I won't leave him." In other words, Parth is not going to let go until he wins.

Buoyant with confidence, Parth enters a fugue state in the fourth game. Time dissolves into the pure, clarified present. Each stroke is facile and free; each point is joyful. He glides across the court, frictionless. His lobs are rainbows. His rails are bullets. The crowd next door roars as Kelly vanquishes Andres in five. Parth doesn't hear it. He doesn't absorb the noise. Euclidian geometry and the infinite merge. The ball is huge, the angles perfect. The world is a floating sea of wood, carbon, rubber, graphite, and he is a liquid flowing downhill— he has deliquesced.

With a few passing waves of his magical wand, he wins the game 9–0. He wins the first three points of the fifth game. He has just won nineteen unanswered points in a row. In crew parlance, he has rowed through Letourneau.

Showing incredible fortitude and sangfroid, Letourneau fights back. He has just blown an enormous lead. He was two points away. Two points. Yet he doesn't give up when it would be easy to give up. The storyline is that he blew it. No one writes that he blew it and then came back and then he blew it again. But Letourneau bravely inserts himself into the story again. He knows about saving match points—last year Manek was up 2–0, 8–0 and Letourneau scrambled back, saving multiple match balls to win the third game and push it to a fourth.

The score knots: 3–3, 5–5. Letourneau has better racquet skills, so Parth doesn't want to try to go shot for shot. Instead, he keeps the ball tight and refuses to go for a winner unless it's 100 percent open. It's 7–5 in favor of Parth. Then he tins two balls, one on a backhand drop and one on a forehand boast. He smiles: *Why can't you make this easy? Why does it always have to be tight?* Suddenly, the roars from next door seep in to Parth's mind. He realizes that he has to win or the streak ends.

It's 7–7.

Letourneau is serving, again two points away from Princeton's elusive fifth victory. Like they did an hour ago, the crowd gathers above the wall. Guys whip out their cameras and cell phones so they can record the climactic moment. Princeton team members populate the first couple of rows and lean forward, ready to leap into the court.

Parth thinks, *One final push. Get everything—no ball bounces twice.* I always like to tell them that unless their legs are cut off, they cannot let the ball bounce twice. Parth runs like a cheetah and quick-twitches to everything Letourneau offers. A long rally ensues. It is the most intense of the match. It lasts more than three minutes, with a helter-skelter frenzy that is almost unbearable to watch. Letourneau plays a good drop; Parth retrieves it but doesn't do much with it, and

Letourneau has a glimmer of an opening in the center of the court. He tins it. Parth gets the serve back, still at 7–7.

The crowd presses. It is impossible to see. After each point, the players down below in the tunnel try to guess whether they hear a Trinity roar or Princeton roar. James is leaning against a wall, his eyes closed, his lips moving in a silent prayer. Frustrated, Belinda Terry, our most avid supporter, and Nour Bahgat, a player on the Trinity women's team, leave the tunnel and go into an empty court next door. After each point they gaze up through the white netting at the scoreboard in the top corner of Parth's court and during the point they watch the faces of the people in the gallery.

Mercury for the Trinity team, this afternoon Belinda is sending messages to scores of alums like Michael Ferreira, parents in India, cousins in Iceland. This is the first year, with the proliferation of third-generation mobile telephones, that fans are divided between watching the match and bending over their BlackBerrys or iPhones, a blue underworld glow on their chins, sending out messages to the world beyond. One person on Belinda's list is Colleen Stewart, the director of Trinity's access control system. Just before the dual match Colleen's cell phone fell into the toilet. When her mother came over to help with her newborn baby, Colleen was in tears: "I dropped my phone in the toilet," she sobbed. "I'm never going to get the results." Her mother lent Colleen her phone and she got the new number to Belinda just in time.

Belinda is working as hard as any player. All her correspondents are sending her replies, asking about the latest score and what the referee is saying. Ferreira texts encouragement every two seconds: "C'mooooooooooooooooooooooon kid, dig deep." Her iPhone, set to vibrate, is jumping out of her hand, so many messages are pulsing in.

Another protracted point. Parth hits an unorthodox shot, a forehand drive with topspin, one inch above the tin. It is too close to tell whether it's in or out and Madan has them play a let. This time Letourneau tins a drive that he had trouble peeling off the wall.

It's 8–7. Belinda sends off another text. Twenty more come in.

Parth thinks, *Okay, match point. Let's not have a long rally.* Again, he hits a wall-hugging drive. Letourneau scrapes it off and the ball comes into the middle. All match, Parth's drops have not been working, and he's reluctant to try another. But here is a 100 percent open ball. It is match point. He's got to go for it. He has to hit a drop shot. He bends down very low, almost to the height of the tin, to make sure he doesn't hit it too low. He lets the ball sink, holding his racquet above it like an executioner. He slaps a straight backhand drop. It is a little too high—he factors in a margin of error—but luckily it's sticking to the wall. Letourneau scrambles after it. When he gets there, all he can do is chuck it up in the air. The ball rebounds off the front wall and comes very close to him. Parth stops, unable to hit the ball.

After a moment's pause, Madan says, "Stroke to Sharma. Game and match to Trinity." Parth grabs his shirt, around the chest, and tugs it out, his head nodding, as if to say, *Here is where this performance came from.* It was all heart.

It's 4–4.

CHAPTER NINE

Character: Baset

He was wearing new blue jeans, an Oxford shirt, and a jacket. He had two suitcases on wheels and an oversize, bulging squash bag. He was tall, six feet five. He was at the airport in Kiev, in a tunnellike waiting room. There were no chairs, so he stood for a good while and then slumped on the ground. In the room were men with gold teeth, women in black robes and woolen shawls, a few silent children.

He had been traveling for more than forty hours and was just two times zones away from home. It would have been quicker by bicycle. He had booked his ticket at the last moment because he had just received his visa yet had only a few days to get to his destination before the visa became invalid. It was a situation out of Kafka. So was his itinerary: Lahore to Karachi, two-hour layover, Karachi to Dubai, eight-hour layover, Dubai to Kiev.

It was late August. He had nothing to read: no books, magazines, or newspapers. He had nothing to listen to, no iPod. In Dubai he had roamed from shop to shop in the airport, busying himself by looking at every item, one by one until he shuffled his bulky burden of bags to the next shop. He bought a couple of bottles of duty-free cologne. In Kiev he had no shops to kill time in because he had been shunted by a gruff, Russian-speaking security officer into a room for passengers in transit. It was the ultimate test of modernity: Could you survive the boredom of a seven-hour layover in a single room in Ukraine?

The flight left. It was a huge relief to be moving again. He cocooned in his seat, although as always, he had trouble unfolding his six-feet-five frame and his knees flattened on the seat in front of him. It was another long flight, more than ten hours. But he slept most of the way. He was a good sleeper.

He landed. He easily went through security, another relief. He grabbed his three bags and took a car service from the airport for the hour-and-a-half drive up country. He came through the iron gates. It was dark, past twilight. He got out and saw two students, who kindly guided him to campus security, who let him in to his dormitory. His room was bare, nothing on the walls, nothing in the bureau or closet or on the table. His bed had no sheets, no pillow, no blankets. He put down his three bags. He turned out the light. He lay down on the bare mattress, still in his clothes.

He slept for fourteen hours.

When he woke up, he showered and had a meal at the cafeteria. It was all new: the worn patter of the servers, the smells of egg salad sandwiches and tater tots, the smorgasbord of the salad bar. He went back to campus safety and asked, three days after he had left his home in Lahore, if they could call the squash coach and let him know he had arrived.

I was frantic with anxiety. We had seen odd arrivals before. In the late summer heat, the American players arrived in Hartford. Dressed like L.L. Bean models, they came to the campus in hulking SUVs loaded to the hilt with bags and boxes. But the overseas guys, coming by airplane, often arrived unprepared, like Simba Muhwati walking through baggage claim in midwinter wearing flip-flops.

Our custom with overseas players was to fully orchestrate their first few days to accelerate the process of acclimatization. Their first stop on campus was the squash courts and inevitably it was during practice. The newcomer had usually been emailing and Facebooking with guys on the team, so they were not totally unfamiliar with one another. He would come into the gym and we would cloak him in a warm, welcoming whirl of hugs, high-fives, and hellos. We would make sure that he began the Trinity journey with his squash family already intact. We would then assign an upperclassman to start all the paperwork to turn this kid into a Trinity student.

Baset Ashfaq Chaudhry was special. (His surname was Ashfaq; Chaudhry was a ceremonial clan name that no one used.) He was the most celebrated recruit in the history of intercollegiate squash. In January 2005, he won the British Junior Open to claim the Drysdale Cup, squash's oldest junior title. He played on the Pakistani boys team that won the world junior team championship in 2004. He comfortably held a spot in the top echelon of juniors—six of the nine other winners of the Drysdale Cup since 1999 were in the world's top ten a decade later. He finished high school just before the British Junior Open triumph, and upon his return to Pakistan he took university-level courses, lived at home, and played in a few pro tournaments in India, Malaysia, and Egypt (never winning prize money that exceeded his expenses). In June 2006, he was ranked sixty-first in the world.

No Drysdale Cup winner had ever played American collegiate squash except Anil Nayar, from India. Nayar showed up in Cambridge in the fall of 1965 unbeknownst to the Harvard coach, Jack Barnaby. Both Nayar and Barnaby loved to tell the story. Nayar had applied and been accepted at Harvard completely unrecruited, a situation hard to imagine today but more commonplace in an earlier era when squash did not have a significant profile, even at Harvard. One day, Nayar came by the courts and requested to join the team. Barnaby asked if he had ever played before. Nayar proudly said that why, yes, he had actually won the Drysdale. Barnaby quipped, "Come back tomorrow and I'll have a red carpet rolled out for you."

No one thought to roll any carpets for Baset. He was considered beyond American collegiate squash—too good, too talented, too old. But he was tiring of the pro tour. One incident stuck in his craw. In New York, with Amr Shabana, he tried to hail a taxi at rush hour. None of the cabbies recognized Shabana. He was anonymous. Here was Shabana, the greatest squash player alive, and yet he couldn't catch a cab.

One night while surfing the Internet, on a whim he contacted two coaches: me and the Harvard coach. I happened to be online. I quickly scrolled through his player biography on the pro tour website, saw that he said "studying" was one of his interests, and within two minutes I emailed him back.

Half a year later, he made his most singular peregrination around the world. His father called my office from Lahore. I was giving a lesson when the phone rang, so he left a message. "Please, sir, this is Muhammed," he said, in a mellifluous accent. "Can you find my son, Baset Ashfaq?"

I wrote down his number and called him back. His father didn't have an itinerary. Neither did I. His father mentioned something about the Ukraine—or was he just saying it was insane? Was that Uzbekistan, not Ukraine? There was something in an email about a country starting with U. But why would he fly to Ukraine? I looked at some maps online and couldn't figure it out. I called every airline that landed in New York City. I called security at all three of New York's international airports. Nothing.

The phone rang. It was Muhammed. He politely introduced himself, explaining that his son was Baset Ashfaq, that he was coming to Trinity College in Hartford, Connecticut, to enroll as a university student. It was as if we had not just spoken a half hour before. (The Ashfaqs were the most polite family I had ever met.) I told him what I knew. We hung up. He called back four more times within the hour. Each time he went through the entire spiel, graciously establishing again and again who he was.

Finally, Ukraine Airlines said someone with the name Baset Chaudhrey had arrived the day before on a flight from Kiev. *The day before.* He had cleared customs, someone else told me. This was good news, because I always worried about my subcontinental players coming to the United States after 9/11. But if he had landed yesterday afternoon, where was he?

The phone rang again. It was campus security, telling me that there was a kid in their office who said he was on the squash team. "Don't let him move," I shouted, and ran out the door.

"I don't know whether to hug you or kick your ass," I said, after giving him a hug.

We went back to my office. I called my number one tennis player, a kid from India—this was one of the first things my players learn, that the cultural rivalries from home meant little here in America—and told him to come help me: "Baset is here. Get him registered, get his ID card, his email account, a cell phone—something."

Baset looked around the office. As if on cue, the phone rang. It was his father. They talked for a couple of minutes in Urdu, a labyrinth of consonants and glottal stops. As Baset stood at my desk, he mindlessly fiddled with the Trinity national championship rings that lay in a little bowl: the gold, diamonds, the slogans (TOO STRONG and NEVER FEAR, NEVER RETREAT emblazoned in diamonds), the finger-dropping weight.

He stopped and put his hand on the phone's mouthpiece.

"What are these, Coach?" he asked.

"Those are the eight national championship rings. We make one after winning the national title."

"Order four more."

Character can be built. Very often our true selves are covered over by a scrim of self-doubt, insecurity, or overzealousness. It's the coach's job to tear away that scrim, to allow for new growth.

I overestimated Baset. Deep in my mind, I knew from my experience with Marcus that it would not be easy, but I really wanted a clean run. I wanted to insert him into the squad at number 1 then sit back and watch him go undefeated for four straight years.

A day after his unorthodox arrival, I got a text message from Goose. "Just hit with Baset. Real deal."

He was the real deal. He hit a heavy ball: zinging pace, superb length and width, and a violent velocity that I had never seen in my thirty years of collegiate squash. He detonated the ball. And yet he had soft hands and was surprisingly agile and fluid, especially considering his height. He had unbelievable deception for a college player. He could shape as if he was hitting a drive and then, with a quick flick of his wrist, sucker punch the ball crosscourt.

He got on well with everyone and spoke Hindi with the Indians on the team, Hindi that he had learned from watching Bollywood films as a child. But his game, with the sudden decrease in training and his attention being drawn elsewhere, had deteriorated. That fall in qualifying for the U.S. Open, he tumbled to Tom Matthews, an Englishman. It was not pretty. Baset had no imagination. He lost points he should have won. He tinned the ball when he should have driven it halfway up the wall. He lobbed out of court. He looked forlorn between points. He lost the first game and the zip went out of him completely. Afterward, he barely could conceal his disappointment. He had always beaten Matthews. He had trepanned him 3–0 in the qualifiers of the World Open six months earlier, and he had been ranked a dozen places above him when he had quit the tour and moved to the States. Now, after two months of college, he was losing to him. A couple of former players had come to watch the match. They said to me, "I thought you said this guy was incredible." Baset was intellectually prepared to leave pro squash behind and pursue a college degree, but he had not calculated how his pride might get temporarily injured.

An early challenge match between Baset and Shaun Johnstone, a senior, showed me how much trouble our Drysdale Cup winner was in. Baset had crushed Shaun in the opening challenge-match tournament, but a few weeks later they played again, and Shaun ambushed him. Baset lumbered onto the court, a bit chunky and a bit slow. Shaun played like a man possessed. He brought Baset forward every time he could, rattling the ball around the front corners, making Baset stretch and twist and turn his six-five frame on every point. Everything was misdirection. He was annoyed, his eyes flickering the suggestion that he was not mentally prepared for a dogfight. Shaun won the first and took the second game 9–5. Baset hurled his racquet at the front wall. Everyone looked at me. I said, "That was a sign of weakness." The third game was brutal. Baset was fully in it, trying to inch his way back into the match, but the ball was ricocheting out of his reach. Shaun won 10–9.

Shaun was politely elated. This was still his team. No freshman was going to change that. Baset was gutted. I walked straight from the bleachers to my office, not saying anything, following my Russ Berkoff rule of not talking to players after they lost. Instead, I sat down and sent him an email, knowing he would not get it for a couple of hours. I got his reply late that night: "Coach, I really apologize. I wasn't ready. I wasn't hungry. I will look to take revenge, Inshallah. Baset."

The next morning at seven thirty Baset was in the courts, doing wind sprints.

It was pretty electric at his first home match against Yale. The kids were chanting "Bee Sting" and "Killer Bee," and you could not hear his name when he was announced. He hammered Nick Chirls, the Eli number 1, 9–1, 9–1, 9–1. A few days later he crushed his Connecticut College and Penn opponents, losing just ten points total. Against Williams, Baset won his match against Tony Maruca, 9–2, 9–2, 9–1. It was a smooth, easy half hour, virtually the same as his other matches. But in between games when I was coaching him, Baset was somewhere else. I could not reach him. He looked away at the floor, covering his eyes with a towel.

After the match, I took him into my office. "Let's talk," I said. "You're a great kid. But you know something? Let's look at your reality. A year ago, your life was so different. You were living in Pakistan, seeing your friends, training twice a day, taking a class or two, watching Bollywood videos. Now you are in America—new food, new culture, new weather, new schedule." Baset was raised Muslim and grew up praying five times a day and going to the mosque every Friday for prayers. "The only thing that is the same is squash. And now the squash isn't going so well in your mind. Why is that? It's because you can't train twice a day. You've got too much going on. But so what? You had a 3.8 freshman fall. You're studying. You're making friends. Listen, you get to choose being happy or not."

"But my squash is so terrible," Baset said, after a pause to wipe his brow.

"You just beat a good player there, and you beat him three love.

Maruca's a good player. He's been playing for nine years, summer camps, tournaments. He's good."

"Really, Coach? He's a good player?" Baset could not see it. He had no perspective.

"Yes, Baset," I said slowly. "You don't get to the write the story but you do get to live it. You've got to enjoy this time."

Smiling weakly, he walked out of the office. I felt useless. I had not reached him. The expectations of being this famous recruit had seeped into his hardwiring and shorted out a couple of connections. The gossip was getting to him. He had forgotten who he was.

He lost a second challenge match, to Goose. Like Shaun, Goose played a hard, grinding first game and won it 9–5. Baset went into a shell and had barely any life in him as Goose ran it out 9–4, 9–4. In the next challenge match, Baset beat Supreet, our number 4. If he had lost that, I told James Montano, I would have quit.

Slowly he reemerged. In January he beat Goose to get back to number 2 and then Shaun to get to number 1. His mental side improved. But he had shin splints, which might have been caused by the new sneakers he was wearing. A week before the national intercollegiate teams, he sprained his right ankle during a drill. It swelled up. James got ice, fetched crutches, and called the trainer. Baset wore a boot for a couple of days and the ankle swollen and looked awful. I kept him out of the first round of the nationals but he played against Yale in the semis and then Princeton in the finals, when he had an earthshattering victory over Maurico Sanchez of Princeton.

Watching Maurico was like reading Shakespeare by flashes of lightning. He was a mercurial player with quick feet and even quicker hands. Baset's win was Maurico's first loss all season. The match started out slowly, with Baset trying to control the pace and Maurico straining to create distance between the ball and the tall Pakistani. Maurico came out on top 9–4. I told Baset after the first game, "Win every point three or four times. Hit the ball tight, with good length; wait for something to open up. Be patient. When you get an opening, get between Maurico and the ball and crack it. But don't start shooting too quickly. He is too fast and will get to it unless he's behind you." Baset rolled through the next three games, 9–2, 9–2, 9–1.

In those three games, he showed that he was a member of a phylum of creatures rarely seen in the squash ecosystem. He really could play pro squash rather than college squash. He could keep it air-lock tight, no matter how much duress Maurico put him under. It was little noted in Trinity's dual-match victory, but his match with Sanchez was a seminal moment.

A week later, he fell in the semis of the intercollegiates. A week or two lay between the end of the national teams and the start of the intercollegiates, the tournament for the top sixty-four players in the nation. It was an odd time. I saw the guys every day, but I did not coach them. That was the culmination of my core statement that this was a team sport. The tournament was an individual event. I left them alone.

He played well on Saturday morning, dispatching a pugnacious Kimlee Wong in the quarters. But that evening in the semis, he looked forlorn and ordinary, the pressure of expectations clearly weighing on him. The crucial moment came in the middle of the opening game. Sid Suchde of Harvard coughed up a loose ball. Baset stepped up and crushed it. Sid asked for a let. He got it. All of a sudden, Baset was confused. It was not a let, at least in the way that some international players would have seen it. The referee, Meherji Madan, saw the rally differently than Baset, who did not take it in stride. He had to make an adjustment—it was like a pitcher learning to adapt to a minor league umpire's strike zone—but it rattled him. He started running into Sid when going for short balls in order to emphasize that he could get to Sid's drop shots and secure a let. It was getting unnecessarily physical.

Between the second and third games, we talked. I calmly told him he needed to finish the points earlier. Baset, like most elite athletes, would resist my suggestions if I seemed caught up, too. He took advice personally. I evenly told him that I was not emotionally involved. "Look, my temperature right now is the same as it was when you began the match. The same cannot be said for you, and therefore, you cannot truly measure what is happening out there." He did not believe me. He thought he had to hit the ball harder.

Sid took over and won convincingly 9–7, 9–5, 9–6.* I should have realized that anytime a guy is that big, there will be jostling—he just filled up too much space—but Baset didn't like it when he couldn't get lets. He was a gentle giant and didn't like to stamp up and down the court like a dinosaur. He had again forgotten who he was.

Coaching is akin to being not a parent but a grandparent. You offer skills, guidance, support, and love. You can spoil the kids. You can make mistakes. At the end of the day they go home to someone else. You can slightly modify behavior, but their values and perspectives are formed elsewhere, and you can't do that much to change them. They build their own walls of delineation, and you work within the rooms you're let into. A lot of angst floats like a halo around my players—and their fathers. I always say that I would rather coach a team of orphans.

I remembered giving a tennis clinic for eight-year-olds my first day on the job at Apawamis, the country club outside New York City where I worked after leaving West Point. The first day of every clinic naturally involved more talking and explaining than the ensuing sessions. I laid out the ground rules: timeliness, courtesy, patience; how to hold the racquet, how to pick up balls. Around the fence were probably a dozen mothers, who watched attentively. Their sons and daughters seemed to enjoy the clinic. I was really in my element, moving kids around the court like chess pieces, talking, gesticulating, and making strong points about sportsmanship and courtesy. I was quite sure that I was doing a masterful job.

When the class was over, the little ones ran off to their mothers. One mother walked up to me and said, "Do you realize that Charles hit six balls today?"

---

* Interestingly, Sid went on to beat Maurico Sanchez in the finals in four games to claim the title. Sid had lost in the finals the year before, so on a personal level, as a graduating senior that never won a national championship, it was nice to see him go out on top.

I wasn't quite getting her drift, but she then proclaimed in a loud voice, "I just paid ten dollars per hit today." That day I implemented a policy of not letting parents watch practices, something I have applied ever since.

Baset's parents loved him dearly. His father, Mohammed, was a first-class cricketer until he injured his shoulder, at age nineteen; he never recovered his bowling or batting form. Mohammed returned to work in his father's importing business (industrial chemicals). Baset's first love was cricket and he yearned to become a professional, but his father steered him away from it because he had seen insidious intrigue around who got selected for what team. For the first three or four years that Baset played squash, he didn't like the sport and played it just for the sake of his father. After a lot of losses, he started training seriously. His club, the Punjab Sports Complex, was considered the biggest club in Lahore, but it had pretty average facilities: two indoor glass-and-wood courts and five open-air cement courts. The indoor courts got too slippery because of humidity, and the outdoor courts flooded when it rained.

At sixteen, he ran into injuries—he sprouted up beyond six feet, which bothered his back, and he then strained his hamstring and was out for three months—and when he came back from his injuries, guys he used to trounce were now beating him. This angered him so much that he started training five or six days a week.

When he was eighteen, because of injuries, he had missed the trials for the Pakistani team heading to the British Junior Open and wasn't selected. Just what his father had feared in cricket now happened in squash. Mohammed asked the Pakistani squash federation secretary if he could enter Baset's name. The secretary said no. Annoyed, his father called a friend high up in the government, who went over the secretary's head and got Baset registered. The secretary relaliated by banning Baset from the Punjab Sports Complex. Baset reached the quarters British Junior Open, beating one of the selected kids from Pakistan in the third round. The following year, he won it.

In his sophomore year, Baset was a different guy, more mature and settled. He spent his summer back in Pakistan and came back to campus on Labor Day weekend more at peace with his family and himself. He had lost twenty pounds. In a guy who was six feet five, this was enormously encouraging, as he needed all the help he could get to accelerate around the court. He seemed stronger mentally, too. He was spreading beyond his roots. He started to see himself staying in the States after graduation. His studies were on track: he was majoring in economics and was an honors student.

In our dual match against Princeton, Baset faced Maurico again. Everyone had heard that Baset was a renewed player. Maurico was known as the hardest worker in the college game. He trained all year, pushing his lithe body to the extreme. He was a runner: he didn't have much shot-making ability, but he got to every ball. A native of Mexico City, Maurico had spent a postgraduate year at Lawrenceville Academy down the road from Princeton, and for four years he had been one of the best players living in the States.

On the first point of their match, Maurico tried to make a statement. Baset served. Maurico cracked a shot into the right corner— immediately trying to end the point. He was successful, but the notion was wrongheaded. It showed impatience to shoot the first time you touched the ball. He was worried he would not last.

He did not. Baset chopped him up in three, 9–2, 9–2, 9–0. It was the most lopsided win I had ever seen in a number 1 match between the two top-ranked teams in the country. Those guys carried enormous egos to go with their talent, and they simply never let a match slip away that completely. At the nationals, Baset beat him 3–1. At the intercollegiates, he trounced Goose Detter in the finals.

In 2009, everything went smoothly for Baset until he lost to Maurico on Valentine's Day. As he went on court, Baset knew the score of the dual match, that we were up 5–3, so a tiny puff of indifference wafted across his mind. His match didn't matter to the team's score. He went

out a little off speed and Maurico rushed pell-mell to take the first
two games. Baset revved up his game and he won the next two, the
latter in a tiebreaker that included a match point for Maurico. Baset
flew to a 2–0 lead in the fifth, and then Maurico, using his superior
quickness, went on a tear and captured the next nine straight points
to take the match.

Today, all hell is breaking loose. Princeton's courts are bouncier
and the ball comes out more, especially with the heat of five hundred
people in the gallery. In the players' nomenclature, it's hard to lay the
ball down. This makes for a distinct advantage for a finesse player
like Maurico, especially against a power hitter like Baset. Baset loses
the first game in a tiebreaker. He's up 4–1 then down 8–4—a trouble-
some streak. He saves one game ball, but in the tiebreaker, Maurico,
jerking him around the court, eventually takes the first.

He settles down and handily snags the next game. He goes up 7–0
in the second and wins it, although it took more than twenty-seven
minutes to put it away. *He is fine*, I think. In the third, it is tighter and
they have a ten-minute standoff at 5–4 before Baset slides ahead. The
play gets physical again, but unlike the match against Sid three years
ago, it's Maurico who's doing most of the pushing and bumping as he
tries to slalom around Baset.

After Baset wins the third, the air goes out of his sails in the fourth.
Maurico pushes forward and there is no resistance. He goes up 5–0.
Baset tacks back to 5–2, but Maurico cruises to a 9–2 win in just
eleven minutes.

Collegiate squash, in its long history (the first intercollegiate match
was Harvard versus Yale, in February 1923), has had some epochal
nail-biters in which the dual match was at 4–4 and the last match
on court went to five games.* Before the start of the national teams

---

* Some of the 4–4 dual match classics: In 1953, Harvard's Steve Sonnabend,
at number 9, was down 2–0 against Princeton before winning in five; three years
later Lee Folder, Harvard's number 5, was down 2–0 before winning 15–9 in
the fifth (using fifteen-point scoring); in 1958, Harvey Sloane of Yale and Gerry

in 1989, there was no play-off system, and thus, while the excitement of these 4–4, fifth-game matches was fever pitched, there was always a sense that even if a team lost, perhaps they could win another day, there was perhaps another way to still claim the title, or perhaps it really didn't matter. In 1987, Yale beat Princeton 5–4 on a double match-ball point at 4–4—it couldn't get closer—and yet the following week Harvard crushed Yale 9–0.

To become a national champion today, you had to win the nationals—the regular season was largely irrelevant aside from helping to seed the sixty teams that came. Since 1989 the finals had never come down to a 4–4, 2 all scoreline. This was the equivalent of the finals of the NCAA basketball tournament going into overtime (which it has, seven times, including in 1957, when North Carolina beat Kansas in triple overtime, and in 2008, when Kansas beat Memphis State).

During the break before the fifth game, we talk to Baset. James tells him, "No one left but you. Remember, you win, we win the national championship." Baset misinterprets it. He thinks we have already won the dual match at 5–3.

At first, Maurico keeps the momentum going, hunting down the

Emmet of Harvard were tied 13 all in the fifth (Sloane won); in the 1960s, Harvard's John Francis, at number 9, was down 11–6 in the fifth at Yale before he reeled off nine straight points to win; a year later against Princeton, Francis survived four match points to win in a fifth-game tiebreaker over Bunting Hayden-Whyte; in 1970, Eddie Atwood of Harvard was down 2–0 before winning in five; in 1987, Yale's Bill Barker, at number 6, and Joe Lubin of Princeton were tied at 17–17 in a fifth-game overtime—double match ball—before Barker won it on a drop shot (curiously, Princeton had the dual match originally won at 5–3 but Bob Callahan defaulted a match when it was revealed that a Tiger had popped the lenses out of his protective eye goggles—Barker and Lubin learned this after their third game; Barker also fractured his racquet, down 5–0 in the fifth game, shouting, "Are you going to try or what?" and played with it the rest of the way, too embarrassed to change it); in 1990, Yale's John Musto, at number 1, won 15–13 in the fifth over Harvard's Mark Baker; and in 1995, Tal Ben-Shahar of Harvard, playing at number 3, won 18–17 in the fifth over Yale's Jamie Dean.

volleys at every opportunity. He dashes out to a 5–0 lead. Baset has just lost nine points in a row. He is asleep at the wheel and the truck is about to crash. Everything is in Maurico's favor. He hasn't lost a point in half an hour. He has the home-court advantage, with a screaming crowd ("Let's go Mo!"). It is getting very intense. Every negative call is contested, and a cascade of jeers and boos and groans of displeasure rains down on Hunt Richardson, the referee. I start to mentally write my concession speech.

At 5–0, it oddly becomes quiet in the gallery. You can clearly hear the *thwap* of the ball coming off the strings and the peppering concatenation of the ball rebounding off the walls. People are stunned that the fifth game is so one-sided, that they are seeing the collapse of a great champion. Ever since schoolboys smacked the first squash ball a century and a half ago, there's just one question people universally ask about a five-game match: "What was the score in the fifth?" Everything else pales. It doesn't matter if you saved match points in the third game or played beautifully in the fourth. The question is: What did you do when the match was tied at the end, when either of you had the chance to win it? What did you do at crunch time? The score in the fifth is a talisman. It's thought to reveal character. And here, Baset is showing none of the remarkable resilience we had seen from him before. He is getting chopped up.

Sitting next to me is Reggie. Without moving his legs or torso, he leans his head over so that it is almost touching my shoulder. He whispers, "Do you think he can come back?"

I don't know what to say. You never give up hope. You have to be honest, you have to face facts, and you have to learn to accept defeat. But character can be built. You can instill courage. With Matthew over the years, this has been my mantra. You never give up. You never relinquish that last tiny droplet of light in your heart.

The thing about light is how it interacts with darkness. In the end, darkness can never extinguish light. Night can come on and yet if there is a television, a computer, a lightbulb on, a baby monitor's battery glow, you can still see something. On the other hand, light always extinguishes darkness. When the wick of a candle catches fire in a dark room, a bit of the darkness disappears.

I light a candle.

"Yes, he can do it," I murmur back to Reggie. Baset is not playing well, but he can still win. The true test of a champion is winning when you are not playing well. National titles are not *won*, they are *not lost*. At this level, players have to recognize tiny deviations from their norm and compensate for them. There is almost a science of managing failure.

Baset's match reminds me of the time I watched Mark Talbott win a squash tournament. At the time, Talbott was peaking as an athlete, the greatest American squash player in history, in his prime. He was strong, talented, devastatingly tough. He captured title after title. In the match I saw, he played his usual smooth game. He floated around the court, never rushing, never hurrying. He cut the ball with ease. He walloped his opponent, his longtime rival Ned Edwards, in three quick games. It was a brilliant display of dominance.

Afterward, I congratulated Talbott on the win. "I struggled the whole time," he said. I suddenly saw that his face was drained and his eyes were tired. "Nothing was going where I wanted. I felt like I was swimming through wet concrete there." I had seen none of it.

Today Baset is swimming through concrete. The question is whether he has developed the internal fortitude to gut it out. Baset is such a natural genius at the game that he doesn't have an assassin's attitude. With his imperial bearing, he has coasted. He's not as mentally tough as some of the other guys. He has not gone through the tempering fire of repeated close matches. He has lost just twice in his college career. Most of the time he has won because of his talent. He likes squash; he respects squash; but he doesn't use it to power his ego or get girls or anything. He doesn't *need* to win. He wins because he is good. But now, unlike a week ago, when he backed down in the fifth game, Baset suddenly discovers an instinct to fight.

In the tunnel, players are lying in lifeless clumps, heads buried in their hands. John Lingos-Webb, a bombsquader, has a Trinity flag that he has been waving all afternoon. It is furled up. A Princeton parent comes up to Roosh and says, "Son, it happens. You were beaten by a better team," and shakes Roosh's hand. He leaves and Roosh stares at him, not sure whether the parent is being patronizing. Another bombsquader, Will Burchfield—who goes by Burchy—is standing near the glass back wall. He is the only one who hasn't given up. He is shouting out scores to his teammates down in the tunnel.

Baset gets the serve back on a whirling-dervish point but loses it again. A long point. Maurico is almost frantic. He is all over the court, hitting the ball as hard as possible, but the points don't end quickly. Instead, the court seems to shrink and the two of them nervously bump into each other, leading to let after let. The match is now raw and instinctual. There's 672 square feet of space on the floor, and neither Baset nor Maurico, their aggression coiling and uncoiling like snakes, is giving up a foot. Then Baset crushes a drop for a winner. Then he passes Maurico and is finally on the scoreboard.

Burchy shouts out, "One–five." Baset, reaching into a reservoir of courage he didn't know he had, has started to come back. Upon hearing Burchy's call, Roosh, prostrate, yells out, "Don't move" to everyone in the tunnel. A few boys have started to rush toward the court. "We can watch or we can win," Roosh says. Superstitious, he wants everyone to stay where they were when Baset won his first point. A couple of Williams players saunter through the tunnel. Roosh doesn't let them pass. The tunnel is now filled with motionless, silent, anxious people.

Belinda is in the stands. Stashed in our conference room is a bag with forty new baseball caps, ELEVEN emblazoned on the front and NATIONAL CHAMPIONS on the back She thinks she's going to have to send them to Nicaragua. I catch her eye and smile. It's a good smile, not "it's been a nice run" but more "I am not worried yet." A couple of the players look over at me. I again try to radiate calm, as if I am enjoying this.

Belinda's iPhone, fully charged in the morning, is losing power because of all the messages going in and out. The green area in the battery symbol is shrinking. Then the phone reports that she has 10 percent power left.

A friend texts her: "What is the score?"

She types, "1–5 in the 5th."

The friend texts back, "OMG, OMG. More mojo needed."

At the end of a short, well-constructed point, Baset hits a feathery backhand boast for a clean winner, 2–5.

Maurico is visibly agitated. He swings wildly, his follow-through almost carrying him across the court.

"I will spill bottle of wine, blood of goat."

"Sharpen knife for goat. 3–5."

In literally eighty-odd seconds, Baset has won three points. He has stopped the skid. The comeback has begun. Lingos-Webb unfurls the flag again. Belinda is furiously texting, her fingers flying across her black phone: "Prayers to sports deities, blood of goat and dog spiritually sent. Do we need real blood?" An epic rally, lasting seventy strokes, comes next. Baset wins it with a stroke.

"I will cut finger. Already biting tips. 4–5"

At 5–5 Maurico starts to get desperate. He trips over Baset's feet and dives like a soccer player into the penalty area. On the next point he runs into Baset while going for a faraway rail and drops his racquet for emphasis. Richardson says, "No let." Maurico tins quickly. The gods have turned on him.

At 7–5, the match gets becalmed. Maurico finally wins a rally and gets the serve. He tins, Baset tins. Baset gets an obvious stroke. Then a fantastic rally ends with a dud. Baset makes some preposterous gets only to flub an easy sitter right into the middle of the tin. It's like a golf pro missing a ten-inch tap-in. Baset doesn't fling his putter. He gets the serve back with a nick volley. Then he loses the serve.

Maurico does his usual service routine, bouncing the ball from his racquet to the floor and into his hand. Racquet, floor, hand; racquet, floor, hand. He does it eleven times. It is the last time he'll serve.

Baset creams the ball, leaving Maurico sprawled on the ground.

After nearly eight minutes of tension, the score finally changes.

Baset hits a rail that clings to the wall. The Trinity crowd stands up and chants, "Killer B, Killer B."

It's 8–5. Another let. Then the final rally of the match. After 117 minutes, after 6 hours, after 4 months, after 11 years, it comes down to this point. It will last only ten strokes and about a dozen seconds, but it beautifully illustrates why Baset is a champion.

Baset hits only crosscourts—it is match point and he wants to avoid a stroke situation, which happens much more often on straight drives, when the ball niggles the side wall and comes out into the middle. He serves. Maurico hits a forehand rail off the serve. Baset cuts it off and sends it crosscourt. Maurico chops a backhand rail. It isn't that good and pinballs off the side and back walls. Baset serenely cracks it crosscourt. They exchange crosscourts, *bam, bam, bam, bam*, Maurico's forehand to Baset's backhand to Maurico's forehand to Baset's backhand. The last two are volleys. There is a fluid rhythm here—it is almost like they are warming up.

This is where Baset shows that he's the better player. Maurico's first crosscourt is too wide and bumps the side wall; his second one isn't wide enough and comes down the middle of the court. Baset gobbles up the last one and rips it crosscourt, past Maurico. Frantically following it, Maurico tries to flip the ball off the back wall, a last-ditch desperation effort. He makes contact, but there is not enough on the ball and it floats, ever so slowly, in a high-arcing parabola, toward the front wall.

Before it lands on the floor, it is obvious it will never make it.

Baset howls and hurls his racquet into the air far above him. Maurico, for a second, stands in the back corner in disbelief. Burchy yells, "We did it," and the entire tunnel is transformed into a seething mass of players, released at last by Roosh. Everyone is sprinting to the court. Tears rolls down faces. They mob Baset. They cry into one another's arms, the utter relief finally coming out. They bob and sway. They look like kids at a Sweet Sixteen doing the hokey-pokey. They look like the 1980 U.S. hockey team after beating Russia. They look like pure joy.

I am numb. I turn to Reggie and ask, "What just happened?" We hug and head to the court.

Belinda is the only person in the stands who has not moved. Her phone, the battery dying, is vibrating with dozens of incoming messages. She ignores them. Her fingers tap out a simple message: "We won."

She hits send. Then her phone goes dark.

Epilogue

In the past ten years, he has entered eleven rehab centers. They had varying lengths of required stay, many of which were ninety days, after which you could move to a halfway home. Ten times, Matthew got kicked out before the terms were up. Twice he got kicked out in the first week.

Once he made it through the ninety days and moved into a halfway home. He was on Suboxone, a new drug that heroin addicts could take instead of methadone (which Matthew had been on twice). It worked. He was sober. I went to a counselor with him every week. The people at the halfway home told me he was doing well, that he was the smartest person they had ever had in the home.

The halfway home had cinder-gray shutters and his room was bleak, but he was sober, he was strong, he was clear-eyed. He took a job working on a construction site at a mall. I got my hopes up for the first time in years. This was the Matthew that we had lost in 1993. "I'm over drugs. I'm sober," Matthew said. "I'm fine. Every day is a battle, and I am winning it."

One day I showed up at the halfway home to ferry him to our therapist. "He's not here," the woman said. "We don't know where he is." It turned out he had tested positive for drug use and had been kicked out of the halfway. I thought I might get a phone call from him, asking for money, but the hours stretched to days. I talked with my sister, Michelle, who was always a beacon of nonjudgmental support. She told me to wait. He finally reappeared by way of a telephone call from Omar, the security guy at the front desk of the gym: "There is someone here claiming that you're his father."

I went down. Matthew was there, brooding in the corner of the hallway like a hayrick. He looked terribly old. His skin was wrinkled like a peach stone. His hair lay matted on his skull. His expression was baggy with patience, as if he had no plans, nowhere else to be. I could tell it was a front. It was the look of drugs. "Matthew, I am going to call the police. I can't have you here. This is where I work. I have a job. I can't have you coming here."

"But, Dad . . ." There was an accusing shadow in his eyes. He was sad. The sorrow loomed like a mountain behind the city of his face. It was always there. And his words sounded odd. He talked like an eighteen-year-old, fast, furious, elliptical, full of hyperbole. It was as if his brain had stopped developing once he had begun injecting heroin, and he had a mid thirties body and a teenage mind that was challenged by the daily decisions of life: *Do I get up out of bed, do I go to work, do I do the right thing, or do I give in to this moment?*

Two days later, I got a call from the Bridgeport police. He had been arrested for armed robbery as he tried to steal from a convenience store.

Helping an addicted person, a true addict, doesn't work. There are three outcomes: he will find his own way to help; he will continue to manipulate you and use; or he'll die. I wanted to believe so badly that the old Matty was back. He was sober. He was working. He was smiling. But I was deluded. It was always a lie.

"Let him flounder, leave him alone," said my father. "You are enabling him. You need to let him find his own way. You have got to let him do the right thing." That was the phrase in the air at the rehab centers: let him do the right thing. My father saw it as black and white. "Addicts—you can never carry the water for them."

My mother said, "I will never ever leave my grandson alone. I will never walk away." She was right. He was right.

Now I give Matthew the gift of time. I don't give him money or support. Just love. I have no ownership of the process. We see each other. He is in jail right now, in Enfield, Connecticut. He is thirty-four years old. Hardly anyone has survived with a heroin addiction for as long as he has. For years everyone has said that he must hit rock bottom. The problem is that he is too strong. He is an Assaiante, and his rock bottom is fathomlessly deep.

Something has kept him alive and I try to nurture that something, just in the hopes that it may someday grow again and he may be at peace.

At the moment Baset Ashfaq wins the last point of the dual match, Will Burchfield hurtles into the court. He comes in an unorthodox way. He climbs over the glass wall.

In 2004, Burchy was a little freshman at Lawrenceville Academy, playing number 7 on the team. In the national high school team championships at Exeter, Lawrenceville faced Brunswick Academy in the finals. The dual match was tied, and the decider was Burchy against Robby Berner, a freshman at Brunswick. Berner went up 2–0, Burchy climbed back into it and managed to win 9–5 in the fifth. When he clinched it, his teammates poured over the glass back wall, like East Germans in Berlin in 1989. It was a moment he never forgot, and five years later he spontaneously reenacted the highlight of his high school career at the highlight of his college career. Luckily no one else followed him.

At the awards ceremony, Roosh says, "Oh, Baset, thanks for saving us," and gives him a huge hug.

"What do you mean, saving us?" Baset asks.

"It was 4–4, man. Amazing."

"What, are you kidding?" He really didn't know that everything had been riding on his match.

We don't leave Princeton that night until around ten o'clock. We come out into the parking lot. It is cold, about freezing, with a nippy wind. The sky is clear. The lot is empty and quiet, save for one corner, where our cars are parked. Guys are hanging out of sunroofs, stereos are blasting "Stand Up (For the Champions)," the Right Said Fred anthem—"*I was built to be the best / Number one and nothing less. . . .*"

It's smooth sailing and we get back to Hartford with ease. At the exit for Asylum Street off Interstate 84, we pull over at the TRINITY NATIONAL CHAMPIONS 1999–2008 sign. For a minute it is a primal scene: we scream and hug and take a photograph and dance like crazy men around a campfire.

We pull into the Ferris parking lot around half past one. A crowd of fans are waiting for us with signs and banners, car horns honking like it's VE Day. More singing, more mayhem.

The boys go off to Psi Upsilon for more singing and carousing. Everyone goes home at dawn.

Three hours after getting home, I am on my way to tennis practice. It is a Monday in late February and my tennis team has already begun its season.

After parking my car at the gym, I send off an email. Today, I tell them I am proud of them. Nothing has changed for them as people. They are the same as they were when we left for New Jersey on Thursday afternoon. But they are now a part of the best college squash team in the world. And, I add, they had participated fully and beautifully in what was the greatest dual match in college squash history.

And then I add the postscript: 12.

Spring comes. We have our annual team banquet. We order the championship rings. The team votes on the various awards. Binnie gets Most Improved and Parth the Most Valuable Player award. All the freshman win the George Dickle Award for participation.

Goose, Manek, Roosh, and Charlie graduate. Goose goes to Arkansas to take a job in banking. Based in Little Rock, ironically he is living in the state with the fewest squash courts in the nation. Manek becomes a teaching pro at a club in Greenwich. Roosh finds a job in Singapore and pines away for his Trinity friends. Charlie travels around New Zealand, sleeping in a van.

The following year is different. It always is. We bring in a couple of freshman. One is Goose's younger brother Johan; another is Antonio Diaz from Mexico who lands at number 6, and a third is a South African, Reinhold Hergeth, who came in at number 9.

We cruise through our regular season, the main hiccup being that both Vikram and Supreet suffer concussions that require long convalescences. We beat Yale 8–1, though there is a tense moment in the beginning. Reinhold (he instantly became Rhino) is losing to Rob Berner; Supreet at number 3 is up 2–1 but struggling; and Diaz is down 2–0, 11–10—match point. We're about to be down 2–1 or even 3–0 in the dual match. Instead, Diaz pulls it out in five, Supreet wins in four, and Rhino ends up losing our only match.

In our last dual match of the regular season, we have our rematch with Princeton. We win 9–0. Baset goes to five against freshman Todd Harrity, a Philadelphia boy with great promise. Of the returning lettermen, Supreet goes down 2–1 against Christopher Callis but survives in five. Vikram, at number 4, destroys David Canner in three. Randy Lim, at number 5, beats Kelly Shannon in four, and Andres, at number 8, takes care of Peter Sopher in three. The most interesting match is the one that reprises last year's matches: at number 2, Parth versus David Letourneau. Parth hauls it in, 8–11, 11–4, 11–9, 11–9.

At the nationals, we again face Princeton, this time in the semis. Baset chops Harrity in three. Parth and Letourneau face each other for the fourth time in twelve months; Parth wins in three. Two matches go deep into the fifth game, with Trinity capturing both: Randy Lim over Santiago Imberton and Chris Binnie over Peter Sopher. Trinity wins 7–2.

In the finals, we beat Yale 6–3. The clinching match, as it was last year, is Baset's. He is playing a freshman, Kenny Chan, from Singapore. Drilling a low, hard forehand rail—perhaps Baset's signature stroke—he completes a 11–6, 11–6, 11–4 win. The senior cocaptain has just secured Trinity's twelfth straight national title and 224th consecutive win.

Instead of shaking Chan's hand and exiting to a swarming mob of teammates and alums, Baset does something unexpected: he stoops down, and for three or four seconds, yells at Chan, who is about a foot shorter. He then leaves the court and embraces some teammates and his parents. Seeing Chan exiting the court behind him, Baset turns and yells at him again. Immediately, his teammates and supporters, led by Simba Muhwati, jump in between him and Chan. The celebration moves away from the court's door and Chan soon exits.

The whole incident lasts about fifteen seconds.

The story goes viral. The video of the match reaches ESPN, who places it in heavy rotation on *SportsCenter*. Hundreds of thousands of people view it on YouTube. People comment on websites. People comment on the comments. It is on local news broadcasts. It is in *USA Today*. Dave Talbott and I go on ESPN for a ten-minute discussion of the incident. For about five hours on the Friday after the incident, there are just four items on the ESPN ticker at the bottom of the screen: one about Tiger Woods, another about Lindsay Vonn, a third about the U.S. Olympic hockey team, and a fourth simply saying "Baset Chaudhry withdraws from singles championship." That is it. He has become such a household name (his wrong surname, too) that ESPN assumes its viewers know who he is. In the first sixty hours after the incident, I get more than five hundred emails from people I don't know. Twelve straight titles and Trinity Squash has never gotten this much attention.

For all of us, it is a sad ending to a magnificent career. Baset was a wonderful and sensitive kid and feels badly and we feel badly. This put a big strain on everyone, but after my experience with Marcus Cowie more than a decade before, I know I have to be proactive. I can't just let this slide. We talk for hours about the past and the future, placing this incident in context of his family, his culture, his pride, his journey.

One day in the late spring, I talk to Baset on the phone while driving away from the campus. He is graduating in a few days. He is strong again, in fact stronger than ever. He has a job waiting in New York. He has learned about character. He has learned about ego. He has learned about ownership. Together we have learned to run to the roar.

I hang up the phone. I drive past the Trinity squash highway sign. It has a new date, 1999–2010, next to NATIONAL CHAMPIONS. All those stories, all those emotions, all that hard work, distilled and shrunk into eight white numerals. I call Kristen. She is now working at the

NYU Law School in event planning and getting a master's degree in education at NYU's Steinhardt School. Someday she'll be my boss. We talk for a few minutes. I then call Scott. He's doing well. He has a wonderful marriage and two beautiful children and I tell him that he teaches me every day how to be a good father. Both conversations are short but meaningful.

I drive north to Enfield, Connecticut. I pull in through the gates at the Robinson Correctional Institution. Inside, I go through security and walk into the visitor's room. I've done this fifty times before, but I never get used to it. I sit in a chair and stare at a covered window.

The cover goes up. On the other side of the bullet-proof glass, I see, through the tears in my eyes, prisoner number 339914. I pick up a phone and say hello to my son.

AFTERWORD

Squash is to Trinity College what basketball is to Duke, swimming to Kenyon, or football to Penn State: the sine qua non of collegiate athletics, the highest standard-bearer, a source of pride for the college, and a lightning rod for those who might, for whatever reason, wish to hurl invidious comments and even accusations, a "success tax" known all too well by any who are winners over the long haul.

Paul Assaiante, who has led the squash miracle at Trinity, has written an important book that is an admixture of many stories that meld together into one fabric. His book is that unique combination of history (squash in the United States, borrowed from abroad and then transformed); of squash at Trinity (from a relatively inconsequential silo within our athletic programs to the longest unbeaten record in American intercollegiate sports); of his own life's journey from a teenager interested in gymnastics to the present day as a veteran squash guru; and from his fatherly devotion to his players ("my boys") to the tragic, and the brutally honest, account of his self-proclaimed failure as a father to his own troubled son. *Run to the Roar* is therefore many things (as any really good book should ideally be simultaneously).

But at the end of the day, this book is about the unremitting pace of change: how an imported sport gets transformed in this country, how squash then goes on to attract to the United States some of the best squash players in the world, how one sport could become the lingua franca of athletic excellence unparalleled at a small liberal arts college in Connecticut, how the lives of the players interact with the life of the coach responsible for their experiences on our campus, and ultimately how one man's devotion over the years to his players shines forth for everyone else to see, while that same man watches as his own son becomes himself a pawn in the hands of the most dreaded drug of them all: despair.

Tuesdays with Morrie is Coach Assaiante's favorite book. His own readers will perforce understand why after having read *Run to the Roar.* This is ultimately a story of triumph against all odds. It is the story of making concrete a never before dreamt of possibility and fastening that possibility to the essence of an academic institution. Like those privileged few, however many, who have watched in amazement over the years as Trinity squash made history, *Run to the Roar* ultimately makes one want to stand up and cheer.

When that inevitable day dawns and Trinity's winning streak is at long last broken (the mathematical odds are so acutely against any continuation ad infinitum of such an historic feat), Paul will sit down quietly with his boys to discuss what the end of the streak means for them and for Trinity. He will talk to them "man-to-man" (as trite the cliché may be, like all clichés, it betokens profound truth) about life's biggest lessons, he will insist that the boys congratulate the opposing team like the gentlemen he expects them to be at all times, and then he will undoubtedly ask them to join him in cleaning up the trash and other debris left over by the spectators who have flocked to the defining match. (As he constantly tells his boys, we do not want to burden the housekeeping staff by having them clean up what we are physically so capable of tending to ourselves.) He will tell them not to take their privileges and blessings for granted. He will hand out plastic trash bags to each of them, and then he will lead them to their appointed trash-collecting rounds. Responsibility taught by example. We are all fellow human beings. We care about one another and those around us. We want to help. We want to set examples not because someone tells us we should, but because we know that this is the right thing to do. Such is education writ large, and education at its best.

This graceful and insightful book will be a delight for years to come.

—James F. Jones Jr.
President, Trinity College

ACKNOWLEDGMENTS

In the spring of 2004, Paul Assaiante called me out of the blue. I had known Paul for two decades. I had sometimes crossed paths with him, especially when I was in college and we played against Williams and then immediately thereafter, when we both were living in Baltimore, I had followed the rise of the Trinity dynasty with interest. In the summer of 1998, I wrote a cover article for *Squash Magazine*, breaking the story on Trinity's first great recruiting class and the start of what was going to become the streak.

But until Paul called me, I was under the impression that it was the players, not the coach, who were revolutionizing American squash—his journeyman résumé and his quiet, self-effacing demeanor had fooled me. We began getting together on the telephone, every week for an hour or two, not knowing where our conversations were leading. We kept on talking, year after year. I tracked the team each season, learning about the behind-the-scenes work that went into producing a champion. During our conversations, I pieced together Paul's career and the development of his philosophies. I learned about the mistakes he made on and off the court, about the personal travails he endured, and how those experiences had made him the master coach he is today.

After six and a half years of talking, we now have this book. But like what Paul teaches his players, our collaboration has always been about the journey, and I am deeply thankful to Paul for making it so special.

When we decided to pivot the narrative around the finals of the 2009 nationals, the 2008–09 Trinity squash team graciously allowed me into their lives. They agreed to repeated interviews in person, on the telephone, and by email, and their extensive contributions form the heart of *Run to the Roar*: Baset Ashfaq, Christopher Binnie, William Burchfield, Gustav Detter, Gedd DiSesa, Daniel Echavarria, Travis Judson, Randy

Lim, John Lingos-Webb, Ian MacGregor, Vikram Malhotra, Manek Mathur, Parth Sharma, Supreet Singh, Derek de Svastich, Andres Vargas, Charlie Tashjian, Rushabh Vora, Andrew Weisz, and Wesley Wynne. The assistant coaches that year, James Montano, Simba Muhwati, and Reggie Schonborn, were exceedingly helpful, sitting for multiple interviews and generously providing insight into the history of the program and the personalities of the players. James in particular was the glue for the program for these twelve championship seasons and his perspectives were critical for each chapter.

The greater Trinity community contributed wonderfully. Jimmy Jones wrote the splendid afterword and was always a keen supporter. In addition, I gained immeasurably from the assistance of Rick Hazelton, the athletic director; Wendy Bartlett, the women's squash coach; Dave Kingsley, the director of sports communication; Chris Gordon, assistant coach; and Colleen Turner of Buildings and Grounds. I was blessed to have the expertise of Dick Druckman of Gold Medal Impressions for the photographs that adorn the cover and the table of contents. Luke and Belinda Terry told me their many stories, and Belinda provided her breathtaking account of the Princeton dual match.

Moreover, many Trinity squash alumni from the past fifteen years sat for interviews and/or wrote detailed memoirs of their experiences: Yvain Badan, Nick Barquin, Rohan Bhappu, Jay Boothby, Christian Bullitt, Ashton Crosby, Steve Gregg, Michael Ferreira, Shaun Johnstone, Patrick Malloy, Ryan O'Connell, Duncan Pearson, Preston Quick, Lefika Ragontse, Thad Roberts, Bernardo Samper, Charlie Saunders, Coly Smith, Jonny Smith, Jacques Swanepoel, Chase Toogood, Eric Wadhwa, Noah Wimmer, and Tommy Wolfe. In addition, Brian Marsden, a tennis team alum, added his poignant story, and Neil Robertson dug up a rare copy of the Atlas Lives match.

For the West Point scenes, I had the vivid recollections of Russ Berkoff, Roland Nordlie, Walter Oehrlein, and Charles Oliver; in addition, Roland kindly sent me a bountiful archive of material on his father.

Many collegiate players and coaches provided vital background and perspective, in particular Bill Doyle, Daniel Ezra, Eric Pearson, David

Talbott, Mark Talbott, and Tim Wyant. Above all, Bob Callahan provided video from the dual match and reconstructed each match from that painful day. There is no one in the game who is more of a gentleman than Bob. In addition, both referees at the dual match, Meherji Madan and Hunt Richardson, supplied more video and expert analysis and commentary on the matches they handled.

I also want to thank Kristen Assaiante, Scott Assaiante, and Julia Assaiante, who sat for interviews, read multiple drafts of the manuscript, and commented and advised. I was also helped by the thoughtful manuscript comments and collaborations from Michael Bamberger, Jack Davis, Lucy Ferriss, Leah Flickinger, Jeremy Katz, Sean Khosrowshahi, and Joseph Regal.

Two years ago Tom Wolfe read an early draft, and it was his enthusiasm that led us to David Black, our outstanding literary agent, as well as to writing his brilliantly exuberant introduction. At Penguin, Adrian Zackheim led us with uncommon grace. Courtney Young edited with wisdom and rare attention, and we benefited greatly from the work of Emily Angell, Nick Owen, and Jaime Wolf.

Deepest thanks go to my family: my sisters and in-laws, Colby Loud, Jane Sismaet, and my parents, Jim and Debbie Zug, who religiously read each succeeding draft and never lost faith in the project. Lastly and most joyfully, I thank Rebecca Zug and our two children, Livingston and Collier, to the moon. And back.

—James Zug

INDEX